Teaching With Documents

THE COLONIAL PERIOD to 1879

National Archives Trust Fund Board
National Archives and Records Administration

A B C · C L I O

ABC – CLIO, Inc.
Santa Barbara, California
ISBN 1-85109-489-X

Teaching With Documents is comprised of four volumes:

Teaching With Documents: The Colonial Period to 1879

Teaching With Documents: 1880–1929

Teaching With Documents: 1930–1949

Teaching With Documents: 1950–1975

To order, contact ABC-CLIO:
Phone: 800-368-6868
Fax: 805-685-9685
http://www.abc-clio.com/schools

Published for the National Archives and Records Administration
by ABC-CLIO through the National Archives Trust Fund Board
2002

Library of Congress Control Number: 2002110141

Table of Contents

Foreword — i

Acknowledgments — ii

Publisher's Note — iii

Introduction — iv

Articles

1.1	"The Alternative of Williamsburg": A British Cartoon on Colonial American Violence, 1775	1
1.2	Navigation Act Broadside, 1785	6
1.3	Delaware's Ratification of the U.S. Constitution, 1787	10
1.4	The Wording of the First Amendment Religion Clauses, 1789	15
1.5	Jefferson's Letter to Washington Accepting the Position of Secretary of State, 1790	19
1.6	The 1820 Census of Manufactures, 1820	21
1.7	Maps of Salem, Massachusetts, 1822	26
1.8	Census of Cherokees in the Limits of Georgia, 1835	29
1.9	U.S. Court of Claims Deposition of Kish um us tubbee, 1837	33
1.10	General Orders Pertaining to Removal of the Cherokees, 1838	40
1.11	A Ship's Manifest, 1847	46
1.12	Lincoln's Spot Resolutions, 1848	48
1.13	Lincoln's Letter to Siam, 1861	53
1.14	Robert E. Lee's Resignation from the U.S. Army, 1861	58
1.15	Letter to Giuseppe Garibaldi, 1861	62
1.16	Circular from the Surgeon General's Office, 1862	67
1.17	The Fight for Equal Rights: A Recruiting Poster for Black Soldiers in the Civil War, ca. 1862	70
1.18	The Homestead Act of 1862, 1862	75
1.19	*Ex parte Milligan* Letter, 1864	83
1.20	Civil Rights Mini-Unit, 1865–1978	88
1.21	Reconstruction, the Fourteenth Amendment, and Personal Liberties, 1866 and 1874	113
1.22	1869 Petition: The Appeal for Woman Suffrage, 1869	120
1.23	A Bill to Relieve Certain Legal Disabilities of Women, 1872	125
1.24	Glidden's Patent Application for Barbed Wire, 1874	129

1.25	Documents Related to the Disputed General Election of 1876, 1876	*134*
1.26	Native American Education, 1876	*141*
1.27	Alexander Graham Bell's Telephone Patent, 1876	*146*
1.28	Mapping a Mystery: The Battle of Little Bighorn, 1877	*150*

Numbered List of Articles		*154*
Appendix A:	Types of Documents	*156*
Appendix B:	Disciplines and Subject Areas	*157*
Appendix C:	Thematic Chart	*158*
Appendix D:	National Standards for U.S. History	*160*
Appendix E:	National Standards for World History	*167*
Appendix F:	National Standards for Civics and Government	*171*
Appendix G:	National Archives and Records Administration	*178*
Appendix H:	Document Analysis Worksheets	*180*

Foreward

The mission of the National Archives and Records Administration (NARA) is to provide ready access to essential evidence that documents the rights of citizens, the actions of Federal officials, and the national experience. NARA does this in many ways–through our work with Federal Government agencies to manage and evaluate Federal records, through our preservation of Federal records in a nationwide network of records service centers and archival facilities, through our commitment of providing public access to these records in our research rooms and via the Internet, through the exhibition of particularly significant archival materials, and through publications such as this.

Since 1977, we at NARA have collaborated with the National Council for the Social Studies (NCSS) to produce a regular feature article in their journal, *Social Education*, highlighting documents from the holdings of the National Archives. Originally titled "Document of the Month" and now called "*Teaching with Documents*," this journal department features NARA documents, provides historical context for the documents, and suggests ways in which teachers can use the documents effectively with their students. These articles have proven to be one of the journal's most popular departments.

And no wonder–through these articles, teachers and their students have discovered the educational value and the thrill of examining letters, reports, maps, and photographs created by actual participants in significant historical events. In these articles NARA supports the emphasis in most state curriculum frameworks on teaching with primary sources, and the result has been improved teaching of American history and critical thinking skills.

In 1989, we compiled the first 52 articles into a single compilation. In 1998, the second compilation was published. Our "*Teaching with Documents*" articles and the two original compilations have made a difference in history education. We are pleased, therefore, to be working with ABC-CLIO to offer this new, 4-volume *Teaching With Documents* compilation and CD-ROM, featuring 25 years worth of articles in chronological order according to their featured document. We are delighted to be making the articles and the documents even more widely and conveniently available for the use and enjoyment of both teachers and students.

John W. Carlin
Archivist of the United States
2002

Acknowledgments

The *Teaching With Documents* volumes are the result of the contributions of many talented and devoted individuals. Numerous archivists, authors, educators, and editors helped research and write the "*Teaching With Documents*" articles that are compiled in these volumes. Without the expert help of archivists, the search for records would have been far more time-consuming and difficult. The comments and reactions of educators who have written and spoken to us have shaped and improved the document selection and the teaching exercises over the years. The editors at the National Archives and Records Administration (NARA) and the National Council for the Social Studies have reviewed the manuscripts ably.

Special thanks go to the contributors who researched and wrote drafts for "*Teaching With Documents*." Those who are or were affiliated with the education staff of the National Archives since 1977 include Wynell Schamel, Lee Ann Potter, Jean West, Beth Haverkamp Powers, Adam Jevec, Linda Simmons, Walter S. Bodle, Kathryn Gent, Leslie Gray, J. Samuel Walker, Nadine Smith, Mary Alexander, Marilyn Childress, Ce Ce Byers, Richard A. Blondo, John Vernon, and Elsie Freeman Finch. Other NARA staff who contributed to the articles are Stacey Bredhoff and Bruce Bustard, exhibits specialists; Charles E. Schamel, legislative archivist; Lucinda Robb, legislative outreach staff; and Amy Patterson, special media archivist. NARA archivists Nick Baric and David Wallace contributed to the development of the charts linking the articles to national education standards. John Harper, a University of Maryland graduate student; Emily Ray, an author; and Natalie Lloyd, a student at Brigham Young University, wrote articles while volunteering at the National Archives. Teachers Jacqueline A. Matte, Tom Gray, Patricia Baars, Stan Beck, Jean Preer, and Jan D. Schultz also contributed articles.

The careful attention to historical accuracy and educational significance in the work of each of the contributors assures consistent excellence in the teaching materials included in these volumes.

Publisher's Note

Primary source documents have long been a cornerstone of ABC-CLIO's commitment to producing high-quality, learner-centered history and social studies resources. When our nation's students have the opportunity to interact with the undiluted artifacts of the past, they can better understand the breadth of the human experience and the present state of affairs.

It is with great enthusiasm that we celebrate the release of this series of teaching units designed in partnership with the National Archives—materials that we hope will bring historical context and deeper knowledge to U.S. middle and high school students.

Teaching With Documents is a compilation of 113 articles, most of which originally appeared in *Social Education*, the journal of the National Council for the Social Studies. Each article focuses on a National Archives document, providing a brief historical background for the document and teaching activities. The documents span the history and policies of the U.S. government from the formation of the union to Watergate and they include posters, maps, photographs, charts, drawings, and official correspondence and proceedings of the federal government. For more effective use of these teaching units in the classroom, each booklet is accompanied by an interactive CD-ROM which includes digital images of original documents.

The mission of the National Archives is "to ensure ready access to the essential evidence that documents the rights of American citizens, the actions of Federal officials, and the national experience."

These units go a long way toward fulfilling that mission, helping the next generation of American citizens develop a clear understanding of the nation's past and a firm grasp of the role of the individual in guiding the nation's future. ABC-CLIO is honored to be part of this process.

Becky Snyder
Publisher and Vice-President
ABC-CLIO Schools

Introduction

Twenty-five years ago, in the fall of 1977, the National Archives pioneered a teaching with documents program to make Federal records accessible to classrooms and to encourage teachers to use archival sources as learning tools. What began as a small publication project to provide reproductions of interesting and significant documents to secondary school history teachers has evolved into a complex publication and professional development program for teachers and students at all educational levels and across the curriculum.

Early in the program, the National Archives education staff wrote articles for professional journals such as the National Council for the Social Studies' *Social Education* defining primary source materials, formulating a rationale for teaching with primary sources, and presenting lesson plans and document reproductions for classroom use. These articles introduced teachers to the use of primary sources—documents, reports, maps, photographs, letters, diaries, posters, and recordings created by those who participated in or witnessed the events of the past—as a teaching method that exposes students to at least three important historical concepts and skills. First, students realize that written history reflects an author's reconstruction and interpretation of past events. Therefore, students learn the need to evaluate historical accounts carefully to recognize their subjective nature. Second, primary sources enable students to touch the lives of people in the past directly. Third, as students use primary sources, they develop a wide range of important analytical skills.

The next phase in the publication program led to the development of a variety of additional curriculum materials published in conjunction with NCSS, Cobblestone Publishing, The Mini-Page, National History Day, ABC-CLIO, and others. For each publication, education specialists researched archival documents, and wrote background essays and designed teaching strategies for using them. These materials continue to provide primary resources for a wide range of grade levels, abilities, and disciplines.

To assist teachers in developing their own document-based teaching materials, the education staff offers Primarily Teaching, a 2-week summer workshop in archival research and pedagogical instruction in how to use documents as teaching tools. The staff, all of whom have classroom teaching experience, also offers workshops at regional and national professional meetings, in-service programs for school districts providing travel and expenses, and interactive videoconferences.

Similar educational programs are offered nationwide throughout the National Archives system by the Presidential libraries (see Appendix G), the Regional records services facilities (see Appendix G), the Center for Legislative Archives, and the National Historical Publications and Records Commission. Included among the programs are the following: the Harry S. Truman Library in Independence, MO, provides the White House Decision Center—an onsite, simulation experience for students; the National Archives-Northwest Region in Seattle offers summer workshops for teachers; the John Fitzgerald Kennedy Library in Boston offers "learning with documents" workshops for students and sponsors the annual Profiles in Courage student essay contest; and the National Archives-Central Plains Region in Kansas City produces videotape teaching products. In a new outreach program, the National Historical Publications and Records Commission has developed teaching packages of documents related to early U.S. foreign policy and Southern secession in partnership with Jackdaw/Golden Owl Publishing Company.

More recently, many users of the printed materials created by the National Archives education staff have also been identified as high-profile Internet users. In 1996, the National Archives education staff launched The Digital Classroom section of the agency's web site. This section, specially designed for educators and students, is located at www.archives.gov/digital_classroom. The site provides research activities, opportunities for professional development, educational publication information, document-based lesson plans, and links to thousands of digital images of historical documents from the holdings of the National Archives.

The Value of Teaching With Documents

Each facet of the National Archives education program—from the publications to the professional development opportunities, the videoconferences, and the Digital Classroom—emphasizes the value of teaching with primary sources. Far too many students see history as a series of facts, dates, and events usually packaged as a textbook. As students use primary sources, however, they begin to perceive their textbook as only one historical interpretation and its author as an interpreter of evidence, not a purveyor of absolute truth. For example, as students read eyewitness accounts describing the working conditions for children in the early 20th century; as they look at photographs of very young, dirty, exhausted children working in mines, mills, and the streets; or as they scan reports to the Children's Bureau about the effects of work on children's health and schooling, they weigh the evidence from these sources against textbook generalizations about child labor. Through interaction with the surviving historical evidence, students learn much about historical work, that is necessarily an interpretive process.

Primary sources fascinate students because they are real and often personal; history is humanized through them. Using original sources, students touch the lives of the people about whom history is written. They participate in human emotions and in the social values and attitudes of the past. By reading petitions from black Americans in 1892, for example, students confront the language and feelings of persons who were left out of the World's Columbian Exposition in Chicago and other public events and the response or lack of response from Congress. These human expressions provide students with a real and tangible link to history's cast of characters.

Through analysis of primary sources students confront two essential facts of historical work. First, the record of historical events reflects the personal, social, political, or economic views of the participants who created the sources. Second, students bring to the study of the sources their own biases, created by their own personal situations and the social environments in which they live. As students use these sources, therefore, they realize that history exists largely through interpretation–and tentative interpretation at that.

The most important educational benefit of the study of primary sources is the development of broad cognitive and analytical skills. Interpreting historical documents helps students analyze and evaluate contemporary sources–newspaper reports, television and radio programs, and advertising. By scrutinizing primary sources, students learn to recognize how points of view and biases affect evidence, what contradictions and other limitations exist within a given source, and the extent to which sources are reliable and informative. Essential among these skills is the ability to understand and make appropriate use of many sources of information. Development of these skills is important not only to historical research but also to a citizenship capable of evaluating the information needed to maintain a free society.

Perhaps best of all, by using primary sources, students participate in the process of historical work. The teacher can create a laboratory in the social studies classroom, giving students direct access to the tools of the historian or writer and encouraging students to analyze and evaluate for themselves the building blocks of history. Practicing the historian's craft, they conduct research; analyze and interpret sources; identify points of view, biases, contradictions, and limitations in the historical record; and evaluate the reliability and validity of the sources. According to research conducted in secondary classrooms by David Kobrin, author of Beyond the Textbook: Teaching History Using Documents and Primary Sources, the students' sense of "why they might want to work as student historians–their involvement with history–was strengthened and broadened by the experience of working with challenging primary sources." In fact, he reports that students he worked with in the Providence, RI, public schools found "their own reasons to study history using primary sources."

While it is very important to establish a historical context for student use of archival sources in a classroom, their use can be beneficial in many curricular areas, not just history class. The appendices of this volume contain several charts designed to identify the various types of documents included in this four-volume compilation (Appendix A), possible uses of the documents across the curriculum (Appendices B and C), and connections between Teaching activities and national standards (Appendices D, E, and F). The charts, developed by the education staff, are based on current curriculum guides and frameworks and correlate with the National Standards for History and the National Standards for Civics and Government published by the National Center for History in the Schools, 1996, and the Center for Civic Education, 1994.

Early in the program, history and government teachers embraced these materials and opportunities. They were soon followed by educators from other curricular areas, and most recently, this audience has grown to include many technology educators and media resource specialists. As they seek ways to teach students the skills that will ensure their success in the information age, they have found that instruction through primary sources develops many of the most important skills. While primary sources provide students with tangible links to the past, they also

>   Encourage critical thinking
>
>   Make students question where information comes from
>
>   Drive students to determine validity and reliability of sources
>
>   Push students to consider and recognize bias, and
>
>   Enable students to realize the importance of referencing multiple resources for information.

These are the same skills that may ensure student success in the information age—what is past is prologue.

Lee Ann Potter
Wynell Schamel
May 2002

For More Information

The National Archives and Records Administration brings its rich and varied resources to the public through educational workshops and materials, exhibitions, film programs, publications, lectures, genealogy programs, tours, online services, and other outreach activities. For more information on these opportunities contact Education and Volunteer Programs Staff at the National Archives and Records Administration, 700 Pennsylvania Avenue, NW, Washington, DC 20408; or e-mail education@nara.gov.

"The Alternative of Williamsburg":
A British Cartoon on Colonial American Violence, 1775

In the summer of 1774, the Revolutionary crisis in the American colonies moved into its last and decisive stage. The Continental Congress launched an economic embargo against England in September 1774 by adopting the Articles of Association. The terms of this embargo–nonimportation, nonexportation, and nonconsumption–had serious ramifications both in the colonies and in Great Britain.

The year between the summers of 1774 and 1775 proved dangerous to Loyalists who chose not to comply with the rules of the Association. In Virginia many Loyalists encountered the wrath of the Patriots. For example, Robert Shedden, a Scottish merchant in Norfolk, was severely censured for having sent orders for goods to Andrew Lynn of Glasgow. The committee of Accomac declared Arthur Upshur "out of favor with the country" and fined him £100 for a similar offense. Committee members in the port of Yorktown, VA, forced a vessel belonging to the prestigious London firm of merchant John Norton to return to England without unloading because its cargo included a small shipment of tea.

Twelve miles away in the colonial capital of Williamsburg, Patriots erected a scaffold from which they hung a cask of tar and a barrel of feathers. The Patriots compelled several recalcitrant merchants to appear before the threatening scaffold and sign an endorsement of the Articles of Association. That Williamsburg scene became the subject of Philip Dawe's anti-American mezzotint, "The Alternative of Williamsburg," which satirized the widespread use of physical violence in 18th-century American colonial society. Printed in London for R. Sager and J. Bennett on February 16, 1775, the political cartoon has been preserved in the Records of Exposition, Anniversary, and Memorial Commissions, Record Group 148, as part of the records of the George Washington Bicentennial Commission for the Celebration of the Two Hundredth Anniversary of the Birth of George Washington in 1932. An analysis of the events in Virginia and the other British American colonies that inspired the production of Dawe's mezzotint helps explain its contents.

BACKGROUND

Most American colonists believed that the advantages of belonging to the British Empire outweighed the disadvantages until the British Parliament passed a series of laws in 1767, called the Townshend Acts, to tax the colonists in order to pay the increasing costs of maintaining the British Empire. When these unpopular laws were enacted, the Virginia House of Burgesses, meeting in Williamsburg on May 16, 1769, unanimously adopted a set of resolutions. These included an assertion that the right to tax Virginians belonged solely to the House of Burgesses. The following day, Baron de Botetourt, the British Governor of Virginia, promptly dissolved the Virginia assembly. The next day the Burgesses met informally in Williamsburg's Raleigh Tavern and adopted the Virginia Association, a resolution that was quickly copied by the other colonies. The Virginia Association banned importation of British goods, slaves, and many European luxury goods. Maryland followed suit in June, South Carolina in July, Georgia in September, and North Carolina in November. The rest of the American colonies drew up nonimportation pledges or tightened sanctions already in place.

Throughout the colonies, strong-arm tactics were used by the Sons of Liberty–vigilante groups who often disguised themselves as laborers, blacks, or Indians–to enforce these "voluntary" agreements. Consequently, the British repealed the hated Townshend duties (except the tax on tea) by 1770.

The relatively calm period that prevailed following the repeal of the Townshend Acts quickly erupted into violent protest after Parliament's passage of the Tea Act in 1773. Perceiving that the new legislation undercut the colonies' political and economic position, Sons of Liberty bands throughout the Ameri-

Document 1.1 "The Alternative of Williamsburg," printed in London for R. Sayer and J. Bennett, February 16, 1775. [National Archives]

can colonies protested and frequently prevented the unloading of British tea. The most vivid incident was the Boston Tea Party in December 1773. Parliament retaliated the following year with the Coercive Acts (referred to as the Intolerable Acts by the colonists). These acts, especially the first such measure, the Boston Port Act, created economic stagnation and suffering and served to incite the otherwise cautious colonists into active protest. Patriots in Williamsburg, VA, declared June 1, the day set for closing the port of Boston, as a day of fasting and prayer in support of Massachusetts citizens. Furthermore, the Virginia assembly denounced the occupation of the port of Boston by British troops as a "hostile invasion." Fearing similar treatment for any colony that displeased Parliament, all the colonies except Georgia sent delegates to Philadelphia in September of 1774 to formulate a united stand against recent British colonial policy.

This body, meeting in Philadelphia's Carpenters Hall, became the First Continental Congress. It passed the Declaration of Rights on October 14 and the Articles of Association on October 20. The Declaration of Rights fulfilled the resolution of the delegates to "state the rights of the colonies," which they declared to be the same "rights, liberties, and immunities of free and natural-born subjects, within the realm of England." The preamble to the Association asserted, "We, his Majesty's most loyal subjects . . . affected with the deepest anxiety and most alarming apprehensions . . . find, that the present unhappy situation of our affairs is occasioned by a ruinous System of colony administration . . . evidently calculated for enslaving these colonies and with them the British Empire." Fourteen articles list the grievances of the colonists and outline action to be taken by the colonies that, like the earlier resolves made in the separate colonies, included nonimportation, nonconsumption, and nonexportation of British goods. The Association also provided for committees to be "chosen in every county, city and town . . . to observe the conduct of all persons touching this association . . . ," for committees of correspondence in each colony to inspect the customhouses and "to inform each other, from time to time, of the true state thereof . . . ," and for violators to be punished by publicity and boycott. The document concluded with a pledge binding the members to the Association and a recommendation that the various colonies establish regulations to carry out the plan of the Congress.

The embryonic government structure in Philadelphia matured in the crucial year of 1775. Colonists developed effective economic resistance, extralegal institutions of political control, and a revolutionary military organization. According to historian Warren Billings, the colonies "moved from sporadic protests against specific acts to a sustained and concerted movement by a people capable of fighting a long war, forming effective governments, administering extensive territories, and, to some degree, reordering American society."

In Virginia additional provincial conventions met in March, June, and December and became a de facto legislative body to organize military resistance and pass binding ordinances. In July, Virginia established a Committee of Safety to administer the affairs of the colony between sessions of the convention. Both the conventions and the Committee of Safety raised, equipped, and provided training for colonial military forces. On the local level, Patriots in Virginia established county committees to enforce the articles of the Continental Association and to raise forces for local defense. At least 33 counties and three towns, including Williamsburg, established committees by early 1775. These local instruments of resistance rallied much support for the Association and, after the first shots were fired at Lexington and Concord in April 1775, for the Revolution.

The local committees, often self-appointed and usually composed of the Sons of Liberty, loosely interpreted the authorization of the Continental Congress to observe, condemn, and publicize the conduct of those citizens who refused to pledge. In an effort to weed out disloyal or wavering colonists who would not Associate, committee members looked into private papers, monitored individuals' conduct, and reported suspects. The repercussions of engaging in disloyal activities–defined as passing information to known Loyalists, recruiting for the British, assisting Loyalist refugees, breaking the embargo, and even drinking tea–could be severe. Punishments included intimidation, vilification, humiliation, whipping, beating, and tarring and feathering. Historian Catherine Crary commented that "tarring and feathering, followed by a rough ride on a rail or a parade through the town amid the scorn and derision of the mob, was no mild punishment, but an effective one which the Tories seriously dreaded."

The price of loyalty to the Crown in Virginia and the other colonies could be very high, as Dawe's mezzotint suggests. Tar and feathers hang threateningly over the scene as colonists, holding crude clubs, knives, and scissors, coerce merchants and other Loyalists into signing the nonimportation agreement and even into taking an oath of allegiance to the new Continental Congress. The colonists' esteem for John Wilkes, a Londoner and political radical who championed individual liberty and fought for his seat in the House of Commons, is indicated by the gift of tobacco on which the colonists force the Loyalists to sign. The statue of Botetourt, an actual statue found in Williamsburg, represents the relations between the British and the colonies. Botetourt was a popular Governor in Virginia and was mourned and buried with high style in the Chapel of William and Mary in 1770. The "alternative" of Williamsburg, that is, the alternative to refusing to sign the agreement, presumably includes tarring and feathering, clubbing, or worse. Although these and other particulars of the cartoon's contents and significance may be argued, cartoons, in the words of M. D. George, author of "America in English Satirical Prints," provide "immediate reactions to events, . . . trends of propaganda, waves of emotion, common assumptions, myths, fantasies, distorting mirrors, political climates–. . . what is called public opinion." The featured document reveals volumes about British perceptions of events unfolding in the rebellious colonies.

SELECTED BIBLIOGRAPHY

Billings, Warren, John Selby, and Thad Tate. *Colonial Virginia: A History.* White Plains: KTO Press, 1986.

Crary, Catherine, ed. *The Price of Loyalty: Tory Writings From the Revolutionary Era.* New York: McGraw-Hill Book Company, 1973.

Thomas, Peter, ed. *The American Revolution: The English Satirical Print 1600-1832.* Cambridge: Chadwyck-Healey, 1986.

Note: When the First Continental Congress met on September 5, 1774, in Philadelphia, one of its earliest acts was to elect Charles Thomson as Secretary of the Congress. He served in this capacity for both the Continental Congress and its successor, the Congress of the Confederation, for 15 years–until the establishment of the Federal Government in 1789. Thanks to Thomson's conscientious care, the "Papers of the Continental Congress," now in the National Archives of the United States, provide modern historians with a rich record of events during the formative years of the United States. The Articles of Association are included in the Records of the Continental and Confederation Congresses and the Constitutional Convention, Record Group 360, and have been reproduced by the National Archives in a documentary teaching package entitled The Constitution: Evolution of a Government, published by ABC-CLIO. For more information, contact the Education Staff at education@nara.gov, or access the Digital Classroom at http://www.archives.gov/digital_classroom.

TEACHING ACTIVITIES

Cartoon Analysis

1. Use the Cartoon Analysis worksheet (see Appendix H) with your students to analyze the document.

Cartoon Techniques

2. Help your students to define the following techniques: symbolism, ridicule, caricature, metaphor, satire, and puns. Ask them to find examples of each of these techniques in the cartoon. Identify with the class the dominant techniques used by this cartoonist. The most effective cartoons use symbols and other devices that are unusual, simple, and direct. You might invite an art teacher to join in a class discussion on the elements that make a cartoon effective. Direct the students to write a paragraph evaluating the effectiveness of Dawe's use of symbols and each of the other techniques identified in this mezzotint.

Time Line

3. Use the note to the teacher, textbooks, and other secondary sources to make a time line of the events surrounding the topic of this cartoon. Divide the class into groups of three, give each group a copy of the time line, and ask them to create a line drawing to represent each entry on the time line. As an alternative, this activity could be used as an evaluation tool at the end of a unit on pre-revolutionary American history. Give the students a list of events surrounding the topic, and ask each one to place the items on a time line and to draw a representative visual for each entry.

Point of View

4. Write the following questions on the chalkboard for your students to consider aloud: From whose point of view is this cartoon drawn? What evidence do you see of the cartoonist's viewpoint? What traits make you feel sympathetic or unsympathetic to the cartoon's point of view? After discussion, ask them to locate a cartoon, broadside, poem, or pamphlet that takes a different point of view of the events related to this cartoon and then to write a paragraph comparing the similarities and differences of the two opposing items.

Opposing Perspectives

5. Discuss with your students how we know that the cartoon is drawn from the British perspective, what attitudes are expressed by the artist, and what the British might lose in a conflict against the colonies besides economic advantages. Ask students to locate three political cartoons on any subject that they like, analyze the perspective each cartoon takes, and draw a new cartoon that takes the opposite view to one of their selections. Mount these opposing cartoon pairs in a bulletin board display.

National Archives Document Citation

"The Alternative of Williamsburg," printed in London for R. Sayer and J. Bennett, February 16, 1775; Celebration of the Two Hundredth Anniversary of the Birth of George Washington; Records of the George Washington Bicentennial Commission; Records of Exposition, Anniversary, and Memorial Commissions, Record Group 148; National Archives at College Park, College Park, MD.

Article Citation

Harper, John, Wynell Schamel, and Beth Haverkamp. "The Alternative of Williamsburg: A British Cartoon on Colonial American Violence." *Social Education* 60, 4 (April/May 1996): 233-236.

1.2

Navigation Act Broadside, 1785

Although the Treaty of Paris formally ended the American Revolution on September 3, 1783, tensions between the former warring nations remained. The leaders of the former colonies faced the tasks of creating a new government and, at the same time, establishing a presence in the world. Their relations with old antagonists like the British caused special problems.

The British felt no need to cooperate with their former colonies; on the contrary, they pressured the insolvent new government to honor its treaty obligations, which included compensating Loyalists who had suffered financial losses. Pending satisfaction of those debts, British garrisons remained encamped on the western frontier. To add insult to injury, British merchants viewed the new nation as an ideal market for their goods. After the interruption of trade by the Revolution, British merchants flooded U.S. seaports with inexpensive and much-desired goods.

U.S. merchants reacted to this British competition with anger, echoing cries of earlier years. The threat to the healthy markets they had enjoyed during the military hostilities added to their ire. They petitioned their state legislators and the Congress to regulate trade between the new states and international commerce. As before the Revolution, the Massachusetts merchants voiced their concern with great force. By June 1785, under pressure from the merchants, the Massachusetts legislature formally acted to assume responsibility for regulating trade between the state and other nations. The Massachusetts act admonished the Congress to take up the matter and to provide leadership in controlling international commerce for all the states.

The four years between the Treaty of Paris and the Constitutional Convention exposed several weaknesses of the government as established by the Articles of Confederation. In addition to the problem of maintaining a simple quorum at meetings, the Congress balanced precariously between lack of leadership and the ever-in-creasing demands of the states. The regulation of commerce languished as one of the issues awaiting action.

A meeting in Annapolis, Md., in 1786, was initially called to resolve differences between Maryland and Virginia over control of the Potomac River. It evolved to include representatives from five states. The experienced politicians in Annapolis quickly recognized that the problems of trade, both internal and international, were clear evidence of the inadequacies of the confederation. The Annapolis Convention adjourned without resolving the trade issues, but with a call for a convention to reform the governing system established by the Articles of Confederation. Within a year, the meeting called for in Annapolis convened in Philadelphia to revise the Articles of Confederation. Article 1, section 8, of the new U.S. Constitution created by the convention placed control of commerce squarely in the hands of the federal government. The demands of the Massachusetts merchants, as illustrated here, were finally resolved.

The document is from the Papers of the Continental Congress, 1774-1789, item 42, volume 1, page 350, Record Group 360. Thanks go to James Schweiger, Dover High School, Dover, Del., for identifying this document as one of interest to students and of use to teachers.

TEACHING ACTIVITIES

Some 18th-century language and printing styles may confuse students. We suggest that you review this document with students before making any assignment. Be sure to point out the archaic use of "f" as "s" in the text.

1. The word puzzle on page 9 is designed to encourage students to read the document carefully. You may want to use the puzzle as a homework assignment before you discuss the document.

2. To help students understand the document, ask them to answer each of the following

BOSTON. *April* 18, 1785.

The Minds of the People being greatly and juftly agitated by the apparent Intention of the Government and the Merchants of Great-Britain to deprive the induftrious Trader of every Benefit of our Commerce, by the entire Monopoly of the fame to themfelves; and this Apprehenfion being increafed by authentic Advices received by the laft Ships---A numerous and refpectable Meeting of the Merchants, Traders, and others, convened at Faneuil-Hall, on Saturday the 16th Inft. to confider the alarming State of our Trade and Navigation, the following Votes were unanimoufly agreed to :---

WHEREAS *no commercial treaty is at prefent eftablifhed between thefe United States and Great-Britain: and whereas certain Britifh merchants, factors, and agents, from England, are now refiding in this town, who have received large quantities of Englifh goods; and are in expectation of receiving farther fupplies, imported in Britifh bottoms, or otherways, greatly to the hindrance of freight in all American veffels; and as many more fuch perfons are daily expected to arrive among us, which threatens an entire monopoly of all Britifh importations in the hands of all fuch merchants, agents, or factors, which cannot but operate to the effential prejudice of the intereft of this country:*

THEREFORE, to prevent, as far as poffible, the evil tendency of fuch perfons continuing among us (excepting thofe of them who fhall be approbated by the Selectmen) and to difcourage the fale of their merchandize—WE the merchants, traders, and others, of the town of Bofton, DO AGREE,

THAT a committee be appointed to draft a petition to Congrefs, reprefenting the embarrafsments under which the trade now labours, and the ftill greater to which it is expofed; and that the faid committee be empowered and directed to write to the merchants in the feveral fea-ports in this State, requefting them to join with the merchants in this town in a fimilar application to Congrefs, immediately to regulate the trade of the United States, agreeably to the powers vefted in them by the government of this Commonwealth; and alfo to obtain inftructions to their reprefentatives at the next General Court, to call the attention of their delegates in Congrefs, to the importance of bringing forward fuch regulations as fhall place our commerce on a footing of equality.

VOTED, That the faid committee be requefted to write to the merchants in the feveral fea-ports of the other United States, earneftly recommending to them an immediate application to the Legiflatures of their refpective States, to veft fuch powers in Congrefs (if not already done) as fhall be competent to the interefting purpofes aforefaid; and alfo to petition Congrefs, to make fuch regulations as fhall have the defired effect.

VOTED, That we do pledge our honor, that we will not directly, or indirectly, purchafe any goods of, or have any commercial connections whatever with, fuch Britifh merchants, factors, or agents, as are now refiding among us, or may hereafter arrive either from England, or any part of the Britifh dominions (except fuch perfons as fhall be approved as aforefaid)—and we will do all in our power to prevent all perfons acting under us, from having any commercial intercourfe with them until the falutary purpofes of thefe refolutions fhall have been accomplifhed.

VOTED, That we will not let or fell any warehoufe, fhop, houfe, or any other place for the fale of fuch goods, nor will we employ any perfons who will affift faid merchants, factors or agents by trucks, carts, barrows or labor (except in the refhipment of their merchandize) but will DISCOUNTENANCE all fuch perfons who fhall in any way advife, aid, or in the leaft degree, help or fupport fuch merchants, factors or agents, in the profecution of their bufinefs, *as we conceive all fuch Britifh importations are calculated to drain us of our currency, and have a direct tendency to impoverifh this country.*

VOTED, That a committee be appointed to wait on thofe perfons who have *already let* any warehoufe, fhop, houfe, or any other place, for the difpofal of the merchandize of fuch merchants, agents, or factors, and inform them of the refolutions of this meeting.

VOTED, That we will encourage, all in our power, the manufactures and produce of this country, and will, in all cafes, endeavour to promote them.

VOTED, That a committee be appointed to make immediate application to the Governor and Council of this Commonwealth, requefting them, if they think proper, to direct the feveral Naval-Officers in this State, to grant no permit for the landing of goods from the dominions of Great-Britain configned to, or the property of perfons of the aforefaid defcription, until the meeting of the Legiflature.

VOTED, That copies of thefe refolutions be printed and difperfed among the inhabitants, that they may be adopted and carried into execution, with that temper which is confiftent with the character of good citizens.

☞ *ON our public virtue muft depend the fuccefs of the meafures propofed; and relying on that zeal for the public fafety, which has been fo often and effectually exercifed by this town, they cannot fail of meeting the warm and unanimous approbation of the State in general, and of all thofe who are well-wifhers to the profperity and lafting happinefs of America.*

Document 1.2 Navigation Acts Broadside, 1785. [National Archives]

WORD PUZZLE

```
A  S  U  B  R  O  A  D  S  I  D  E
T  I  O  N  A  F  I  N  D  E  A  B
S  U  T  B  A  Y  O  W  R  T  U  O
M  O  S  F  R  I  D  O  P  D  X  Y
B  O  M  O  N  O  P  O  L  Y  U  C
D  O  M  I  S  R  T  A  F  G  H  O
E  R  M  A  F  T  N  A  R  S  I  T
X  O  S  T  H  D  O  G  F  N  M  T
D  F  A  N  E  U  I  L  H  A  L  L
```

Student directions: In the word puzzle find and circle the five words listed below. The words may appear vertically, horizontally, or diagonally.

Boycott _____

Broadside _____

Dominions _____

Faneuil Hall _____

Monopoly _____

Explain in a sentence how each of the terms relates to the document.

questions. Who developed the broadside? Where? When? In a sentence, state the main idea of the document. List the seven actions agreed to by the group. What does the broadside tell you about trade in Massachusetts after the Revolution?

3. One of the actions voted by the Boston merchants outlines a boycott of English goods. Discuss with students the concept of a boycott and direct them to develop a list of international boycotts initiated by the United States in recent years. Consider with students whether or not an international boycott is an effective diplomatic tool.

4. "Isolationism," "interdependence," "free trade," "multinational corporations," "imperialism," "post-industrial," and "monetarism" all describe aspects of the world economy today. Direct students to define these terms and to explain whether or not they can be applied to the world economic situation of the 18th century.

5. The actions proposed by the Boston merchants directly relate to several events described in most textbooks—the navigation acts, Shays' rebellion, and the Annapolis Convention. Assign students to read about one of these events and to explain how the document relates to it.

6. Broadsides such as this served to inform and to persuade citizens in the United States before the widespread use of newspapers. Direct students to develop a broadside of their own design to alert others to an injustice or an issue of special interest. Be sure to encourage students to think about the elements that make up a broadside (e.g., patriotic slogans, visuals, and logical arguments).

National Archives Document Citation

Navigation Acts Broadside, 1785; Item 42, Vol. 1, p. 350; Papers of the Continental Congress, 1774-1789; Records of the Continental and Confederation Congresses and the Constitutional Convention, Record Group 360; National Archives Building, Washington, DC.

Article Citation

Alexander, Mary. "The World Economy: An Early Problem for Young America." *Social Education* 48, 1 (January 1984): 41-43.

Delaware's Ratification of the U.S. Constitution, 1787

On September 17, 1787, a majority of the delegates to the Constitutional Convention approved the document over which they had labored since May. After a farewell banquet, delegates swiftly returned to their homes to organize support, most for but some against the proposed charter. Before the Constitution could become the law of the land, it would have to withstand public scrutiny and debate. The document was "laid before the United States in Congress assembled" on September 20. For 2 days, September 26 and 27, Congress debated whether to censure the delegates to the Constitutional Convention for exceeding their authority by creating a new form of government instead of simply revising the Articles of Confederation. They decided to drop the matter. Instead, on September 28, Congress directed the state legislatures to call ratification conventions in each state. Article 7 stipulated that nine states had to ratify the Constitution for it to go into effect.

Beyond the legal requirements for ratification, the state conventions fulfilled other purposes. The Constitution had been produced in strictest secrecy during the Philadelphia convention. The ratifying conventions served the necessary function of informing the public of the provisions of the proposed new government. They also served as forums for proponents and opponents to articulate their ideas before the citizenry. Significantly, state conventions, not Congress, were the agents of ratification. This approach insured that the Constitution's authority came from representatives of the people specifically elected for the purpose of approving or disapproving the charter, resulting in a more accurate reflection of the will of the electorate. Also, by bypassing debate in the state legislatures, the Constitution avoided disabling amendments that states, jealous of yielding authority to a national government, would likely have attached.

Ratification was not a foregone conclusion. Able, articulate men used newspapers, pamphlets, and public meetings to debate ratification of the Constitution. Those known as Antifederalists opposed the Constitution for a variety of reasons. Some continued to argue that the delegates in Philadelphia had exceeded their congressional authority by replacing the Articles of Confederation with an illegal new document. Others complained that the delegates in Philadelphia represented only the well-born few and consequently had crafted a document that served their special interests and reserved the franchise for the propertied classes. Another frequent objection was that the Constitution gave too much power to the central government at the expense of the states and that representative government could not manage a republic this large. The most serious criticism was that the Constitutional Convention had failed to adopt a bill of rights proposed by George Mason. In New York, Governor George Clinton expressed these Antifederalist concerns in several published newspaper essays under the pen name Cato, while Patrick Henry and James Monroe led the opposition in Virginia.

Those who favored ratification, the Federalists, fought back, convinced that rejection of the Constitution would result in anarchy and civil strife. Alexander Hamilton, James Madison, and John Jay responded to Clinton under the name of Publius. Beginning in October 1787, these three penned 85 essays for New York newspapers and later collected them into 2 volumes entitled The Federalist, which analyzed the Constitution, detailed the thinking of the framers, and responded to the Antifederalist critics.

They successfully countered most criticism. As for the lack of a bill of rights, Federalists argued that a catalogued list might be incomplete and that the national government was so constrained by the Constitution that it posed no threat to the rights of citizens. Ultimately, during the ratification debate in Virginia, Madison conceded that a bill of rights was needed, and the Federalists assured the public that the first step of the new government would be to adopt a bill of rights.

We the Deputies of the People of the Delaware State in Convention met, having taken into our serious consideration the Federal Constitution proposed and agreed upon by the Deputies of the United States in a General Convention held at the City of Philadelphia on the seventeenth day of September in the year of our Lord one thousand seven hundred and eighty seven, Have approved, assented to, ratified and confirmed, and by these Presents Do, in virtue of the Power and Authority to us given for that purpose, for and in behalf of ourselves and our Constituents, fully, freely, and entirely approve of, assent to, ratify and confirm the said Constitution.

Done in Convention at Dover this seventh day of December in the year aforesaid, and in the year of the Independence of the United States of America the twelfth. In Testimony whereof we have hereunto subscribed our Names.

(signatures of Delaware delegates by county: New Castle, Kent, and Sussex Counties)

Document 1.3 Delaware's Ratification of the U.S. Constitution, 1787. [National Archives]

It took 10 months for the first nine states to approve the Constitution. The first state to ratify was Delaware, on December 7, 1787, by a unanimous vote, 30-0. The featured document is an endorsed ratification of the federal Constitution by the Delaware convention. The names of the state deputies are listed, probably in the hand of a clerk. The signature of the president of Delaware's convention, Thomas Collins, attests to the validity of the document, which also carries the state seal in its left margin. Delaware's speediness thwarted Pennsylvania's attempt to be first to ratify in the hope of securing the seat of the national government in Pennsylvania.

The first real test for ratification occurred in Massachusetts, where the fully recorded debates reveal that the recommendation for a bill of rights proved to be a remedy for the logjam in the ratifying convention. New Hampshire became the ninth state to approve the Constitution, in June, but the key states of Virginia and New York were locked in bitter debates. Their failure to ratify would reduce the new union by two large, populated, wealthy states, and would geographically splinter it. The Federalists prevailed, however, and Virginia and New York narrowly approved the Constitution. When a bill of rights was proposed in Congress in 1789, North Carolina ratified the Constitution. Finally, Rhode Island, which had rejected the Constitution in March 1788 by popular referendum, called a ratifying convention in 1790 as specified by the Constitutional Convention. Faced with threatened treatment as a foreign government, it ratified the Constitution by the narrowest margin, two votes, on May 29, 1790.

The Delaware ratification is taken from RG 11, the General Records of the U.S. Government.

TEACHING ACTIVITIES

1. Prepare students to work with a 200-year-old document by discussing such unique qualities as handwriting, spelling, formation of the letter "s," vocabulary, style, and the use of parchment and iron-based ink (which bleeds through in time). Distribute copies of the document. Read aloud the first two lines of the transcription as the students read the document silently. As a group activity, the students should continue reading the document aloud. You may help them if they stumble. Discuss the advantages and disadvantages of working with a handwritten original source.

2. Provide a copy of the Constitution for each student. Ask students to consult articles 5 and 7 along with the Delaware ratification document and compare point by point the procedures for ratifying the Constitution with the procedures for ratifying amendments to the Constitution.

3. Instruct the students to research the arguments of the debate over ratification. You could share the information in this article with your class. Ask the students to list the arguments of the Antifederalists and the counterarguments of the Federalists and then write a paragraph in response to these questions: What has been the outcome of these arguments? Are the arguments significant today?

4. Consider the Constitution as a framework of government. On the chalkboard make a list with your students of practical steps needed to activate the Constitution and institute a government, beginning with the ratification procedures, election of the President, selection of a capital site, etc. The resolution of the Constitutional Convention on September 17, 1787, sometimes referred to as the fifth page of the Constitution, is a good resource for this activity. In a discussion of these steps, lead your students to recognize the difference between the theory in a document written to describe a government and the reality of putting a government into action.

5. Assign your students to research the ratification story in specific states (their own home states and states selected as case studies). Set up a story-telling day in which each student tells the best stories they found in their research.

6. The delegates of the Delaware convention whose names appear on the ratification document provide an interesting sociological study. Ask your students to look carefully at the names and describe the patterns or categories they recognize. Note: Your students should observe the emerging patterns of ethnic groups, the sex, and the origin of the names listed.

Order	State	Date	Votes for	Votes against
1	Delaware	December 7, 1787	30	0
2	Pennsylvania	December 12, 1787	46	23
3	New Jersey	December 18, 1787	38	0
4	Georgia	January 2, 1788	26	0
5	Connecticut	January 9, 1788	128	40
6	Massachusetts	February 6, 1788	187	168
7	Maryland	April 28, 1788	63	11
8	South Carolina	May 23, 1788	149	73
9	New Hampshire	June 21, 1788	57	47
10	Virginia	June 25, 1788	89	79
11	New York	July 26, 1788	30	27
12	North Carolina	November 21, 1789	194	77
13	Rhode Island	May 29, 1790	34	32

National Archives Document Citation

Delaware's Ratification of the U.S. Constitution, 1787; The Constitution Papers (National Archives Microfilm Publication M338, roll 1); Certificates of Ratification of the Constitution and the Bill of Rights, Including Correspondence and Rejections of Proposed Amendments, 1787-1792; General Records of the United States Government, Record Group 11; National Archives Building, Washington, DC.

Article Citation

Gray, Leslie and Wynell Burroughs. "The Ratification of the Constitution." *Social Education* 51, 5 (September 1987): 322-324.

Text of the Document

We the Deputies of the People of Delaware State in Convention met having taken into our serious consideration the Federal Constitution proposed and agreed upon by the Deputies of the United States in a General Convention held at the City of Philadelphia on the seventeenth day of September in the year of our Lord one thousand seven hundred and eighty seven, Have approved, assented to, ratified, and confirmed and by these Presents, Do, in virtue of the Power and Authority to us given for the purpose for and in behalf of ourselves and our Constituents, fully, freely, and entirely approve of, assent to, ratify, and confirm the said Constitution.

Done in Convention at Dover this seventh day of December in the year aforesaid and in the year of the Independence of the United States of America the twelfth. In Testimony whereof we have hereunto subscribed our Names

To all whom these Presents shall come Greeting. I Thomas Collins President of the Delaware State do hereby certify that the above instrument of writing is a true copy of the original ratification of the Federal Constitution by the Convention of the Delaware State which original ratification is now in my possession. In Testimony whereof l have caused the seal of the Delaware State to be hereunto anexed.

Tho.[s] Collins

Sussex County
John Ingram
John Jones
William Moore
William Hall
Thomas Laws
Isaac Cooper
Woodman Storkly
John Laws
Thomas Evans
Israel Holland

Kent County
Nicholas Ridgely
Richard Smith
George Truitt
Richard Bassett
James Sykes
Allen McLane
Daniel Cummins, Sr.
Joseph Barker
Edward White
George Manlove

New Castle County
Ja.[s] Latimer, President
James Black
Jn.[a] James
Gunning Bedford, Sr.
Kensey Johns
Thomas Watson
Solomon Maxwell
Nicholas Way
Thomas Duff
Gunn.g Bedford, Jr.

The Wording of the First Amendment Religion Clauses, 1789

Although Virginia and Rhode Island guaranteed religious freedom in their state constitutions, and the Northwest Ordinance of 1787 included a bill of rights guaranteeing religious freedom in the territories, the Constitutional Convention did not adopt a statement concerning religious freedom. The only time the subject of religion specifically arises in the Constitution is in Article VI. In setting qualifications for federal office, the delegates determined that "no religious Test shall ever be required as a Qualification to any Office or public trust under the United States." The omission of a bill of rights guaranteeing religious freedom and other civil liberties nearly prevented ratification of the Constitution.

To remedy this shortcoming, James Madison, borrowing heavily from the Virginia Declaration of Rights, drafted a bill of rights, which included a clause on religious freedom, for consideration by the first U.S. Congress. In Madison's original proposal, submitted to the House of Representatives on June 8, 1789, the religion clauses were worded as follows:

> The civil rights of none shall be abridged on account of religious belief or worship, nor shall any national religion be established, nor shall the full and equal rights of conscience be in any manner, or on any pretext infringed.

Madison's proposals, along with amendments suggested by the states, were considered by a select committee of the House, composed of one member from each of the 11 states. On July 28, the committee reported Madison's text in a shortened version as follows:

> No religion shall be established by law, nor shall the equal rights of conscience be infringed.

During the debate in the House, several Congressmen expressed fear that the language might be interpreted to mean that religion should be abolished altogether. The wording as eventually passed by the House on August 24 read:

> Congress shall make no law establishing religion or prohibiting the free exercise thereof, nor shall the rights of Conscience be infringed.

Written as Article 3, this proposed amendment and 16 additional amendments were sent to the Senate the following day.

When the Senate finally took up the subject of the amendments on September 2, the record shows that three alternative wordings were debated in the chamber. Motions were also made and rejected to strike the article completely and to adopt the article as it was worded by the House. In a strong editing session, the Senate slashed wordiness freely, fusing articles and reducing the 17 amendments passed by the House to 12. Articles 3 and 4 were combined to read

> Congress shall make no law establishing articles of faith, or a mode of worship, or prohibiting the free exercise of religion, or abridging the freedom of speech, or of the press, or the right of the people peaceably to assemble, and to petition to the government for the redress of grievances.

The revised articles were sent back to the House on September 9 for concurrence. A conference committee, appointed to settle the differences between the two houses, changed the disputed phrase "establishing articles of faith" to "an establishment of religion," and on September 25 both houses approved the 12 amendments as presented by the joint conference. The final wording, "Congress shall make no law respecting an establishment of religion, or prohibiting the free exercise thereof," was ratified by the states as the First Amendment.

This document is taken from the *Journal of Proceedings of the U.S. Senate, First Session, First Con-*

gress, which was printed in 1820 by Gales and Seaton in Washington, DC, and was based on the original minutes of the clerk of the Senate. The journal is found in the Records of the U.S. Senate, Record Group 46, in the National Archives and Records Administration.

TEACHING ACTIVITIES

Document Analysis

1. Ask students to read the document closely and answer the following questions:

   a. What type of document is this?

   b. When was it created?

   c. Who created it?

   d. Why was it created?

   e. What is recorded in the document about the proposed Constitutional amendments?

   f. Why do you think the First Amendment is referred to as the third article in this document?

   g. What do you think happened to the document prior to this recorded debate?

   h. What do you think happened to it next?

2. Discuss the students' responses, and drawing from the note to the teacher, share additional information about the document.

Writing the First Amendment

3. Direct students' attention to the section beginning "On motion to amend article third. . ." Ask students to write the First Amendment as it would have been worded if any of the three alternative wordings had been adopted. Write on the chalkboard additional wordings considered by the Congress that are mentioned in the historical background. Discuss what the reasons may have been for rejection of the alternative wordings and the pros and cons of the various wordings. Who in the Congress might have supported each of the wordings? Ask for a show of hands for the wording that the students favor.

Background of the Government and Religious Freedom

4. Ask students to review the Northwest Ordinance; the Virginia Declaration of Rights; the Constitution, Article VI, Section 3, and the First and 14th Amendments, and trace the history of the religion clauses in these documents. Assign students to further research, and present to the class ideas about the government's role vis-a-vis religion expressed by John Locke, Sir Henry Vane the Younger, John Winthrop, Roger Williams, Anne Hutchinson, Isaac Backus, Thomas Paine, George Mason, James Madison, Thomas Jefferson, Patrick Henry, William Penn, John Adams, and George Washington. Discuss the similarities and differences between each person's opinion and the position of the present administration as to the role of government and religion.

National Archives Document Citation

Journal of the Proceedings of the U.S. Senate, First Session, First Congress; Printed in 1820 by Gales and Seaton; Records of the U.S. Senate, Record Group 46; National Archives Building, Washington, DC.

Article Citation

Schamel, Wynell. "The Wording of the First Amendment Religion Clauses." *Roger Williams Report* 1991.

poses;" and the bill, entitled "An act to establish the Treasury Department," for his approbation.

Adjourned to 11 o'clock to-morrow.

WEDNESDAY, SEPTEMBER 2, 1789.

The Senate assembled: present as yesterday.

The bill, entitled "An act to provide for the safe keeping of the acts, records, and seal of the United States, and for other purposes," was read the third time, and

Ordered, That it be committed to Mr. King, Mr. Paterson, and Mr. Read.

The third reading of the bill, entitled "An act for establishing the salaries of the executive officers of government, with their assistants and clerks," was further postponed.

The petition of Harman Stout and others, in behalf of themselves and other clerks in the public offices, was read.

Ordered, That the said petition lie for consideration.

The resolve of the House of Representatives of the 24th of August, one thousand seven hundred and eighty nine, "that certain articles be proposed to the legislatures of the several states, as amendments to the constitution of the United States;" was taken into consideration; and, on motion to amend this clause in the first article, proposed by the House of Representatives, to wit: 'After the first enumeration required by the first article of the constitution, there shall be one representative for every thirty thousand, until the number shall amount to one hundred, by striking out 'one,' and inserting 'two,' between the words 'amount' and 'hundred:'

The yeas and nays being required by one-fifth of the Senators present, the determination was as follows:

YEAS.—Messrs. Dalton, Gunn, Grayson, King, Lee, and Schuyler.—6.

NAYS.—Messrs. Bassett, Butler, Carroll, Ellsworth, Elmer, Henry, Johnson, Izard, Morris, Paterson, Read, and Wingate.—12.

So it passed in the negative.

On motion to adopt the first article proposed by the resolve of the House of Representatives, amended as follows: to strike out these words 'after which the proportion shall be so regulated by Congress, that there shall be not less than one hundred representatives, nor less than one representative for every forty thousand persons, until the number of representatives shall amount to two hundred; after which the proportion shall be so regulated by Congress, that there shall not be less than two hundred representatives, nor less than one representative to every fifty thousand persons;' and to substitute the following clause after the words 'one hundred:' to wit, 'to which number one representative shall be added for every subsequent increase of forty thousand, until the representatives shall amount to two hundred, to which one representative shall be added for every subsequent increase of sixty thousand persons:'

It passed in the affirmative.

Adjourned to 11 o'clock to-morrow.

THURSDAY, SEPTEMBER 3, 1789.

The Senate assembled: present as yesterday,

And resumed the consideration of the resolve of the House of Representatives, of the 24th of August, upon the proposed amendments to the constitution of the United States.

A message from the House of Representatives:

Mr. Beckley, their Clerk, informed the Senate, that the President of the United States had affixed his signature to the bill, entitled "An act for registering and clearing of vessels, regulating the coasting trade, and for other purposes;" and to the bill, entitled "An act to establish the Treasury Department;" and had returned them to the House of Representatives;

He also brought up the bill, entitled "An act for allowing compensation to the members of the Senate and House of Representatives of the United States, and to the officers of both Houses;" and informed the Senate, that the House of Representatives had disagreed to the first, second, and third amendments, and had agreed to all the others;

He also brought up the bill, entitled "An act to suspend part of the act, entitled "An act to regulate the collection of the duties imposed by law on the tonnage of ships or vessels, and on goods, wares, and merchandises, imported into the United States." And he withdrew.

The two last mentioned bills were ordered to lie for consideration.

The Senate resumed the consideration of the resolve of the House of Representatives on the amendments to the constitution of the United States.

On motion to adopt the second article proposed in the resolve of the House of Representatives, amended as follows: to strike out these words, 'to the members of Congress,' and insert 'for the service of the Senate and House of Representatives of the United States:'

It passed in the affirmative.

On motion to amend article third, and to strike out these words: 'religion, or prohibiting the free exercise thereof,' and insert 'one religious sect or society in preference to others:'

It passed in the negative.

On motion for reconsideration:

It passed in the affirmative.

On motion that article the third be stricken out:

It passed in the negative.

On motion to adopt the following, in lieu of the third article: 'Congress shall not make any law infringing the rights of conscience, or establishing any religious sect or society:'

It passed in the negative.

On motion to amend the third article, to read thus: 'Congress shall make no law establishing any particular denomination of religion in preference to another, or prohibiting the free exercise thereof, nor shall the rights of conscience be infringed:'

It passed in the negative.

On the question upon the third article as it came from the House of Representatives:

It passed in the negative.

On motion to adopt the third article proposed in the resolve of the House of Representatives, amended by striking out thesewords, 'nor shall the rights of conscience be infringed:'

It passed in the affirmative.

On the fourth article it was moved to insert these words, ' to instruct their representatives,' after the words ' common good.'

And the yeas and nays being required by one-fifth of the Senators present, the determination was as follows:

Yeas.—Messrs. Grayson, and Lee.—2.

Nays.—Messrs. Bassett, Carroll, Dalton, Ellsworth, Elmer, Gunn, Henry, Johnson, Izard, King, Morris, Paterson, Read, and Wingate.—14.

So it passed in the negative.

On motion to insert these words after 'press,' 'in as ample a manner as hath at any time been secured by the common law:'

It passed in the negative.

On motion to strike out the words, 'and consult for their common good and:'

It passed in the negative.

And it was agreed, that the further consideration of this article be postponed.

Mr. King, in behalf of the committee appointed on the bill, entitled "An act for allowing compensation to the members of the Senate and House of Representatives of the United States, and to the officers of both Houses," reported amendments: the consideration of which was postponed until to-morrow.

Adjourned to 11 o'clock to-morrow.

FRIDAY, SEPTEMBER 4, 1789.

The Senate assembled: present as yesterday.

The petition of Thomas O'Hara and others, in behalf of themselves and other clerks in the office of the paymaster-general, praying that their compensation may be augmented, was read.

Ordered, That this petition do lie on the table.

The Senate proceeded in the consideration of the resolve of the House of Representatives of the 24th of August, on " Articles to be proposed to the legislatures of the several states, as amendments to the constitution of the United States."

On motion to adopt the fourth article proposed by the resolve of the House of Representatives, to read as followeth: 'That Congress shall make no law, abridging

Jefferson's Letter to Washington Accepting the Position of Secretary of State, 1790

Following the ratification of the Constitution, the Continental Congress established a timetable to begin the operation of the new government. According to schedule, the States chose electors of the President on the first Wednesday in January 1789, the electors chose George Washington President and John Adams Vice President on the first Wednesday in February, and the new Congress organized and began functioning in New York City on the first Wednesday in March. In advance of his March 22, 1790, inauguration, Washington had taken steps to fill the new cabinet. He chose Thomas Jefferson as his Secretary of State. The featured document, found in the General Records of the Department of State, Record Group 59, is Jefferson's February 11, 1790, letter to President-elect Washington accepting his nomination to the position.

TEACHING ACTIVITIES

1. Duplicate and distribute copies of Jefferson's letter and the Written Document Worksheet (see Appendix H) to each student, and project a transparency of the document. Advise students of the differences between handwriting and tone in the 18th century and now. Then, as a class, read the document aloud, either in unison or alternating students line by line.

2. Direct students to complete the worksheet. Once the worksheet is complete, review the document with the students, noting the purpose of the letter, the difficulties of establishing the Government, the location of the capital, and the conditions of communication and transportation during this time period.

3. Ask students to locate the places mentioned in the letter on a United States map. Have them estimate the distances between the places. Ask one or two students to investigate how much time was needed to travel Jefferson's route in 1790 and today. Allow time for them to share their findings with the entire class, possibly sharing 18th-century illustrations of places along the route.

4. Choose a culminating activity from the following.

    a. Ask students to do additional research on Jefferson and the early years of the Department of State and to write an essay explaining how Thomas Jefferson's innovations and actions shaped the role of the Secretary of State.

    b. Encourage students to study the role of Secretary of State as it has evolved. Ask them to assume the role of a contemporary individual offered that cabinet position and to write responses to the President either accepting or declining the post, giving reasons for their decisions.

    c. Ask students to write essays identifying the actions they believe were most crucial to starting the new government. They should explain their reasoning.

National Archives Document Citation

Jefferson's Letter to President Washington Accepting the Position of Secretary of State, February 11, 1790; (National Archives Microfilm Publication M179, roll 3); Letters Received, Miscellaneous Letters of the Department of State, 1789-1906; General Records of the Department of State, Record Group 59; National Archives at College Park, College Park, MD.

Article Citation

Mueller, Jean West. "Documents and Discovery: Jefferson's Letter to Washington Accepting the Position of Secretary of State." *Heritage Education Quarterly* 3, 1 (Spring 1988): 18-21.

Monticello Feb. 14. 1790

I have duly received the letter of the 21st of January with which you have honored me, and no longer hesitate to undertake the office to which you are pleased to call me. your desire that I should come on as quickly as possible is a sufficient reason for me to postpone every matter of business, however pressing, which admits postponement. still it will be the close of the ensuing week before I can get away, & then I shall have to go by the way of Richmond, which will lengthen my road. I shall not fail however to go on with all the dispatch possible nor to satisfy you, I hope, when I shall have the honor of seeing you at New York, that the circumstances which prevent my immediate departure, are not under my controul. I have now that of being with sentiments of the most perfect respect & attachment, Sir

    Your most obedient & most humble servant

         Th: Jefferson

The President of the U.S.

Document 1.5 Jefferson's Letter to President Washington Accepting the Position of Secretary of State, February 11, 1790. [National Archives]

The 1820 Census of Manufactures, 1820

"Their [sic] are very many young Ladies at work in the factories that have given up milinary d[r]essmaking & s[c]hool keeping for work in the mill. But I would not advise any one to do it for I was so sick of it at first I wished the factory had never been thought of. But the longer I stay the better I like. "

Malenda M. Edwards
Nashua, NH
April 4, 1839

Between 1820 and 1860, thousands of young women like Malenda Edwards left their homes on farms in northern New England to work in the mills of expanding factory towns across the northeast. Towns such as Saco and Biddeford, Maine; Lowell, Holyoke, and Lawrence, Massachusetts; and Nashua, Manchester, and Dover, New Hampshire offered women new employment opportunities outside of the home.

The opportunities grew from regional economic conditions that stemmed from reduced European farm production during the Napoleonic Wars. At that time, demand for American food stuffs increased and New England agriculture expanded. Many farmers took out loans, bought additional land to farm, and initially profited. But when Congress passed the Embargo and Non-Intercourse Acts preceding the War of 1812, the New England farmers lost their overseas markets and found themselves in debt. Significantly, many of these same farmers had daughters whose primary domestic occupations had been spinning and weaving.

New England merchants were also suffering economically from the federal government's attempts to deal with the European conflict. They were unable to import many of the products their customers demanded, including cotton cloth. These circumstances led to the establishment of new mills that employed the daughters of many New England farmers and produced domestic textiles that were not affected by the embargo.

One such mill was the Dover Cotton Factory, incorporated in 1812 on the Cocheco River in Dover, New Hampshire. According to the document featured in this article, in 1820 the factory employed 105 women and girls, and paid them four to six dollars per week with board. These wages were relatively high, most textile mills at the time paid "mill girls" between three and four dollars for a six day, 72-hour work week, and sheltered them in company boarding houses. Although the document does not offer additional information about the women and girls employed at the Dover factory, it is probable that they were similar to mill girls elsewhere: single and ranging in age from fifteen to twenty-nine years old, working in the mill off and on for a period of four to five years.

In 1823 the factory changed its name to the Dover Manufacturing Company. Four years later, the factory changed hands, when the Cocheco Manufacturing Company purchased the property and all its works. Although the initial company failed, the cotton industry in Dover eventually thrived and women–first, the daughters of farmers and later, new female immigrants–consistently played an important role.

In 1828, new rules came into effect at all the textile mills in Dover. These rules prohibited unions, reduced wages from fifty-eight cents to fifty-three cents a day, forbade talking between employees during work hours, and imposed twelve and one-half cent fines for being late. Female workers rebelled and on December 30, 1828, Dover was the scene of the first woman's strike in the United States. Half of the 800 mill girls walked off the job and paraded around the red brick buildings with banners, signs, and fireworks. The mill owners responded by simply advertising for 400 replacements. In fear of losing their jobs, the women returned to work. For nearly 100 years the Cocheco Manufacturing Company was quite profitable, due in large part to the long hours and hard work first of the mill girls and later of children.

No. 7.

Questions to be addressed to the Persons concerned in Manufacturing Establishments, by the Marshals and their Assistants, in taking the Account of Manufactures.

Name of the County, Parish, Township Town, or City, where the Manufacture exists. } Dover, County of Strafford

RAW MATERIALS EMPLOYED.
1. The kind?
2. The quantity annually consumed?
3. The cost of the annual consumption?

NUMBER OF PERSONS EMPLOYED.
4. Men?
5. Women?
6. Boys and Girls?

MACHINERY.
7. Whole quantity and kind of Machinery?
8. Quantity of Machinery in operation?

EXPENDITURES.
9. Amount of capital invested?
10. Amount paid annually for wages?
11. Amount of Contingent Expenses?

PRODUCTION.
12. The nature and names of Articles Manufactured?
13. Market value of the Articles which are annually manufactured?

14. General Remarks concerning the Establishment, as to its actual and past condition, the demand for, and sale of, its Manufactures.

Answers to the above Questions— No. 1.

No 1. Cotton.
No 2. From 3 to 11 Bales Cotton per week.
No 3. Average price about 17 cts. per pound
No 4. Fifteen Men
No 5. One Hundred & Five Women & Girls.
No 6. Five Boys.
No 7. 2000 Spindles. Preparation for the same & 50 Power Looms.
No 8. 2000 Spindles & 110 Power Looms.
No 9. Eighty Five Thousand Dollars.
No. 10. Females, From 4/ to 6/ per week & boarded
Boys — 9/ per week & boarded
Men. From 15 to 26$ per mo. & boarded
No. 11. Uncertain.

Document 1.6a1 Dover Cotton Factory, Dover, New Hampshire;
Census of Manufactures, 1820. [National Archives]

No 12. Shirting & Sheeting
No 13. Sheeting 16 cts Shirting 12 cts & fluctuating
No 14. In good repair

Also a Nail Factory which employs about 7 hands, & manufactures about 200 Tons of nails per year —

Joseph W. Page } Assistant

The document featured in this article is taken from the 1820 Census of Manufactures. Interestingly, this document, like the mills, resulted from the economic circumstances of the 1810s. The U.S. Constitution, in Article I, Section 2, provides for a population count to be conducted every ten years. However, from the beginning, it has left to Congress to determine what specific information should be gathered in a census. Often Congress is influenced by economic factors, and this was the case in 1820.

The economic changes experienced by the nation's economy during the period 1810-1820 include the panic of 1819 (caused in part when thousands of New England farmers defaulted on their loans). Subsequent appeals for aid to manufacturers and trade led Congress to provide for a Census of Manufactures to be taken as part of the fourth census. The legislators believed that if they knew more about the various industries in the country, they would be in a better position to legislate for agricultural, commercial, and manufacturing interests.

Because there was no Bureau of the Census at that time, Secretary of State John Quincy Adams directed a team of marshals and assistants to gather information on manufactures. Information from each manufacturer about raw materials, employees, machinery, expenditures, and production in their establishment was recorded primarily on printed forms. Unfortunately, the results of the census were incomplete and far from uniform. Some manufacturers refused to furnish the desired information for fear of being taxed, and the census takers often interpreted their instructions differently.

A summary of the information gathered, however, was printed as the "Digest of Manufacturers" in the American State Papers in early 1823. Although incomplete, the summary and the individual forms do reveal the types of products that were being manufactured in the United States during the early Industrial Revolution: products such as yarn, cotton sheetings, clocks, furniture, hats, paper, rum, saddles, cordage, flour, and lumber. The summary also reveals important sectional differences, such as that most manufacturing establishments were in the North, most northern establishments were significantly larger than those in the South, and many more women and children were employed by factories in the North than in the South.

Due to the negative reaction to the apparent inaccuracies of the 1820 returns, Congress made no provision for an account of manufactures in 1830. Beginning in 1840, however, manufacturing returns were taken every ten years, and in this century, they have been taken even more frequently, the most recent count having been in 1997.

The document featured in this article is the page from the 1820 Census of Manufactures that records information about the Dover Cotton Factory in Dover, New Hampshire. It is from the Records of the Bureau of the Census, RG 29, National Archives and Records Administration, Washington, DC. All of the returns from the 1820 Census of Manufactures, including the featured document, are available on National Archives microfilm publication M279. Copies of National Archives microfilm publications are available in federal depository libraries and may be ordered by calling 1-800-234-8861.

REFERENCES

Davidson, Katherine H. and Charlotte M. Ashby. *Preliminary Inventory of the Records of the Bureau of the Census (PI 161)*. Washington, DC: National Archives, 1964.

Dublin, Thomas, ed. *Farm to Factory: Women's Letters, 1830-1860*. New York: Columbia University Press, 1981.

Heritage Trails in Dover, New Hampshire: Celebrating 375 Years. Dover, NH: Dover Chamber of Commerce, 1998. (www.dovernh.org/heritage.htm)

Woloch, Nancy. *Women and the American Experience*. New York: Knopf, 1984.

TEACHING ACTIVITIES

Introductory Activity

1. Explain to students that although Article I, Section 2, of the U.S. Constitution provides for a population count to be conducted every ten years, acts of Congress determine the specific information that will be gathered in each census and often the acts are influenced by economic factors. Ask students to read the background article or share with them the information from the background essay about the plight of the New England farmers fol-

lowing the Napoleonic Wars. Direct students to read more about the Embargo, the Non-Intercourse Acts, and the Panic of 1819 in their textbooks. Ask students what information they think might have helped Congress make good decisions about how to help the New England economy at the time.

Document Analysis

2. Distribute copies of the document to students. Ask one volunteer to read aloud the first question printed on the form and another volunteer to read aloud its handwritten response. When all of the questions and answers have been read, lead a class discussion using the following questions: What type of document is this? When do you think it was created? Who do you think created it? What type of information does it provide? Who might use the information provided in the document? For what purpose? (You may use the Written Document Analysis Worksheet in Appendix H.)

3. Direct students to reread questions 4, 5, 6, and 10 of the document. Ask students what the answers to these questions reveal about the workforce in the Dover Cotton Factory in 1820. Share with students information from the background essay about women in the workforce during the period 1820-1860. Ask students to generate a list of questions they have about the women, for example, their working conditions, their housing conditions, and their other activities. Next, ask students to generate a list of sources that they think might exist that would provide them with answers to their questions.

Research

4. Assign groups of three to four students a different New England manufacturing town. Possibilities include Saco and Biddeford, Maine; Lowell, Holyoke, and Lawrence, Massachusetts; and Nashua, Manchester, and Dover, New Hampshire. Direct each group to conduct research on their assigned town's manufacturing history using the questions they generated in Activity 2. Ask a representative from each group to report his or her group's findings to the class.

Role Play

5. Ask students to brainstorm a list of ways in which business owners, government officials, and consumers use economic census data such as the information provided in the document. Possible answers include: to gauge competition, to locate business markets, to locate jobs, to compare working conditions, to evaluate investment opportunities, and to set taxes. Divide students into small groups and ask the members of each group to pretend that they work for the Bureau of the Census. Instruct each group to update the 1820 form to include questions helpful to people today and to historians in the future. Each group should choose a representative to take part in a work session to revise the census form by incorporating the best suggestions from each group.

Compare and Contrast (Internet Activity)

6. Inform students that the most recent economic census was taken in 1997. Direct students to the Web site of the Census Bureau at <http://www.census.gov/epcd/www/ec97frm2.html> and ask them to compare the census forms they created in Activity 5 to the actual forms used by the Bureau of the Census. Ask students to evaluate the real forms, explaining whether they think business people, government officials, consumers, or historians would benefit the most from the information that is requested.

National Archives Document Citation

Dover Cotton Factory, Dover, New Hampshire; Census of Manufactures, 1820; (National Archives Microfilm Publication M279); Records of the Bureau of the Census, Record Group 29; National Archives Building, Washington, DC.

Article Citation

Potter, Lee Ann and Wynell Schamel. "The 1820 Census of Manufactures." *Social Education* 63, 5 (September 1999): 310-313.

1.7

Maps of Salem, Massachusetts, 1822

Map makers have traditionally used various means to represent the three dimensions of the earth in two-dimensional images. Prior to the 19th century, for example, the most common device for indicating relief on a map was through variations of light and shade.

As the use of shading became systematized during the eighteenth and nineteenth centuries, French cartographers referred to these shading lines as "hachures." Hachures represent the slope of the land–the more gentle the slope, the fewer the lines–and the absence of line indicates flat terrain. The illustration on the right side of the document is an example of this system.

The use of contour lines to visually represent different elevations of land came into general use toward the end of the 19th century. An early version of a contour map is seen on the left. Simply speaking, a single contour line corresponds to a single elevation of the land. Because the contour line defines a curved surface (the earth), each line encloses a more or less circular area. The total effect is a pattern of concentric lines. The "base" line or datum for most contour maps is sea level, with each line on the map representing a standard distance above or below the base line. As each line signifies an increase or decrease in the land elevation (in this map, 3 feet), one can accurately calculate height by simply counting the lines from the base line (the water's edge in this instance). The slope of any change in the landscape relief can also be determined by noting the proximity of the contour lines to one another. A high concentration of lines tells the map user that the elevation changes sharply, while widely spaced lines indicate a gradual slope.

The two maps of Salem Neck, Massachusetts, surveyed by George W. Whistler (father of artist James A. McNeill Whistler) and William G. McNeill, topographical engineers for the United States Army, were created for a study conducted in 1822 of fortifications in the area. When the Office of Chief of Engineers decided in 1861 to study the feasibility, of reconditioning the forts, they referred to these maps and the reports accompanying them.

This document is part of the records of the Office of the Chief of Engineers, United States Army (Record Group 77, Fortifications file, drawer 18, sheet 11).

TEACHING ACTIVITIES

In order for students to answer the following questions, they must (a) examine the maps closely, (b) familiarize themselves with the scale and accompanying note (located at the bottom center of the document), and (c) understand contour and hachure methods of mapping. (The exercises can be adjusted to meet the needs of your students.)

Maps as Maps–Basic Map Skills:

1. What evidence is there in this document that tells you that the land area is not an island?
2. What descriptive information contained in the map on the right side of the illustration is omitted on the left?
3. Calculate the length and width of Salem Neck in miles.
4. How are points of elevation represented on each of these maps?
5. Using both maps, try to calculate the height of the area where the Alms House is located. Which of the two maps is preferable? Why?

Maps as Historical Documents:

6. What does this document tell you about mapping techniques in 1822?
7. Is there evidence in the document that the map was used after 1822?

Document 1.7 Map of Salem, Massachusetts, 1822. [National Archives]

8. How might this document have been useful to historians and/or cartographers in the past? How and why might it be used today?

9. Can you find Salem Neck on a contemporary map? Why or why not?

National Archives Document Citation
Maps of Salem, Massachusetts, 1822; Fortifications File, Drawer 18, sheet 11; United States Army; Records of the Office of the Chief of Engineers, Record Group 77; National Archives at College Park, College Park, MD.

Article Citation
"Maps Using Hachure and Contour Methods." *Social Education* 41, 7 (November/December 1977): 640-641.

Census of Cherokees in the Limits of Georgia, 1835

The year 1835 marked the end of an era for 16,542 Cherokee Indians living in parts of North and South Carolina, Kentucky, Tennessee, Alabama, and Georgia. Under pressure from state and federal authorities, a small group of Cherokee signed the Treaty of New Echota with the United States government; it ceded their eastern lands. Under terms of the treaty, the tribe received designated lands west of the Mississippi River and was ordered to relocate within two years. Most Cherokee had to be forced to leave their lands under military escort in 1838 and 1839.

In 1835 the United States government directed the Office of Indian Affairs to take a federal census of the Cherokee. This census served to record the number of Cherokee and to establish the value of their lands. The 66-page tabulation reveals much about 19th-century Cherokee lifestyle.

Census statistics indicate that by 1835 the Cherokee had adapted to the encroaching white culture. Unlike many other tribes, the Cherokee engaged in farming, rather than hunting, as a primary means of subsistence. Of 2,668 families registered in this census, 2,495 (about 93 percent) had at least one farm. The Cherokee economic structure also included black slaves. In 1824, the Cherokee owned more than 1,000 slaves; by the time of this census, the number had increased to 1,500. Light industry was another aspect of white influence on the Cherokee economy. Indian spinsters and weavers manufactured cloth and clothing. Census records of sawmills and gristmills provide further evidence of industries, similar to neighboring white culture.

Perhaps the most striking feature of eastern Cherokee culture was the development of a written language. The 1835 census documents a small, but significant, percentage of literacy among the Cherokee. Sequoya had invented a Cherokee syllabary of 86 characters by 1821; by 1828, the first copy of a newspaper printed in Cherokee and English, the *Cherokee Phoenix*, was in circulation.

The document reproduced here is a portion of page 49 from the 1835 census of the Cherokee. Thirty-eight columns of information fill two pages (numbered page 49). Information is filled in under the following column headings: Heads of Families, Indians, Half-breeds, Quadroons, and Whites; Residence, State and County, and Watercourse; Males, Under 18 years; Males, Over 18 years; Females, Under 16 years; Females, Over 16 years; Total Cherokees; Slaves, Males; Slaves, Females; Total Slaves; Whites connected by marriage; Farms; Acres in cultivation; Houses; Bushels wheat raised; Bushels corn raised; Bushels corn sold; For how much; Bushels corn bought; For how much; Mills; Ferry boats; Farmers over 18 years; Mechanics over 18 years; Readers in English; Readers in Cherokee; Half-breeds; Quadroons; Full-blooded; Mixed Catawbys; Mixed Spaniards; Mixed Negroes; Weavers; Spinsters; Reservees; Descendants of Reservees; Total; and Remarks.

The 18 headings on the right of page 49, not reproduced here, reveal that of the 292 Cherokee listed, there were: 18 who read English, 38 who read Cherokee, 51 weavers, 72 spinsters, 4 mechanics, 169 full-blooded Cherokee, 12 half-breeds, and 9 quadroons. There were also three gold mines on the property of Roasting Fox, Burnt Rail, and Tovesuskee. There were no ferry boats or mills.

This document is from the Census of Cherokees in the limits of Tennessee, Alabama, North Carolina, and Georgia in 1835, Entry 219, Records of the Bureau of Indian Affairs, Record Group 75.

TEACHING ACTIVITIES

Motivator

1. Provide each student with a copy of the Cherokee census and the puzzle. Each answer builds on the answer to the previous question. The answers are: (1) 292, (2) 3, (3) 876, (4) 16, (5) 892, (6) 2, (7) 1784, (8) 41, (9) 1,825, (10) 10, (11) 1,835, (12) the final answer is 1835.

What's in a Name?

2. Direct students to choose for themselves descriptive names to reflect their personalities, interests, or objects important to them. Collect the names in a list and read each name to the class. Ask students to try to match the descriptive names with the persons who selected those names.

Testing a Generalization

3. The worksheet below lists ten generalizations relating to Cherokee Indians in 1835. Students are directed to weigh the validity of those generalizations by using the document. Reproduce and distribute a copy of the document and worksheet for each student. Once the worksheets are completed, review student responses.

Map Skills

4. Direct students to an atlas of the United States and ask them to locate the Cherokee tribe in 1835 by using the geographical information provided in the census. Ask students to answer the following questions:

    a. In what area of Georgia did the Cherokee in this census reside?

    b. What major city is in this area today?

    c. Estimate the number of miles that the Cherokee had to travel to reach the Mississippi River.

Creative Writing

5. Direct students to assume the role of one of the Cherokee recorded on the census list. Ask them to compose a letter to the federal government or to a fellow Cherokee that describes their feelings after learning of the Treaty of New Echota. Ask students to include in their letters how they think life would be different and what they would miss most.

Synthesis

6. Ask students to write a short paragraph describing the lifestyle of the Cherokee based on the information provided in the 1835 census. Students might include such topics as work, family, slaves, and crops.

National Archives Document Citation

Census of Cherokees in the Limits of Georgia, 1835; Entry 219; Census of Cherokees in the limits of Tennessee, Alabama, North Carolina, and Georgia, 1835; Records of the Bureau of Indian Affairs, Record Group 75; National Archives Building, Washington, DC.

Article Citation

Alexander, Mary and Marilyn Childress. "Census of Cherokees in the Limits of Georgia in 1835." *Social Education* 45, 7 (November/December 1981): 564-566.

CENSUS OF CHEROKEES in the limits of Georgia in 1835

HEADS OF FAMILIES, INDIANS, HALF-BREEDS, QUADROONS, AND WRITERS	RESIDENCE, STATE AND COUNTY, AND WATERCOURSE	Males Under 18	Males Over 18	Females Under 16	Females Over 16	Total Cherokees	Slaves Males	Slaves Females	Total Slaves	Whites connected by marriage	Farms	Acres in cultivation	Houses	Bushels wheat raised	Bushels corn raised	For how much	Bushels corn bought	For how much
Eulaulanah	Floyd County Ga. Etowee River	6	1	2	3	12					1	6	2		10	31	30	
The Spirit	"	1	1	6	2	10					1	6	1	1			25	
Nancy Harris	"	1	4	3	2	10					1	2	5		30		12	12
John Fields	"	3	3	3	1	10	1		1		1	20	7		100			
Mills	"	3	1	1	1	6					1	5	2		100	30	15	
Stitch	"	1	2	3	4	10					1	5	3		100			
Sucking	"		1		1	2					1	3	1		50			
Skooblin	"		1		1	2					1	2	2		10			
T. Taylor	"	4	1		1	6					1	15	4		100	10	5	
Figg	"	1		1	2	4												
Don't do it	"	1	5	4	6	16					1	10	7		500	60	25	
George	"	3	1	1	1	6					1	12	3		200			
Tummah tahtakee	"	4	2	1	2	9					1	12	6		200	10	20	
Eua on the Roost	"	3	1	2	1	7					1	5	3		60	10	5	
Buffalo Fish	"	3	2	1	4	10	2	1	3		1	30	7		500	100	50	
Wild Hunter	"		1	1	1	3	1		1		1	10	4		100	30	15	
Swing Snake	"		1		4	5					1	3	1		70	20	10	
Sidney Dunn	"	5	1	1	1	8	1	1	2		1	30	6		30			
Jacob West	"	2	3	1	1	7	8	5	13	1	1	100	15	11	2000		700	
Foug	"	2	1	2	2	7							2					
David Vann	Cedar Ck.	3	1		2	6	7	6	13		1	200	17		2000	100	200	
Sonn	"		1	1	1	3					1	2	2		30			
David Harris	Ballplay Ck.		1			1												
Little Meat	Cedar Ck.		2		1	3					1	1			20	8	11	
Roasting Fox	Coosa River	2	2	1	1	6					1	12	5		10			
Samuel	"		3	4	2	9					1	5	2		50			
Nannenah	"		2	1	1	4					1	7	4		60	6	6	
Jim Foster	"	1	1	6	3	11					1	5			30			
Oolatie	"			1		1					1	6	2		40			
Hoososkee	"	1	2	2	3	8					1	6	1		30			
Sam Spring	"	1	2		2	5					1	6	1		40		2	1 1/2
Ahkechy	Beach Creek	1	1	4	1	7					1	5	2		40			
Chuggooskee	"	2	1	4	2	9					1	10	2		100	15	11 1/2	
Samuel Mills	Coosa River	2	1	1	2	6					1	40	7		100		10	3
David Rail	"	2	1	3	1	7					1	4	2		50		4	2
Warren Smith	"	1	1		1	3	4	1	6		1	40	11		240	50	50	
Tommy Smith	Chattooga Riv.			2	1	4												
Ned Lee	Coosa River	2	1	4	1	8					2	6	2		6		10	5
Sudie	"	4	2	2	2	10					1	2			0		1	4
John Crow	Chattooga Riv.	3	2	1	3	9		3	3	1	1	15	7		200	60	25	5	4
Booin McJim	"		1	1	1	3					1	1	1		20			
Tonal Butler	"		1	1	1	3					1	3	2		30	10	8	
Hich Jailor	"	1	2	2	1	6					2	12	1		100	200	110	
Jim Invadie	"	1	1	1	1	4					1	10	2		50	70	30	
Tom Invadie	"	1		2	2	7				1	1	15	7		250	150	75	
		70	60	76	78	192	22	17	41	3	42	697	173	11	408	346		102	57 1/2

Document 1.8 Census of Cherokees in the Limits of Georgia, 1835. [National Archives]

CHEROKEE CENSUS: A PUZZLE

(1) _____ Find the total number of Cherokee recorded in this census. Indicate this number on the line to the left.

(2) _____ Locate the number of Indians connected by marriage to whites.

(3) _____ *Multiply* answer #1 by answer #2.

(4) _____ How many Cherokee lived near Beach Creek?

(5) _____ *Add* answer #4 to answer #3.

(6) _____ How many persons owned 10 or more slaves?

(7) _____ *Multiply* answer #5 by answer #6.

(8) _____ What is the total number of slaves owned by all the Cherokee?

(9) _____ *Add* answer #8 to answer #7.

(10) _____ How many bushels of corn did Roasting Fox raise?

(11) _____ *Add* answer #10 to answer #9.

(12) _____ Enter your final answer here.

WORKSHEET

Instructions for Students: Below are ten statements about the Cherokee Indians in 1835. Using the census page, decide whether or not the document supports the statement and mark your answer in one of the columns to the left. If you are uncertain, mark the "Need More Information" column.

Yes	*No*	*Need More Information*	
_____	_____	_____	1. Most Cherokee were farmers.
_____	_____	_____	2. The Cherokee tribe was nomadic.
_____	_____	_____	3. The Cherokee sold most of the corn they raised.
_____	_____	_____	4. The federal government only recognized males as the heads of households.
_____	_____	_____	5. The government identified Cherokee residences by the closest body of water.
_____	_____	_____	6. The Cherokee were slaveholders.
_____	_____	_____	7. Floyd County, Georgia, was a good place to grow corn.
_____	_____	_____	8. Very few Cherokee intermarried with whites.
_____	_____	_____	9. Animals were important to the Cherokee.
_____	_____	_____	10. Some Cherokee could read English.

U.S. Court of Claims Deposition of Kish um us tubbee, 1837

The Choctaw were the first American Indians to be affected by the Indian Removal Act of 1830. When tribal leaders signed the Treaty of Dancing Rabbit Creek that year, decreeing the removal of the Choctaw from their southeastern homeland, they did so only after adding article 14 to the treaty. Article 14 gave each head of family an opportunity to remain, select an individual farm or allotment, and become a state citizen. Although more than one-third of the Choctaws decided to stay, the Federal agent handling their claims refused to register their allotment selections, thus allowing white settlers to take possession of the land.

One Choctaw who resisted removal was Kish um us tubbee, whose name means 'one who takes this tree [or branch] and kills.' The featured document is the deposition of Kish um us tubbee that was filed with the U.S. Court of Claims to substantiate his claim to a land allotment under article 14 of the Treaty of Dancing Rabbit Creek. The deposition is one of hundreds of such Choctaw claims, as they are commonly called, on file at the National Archives in the Records of the Bureau of Indian Affairs, Record Group 75. It is entry 270, Choctaw Removal Records, deposition number 254, U.S. Court of Claims case number 12742, Evidence File 1837-1838.

Federal Policy Toward the Indians

In the early part of the 19th century, white settlers who emigrated into the territory now forming the southeastern United States found it occupied by tribes of American Indians who had lived there for centuries. The Creek, Cherokee, Seminole, Chickasaw, and Choctaw Indians saw the land they inhabited become an object of desire as settlers passed through to occupy the Mississippi Territory. Inevitably, this interest in the southeastern Indian lands caused contention, conflict, and the eventual forced removal of the tribes to Indian Territory in what is now Oklahoma.

Almost from the time of its establishment, the Federal Government worked to wrest control of Indian homelands from the American Indian inhabitants. Among the Government strategies instituted was the "factory system," whereby Indians were encouraged to purchase supplies from a factory or merchant on credit and pay for them at an unspecified future date. Although Kish um us tubbee states in the featured document that the Indians paid for such items as knives, axes, beads, clothes, and ferreting with "peltry," buying on credit became common, and factories offered unlimited credit so the Indians would accumulate large debts.

As credit purchases escalated, Indian agents were instructed to offer debt liquidation in exchange for land cessions. Thomas Jefferson stated this Government objective in a letter to William Henry Harrison on February 27, 1803, when he wrote, "We shall push our trading houses, and be glad to see . . . them [the Indians] run in debt, because we observe that when these debts get beyond what the individual can pay they become willing to lop off by a cession of lands." Between 1800 and 1830, the Government approached the Choctaws 40 times to negotiate land cessions. By 1830 more than 13 million acres were ceded.

During the War of 1812, Creek Indians, supported by Spain and England, fought against the Choctaws, Chickasaws, Cherokees, and "friendly" Creeks who supported Americans led by Gen. Andrew Jackson. As a consequence of aligning with the losing side in the war, the Creeks were forced to sign the Treaty of Fort Jackson, ceding some 40,000 square miles of land to the United States. Although the Choctaws, Chickasaws, and Cherokees fought for the United States against the Creeks, they, too, were soon pressured to cede their lands.

After the War of 1812, the Federal Government began to force southeastern Indians to exchange their remaining lands for land in Indian Territory. Most Indians fiercely resisted leaving their ancestral homelands, but with the election of Andrew Jackson as President in 1828, Indian removal was established as a national policy. States quickly passed laws to ensure jurisdiction over Indians living within their borders, and President Jackson informed the Indians that the Federal Government was helpless to interfere with state laws. He told them their only option was to comply with removal.

The Removal of the Choctaws

To coexist peacefully with white settlers, the Choctaw sent their children to schools run by missionaries, built homes and farms, cultivated land, constructed mills, engaged in commerce, and established a representative government modeled on those of the States. They were aware of their rights under prior possession and treaty guarantees with the U.S. Government. Only when the State of Mississippi abolished the Choctaw government in 1830 and imposed fines and imprisonment upon any Indian attempting to hold office in the tribe did the Choctaws agree to cede their homeland to the Government and relocate to Oklahoma.

Although the majority of the tribe opposed the treaty, Choctaw leaders signed the Treaty of Dancing Rabbit Creek in 1830, which guaranteed that once they moved west, they could keep their old customs and govern themselves without interference. To achieve final agreement, article 14 was added, allowing those who did not wish to relocate the opportunity to remain where they were. Many of the Choctaws who wished to remain, however, eventually joined those who had earlier moved west. A few hundred did stay in Alabama and Mississippi, where their descendants live today.

A Rare Account of Indian Culture

Glimpses of Choctaw cultural beliefs and practices are contained in the featured document. Because most American Indians had no written language, the deposition provides a rare account of early contact with Europeans and relates the origin of the Choctaw version of "coming out of Nan a wa ya cave," a creation myth common to many Indian peoples. The Choctaw diet is described, as are hunting practices, a firemaking technique, and the fact that "there was no attempt made to convert them to the religion of the white men."

Near the end of the document, reference is made to a stick representing Kish um us tubbee, with a notch representing his grandson Halubbee, who lived with Kish um us tubbee at the time the Treaty of Dancing Rabbit Creek was signed. Known as the family stick, the device was the established method of signaling to Government officials an intention to lay claim to the provisions of article 14 and recording the members of a family unit. Because family sticks did not note wives, Kelisha, the wife of Kish um us tubbee, was not represented. Sons older than age 10 were represented by smaller sticks attached to the family stick by a string. Daughters older than 10 were noted by notches cut in the middle of the family stick. Younger children of either sex were designated by notches at the end of the family stick.

The deposition of Kish um us tubbee, although created long ago for a specific legal purpose, contains valuable information about the Choctaw culture and the times in which they lived. It exemplifies the versatility of primary sources by demonstrating how much valuable collateral information can be gleaned from a document like this.[1]

[1] See also Jacqueline A. Matte, "Southeastern Indians, Precontact to the Present: An Essay and Selected Bibliography for Teachers," *Social Education* 57 (October 1993): 292.

REFERENCE

Harvey, Karen D., Lisa D. Harjo, and Jane K. Jackson. *Teaching About Native Americans*. Bulletin no. 84. Washington, DC: National Council for the Social Studies, 1990.

TEACHING ACTIVITIES

Document Analysis

1. Distribute copies of the document to your students, and ask them the following questions:

Envelope 6 Jany 1840 See Chishehoma's list [?] No 177 & Yokahayo's list of Fallatown in No [?]

254 Kish um us tubbee — a full Blood Chocktaw aged eighty five years, being interrogated says his name is Tish um us tubbee (that is his War name given him by his white fathers when he went to assist them in their wars) he is also known by the name of Hush to mubbee, Acma to cubbee and Ogle ish tia; that he does not know his age; he has been here all the time: he was about two feet high when he first heard of the Chocktaws coming out of Nan a wa ya Cave from whence they all came he was young but recollects the massacre of the Choc- chuma's — he was grown up before he ever heard of a white man — It seems but a short time since he first heard of one — The first white people he ever heard of were French. he met them on the sea coast about the mouth of Tombig- bee, where they shook hands; there were a great many of them; they came in vessels which were moored at a big bluff at the Confluence of the Alabama and Tombigbee rivers, he does not recollect any of their names. The Chocktaw Towns were then fighting each other with bows and arrows and the white people came to reconcile them and induce them to make peace, He was one of the Warriors, and then belonged to Tala Town Isse; chicha la was his big Chief; he wore a cocked hat given him by the french at this time. one of their private men dis- covered these vessels and told their Chief and they then went to visit them they landed and made a great building of Brick on a bluff named Narraba, on the west side of the Tombigbee and remained there more than a year. they traded with the Indians in knives, axes, beads, clothes Fereting &c. and these were the first ar- ticles of the kind introduced among them:

(left margin: Kish-a-mus-tubbee)

Document 1.9a1 U.S. Court of Claims Deposition of Kish um us tubbee, 1837. [National Archives]

the Indians paid them in peltry, they lived in perfect peace and friendship all the time they were among them. There was no attempt made to convert them to the religion of the white men; they explained to them that the world and every thing in it, was made by a great spirit above: the Indians knew nothing about the great spirit until then: since then they have had preachers, who have informed them upon this subject; they brought no strong water at first, after a while they brought one small keg, and drank it all themselves and gave none to the Chocktaws, no whiskey was introduced into the Country for a great while afterwards and then by the English; the first time he ever saw whiskey was at the french settlement he has named, and he was there informed by the old Chocktaws that it would kill him if he drank it; he does not recollect when it was first introduced in the nation. The Chocktaws had no knowledge of the use of Tools such as axes Knives &c., before the French introduced them at this time. They had no houses but lived in Camps made of Palmeto; they made fire by booring a sharp stick through a softer wood and when the stick passed entirely through the fire would be communicated; they had corn at that time, and worked it with crooked limbs which they obtained from fallen trees. they killed their game entirely with bows and arrows; they were as wild then as now: they killed bear and Buffaloe with their bows and arrows. they had horses but hunted entirely on foot. to make their bows and arrows they used peices of sharp stone. He sayz he has committed an error that they had no corn or grain of any kind until it was introduced by the french at this time; they lived on wild potatoes and game. they were much happier after they became acquainted with the French; the tools and cloths they

Document 1.9a2 U.S. Court of Claims Deposition of Kish um us tubbee, 1837. [National Archives]

2

they introduced among them added greatly to their Comfort.

The first white man's name he can recollect, was Shooleg. He never served under any white officer whose name he now recollects; the English traders succeeded the French; after them the Spaniards and then the Americans. They always continued in Peace with all of them

He had a wife Kelisha at the treaty of Dancing Rabbit Creek: She lived with him then & now; he had no child living with him at that time He has two children living; he has ten wives, and thirteen Children.— He lived at the time of the Treaty, on Tally eo ekona in Talla Town, where he had an improvement a house and Field

   Col Johnson is his Counsel

Ioka haga a full blood Chocktaw a witness for claimant being sworn with uplifted hand deposes as follows

  That he is acquainted with the claimant, Kish um -mus tubbe (Points him out) knew him at the time of the Treaty of Dancing Rabbits Creek and before, he lived about eight miles from him; knew his family and saw them often at that time; He had then a wife Kill ista living with him and still, and one unmarried grand child his name is

1 Halubbee, a male (at home) now eighteen years old living with his grand father at the time of the Treaty. He was born in his house and has always lived with him, and been brought up as his own child; his mother was a daughter of the Claimant, he knew her well but cannot recollect her name she lived with Claimant until her death which happened a short time after Puck she nubbeeg (Doaks Stand) Treaty does not recollect the name of her husband; thinks

Document 1.9a3 U.S. Court of Claims Deposition of Kish um us tubbee, 1837. [National Archives]

thinks it was Ne tu ka   He (witness) was then young. Claimant lived at the time of the Treaty at Tally Lock enna, about ten miles from the Centre of Tala Town, (He belongs to Tala Town) He had an improvement a house and field where he lived at treaty and where he has continued to live ever since. Claimant was at the Council at Spanamingo he made a stick for himself and made a notch in the end, and gave it to him (witness) and told him to give it to Post Oak which he did.

He belonged to Post Oaks Company, He is a full blood Choctaw, and has never been west of the Mississippi

Is not related to claimant.

Is himself a claimant under the 14th Article of the Treaty. The lands claimed in this case has not to his knowledge been sold by Government

He has no idea of the age of Claimant, he is remarkably old

Taken and sworn to at
Louisville Missi. this
28th. April 1838 before
 I. Murray
 P. D. Broom
 Roger Barton

Toka hago his X mark

Document 1.9a4 U.S. Court of Claims Deposition of Kish um us tubbee, 1837. [National Archives]

a. What type of document is this?

   b. What is the date of the document?

   c. Who created this document?

2. Divide the class into three groups, assigning each group to read and analyze the document according to these categories:

   a. Historical references

   b. Geographical location

   c. American Indian customs

   Upon completion, ask a representative of each group to chart information on overlays, on the chalkboard, or on chart paper and present the group's analysis to the class.

3. Ask the students to explain what evidence in the document helps them know why it was written. Compile their responses on the chalkboard. Using the background information given, discuss why the document was written.

Class Discussion

4. Ask your students to identify the branch of Government given jurisdiction over Indian affairs by the U.S. Constitution.

5. Ask your students what stereotypical images come to mind when they think of American Indians. List their responses on the chalkboard. Ask students what they think might contribute to these stereotypes.

6. Using guidelines from *Teaching About Native Americans* (see citation below), lead a discussion about the changes in terminology used over time to refer to American Indians such as Indians, Native Americans, American Indians, and indigenous peoples. Discuss why terms such as Injuns, red man, chief, squaw, papoose, brave, warrior, and redskin should be avoided. The source cited above provides helpful information about each term.

Research Activities

7. Ask students to research and present reports about a tribe that lives or lived nearby. Compare the lifestyle and experiences of that tribe with those of 19th-century or present-day southeastern Indians.

8. Ask students to research and present reports on the southeastern Indian removal experience, often referred to as the Trail of Tears. Students should include the tribe's point of view in their reports. Ask a student to "walk" the trail by mapping the route for a bulletin board display.

9. Ask a volunteer or volunteers to interview an American Indian in person, by letter, or by telephone for a contemporary point of view and summarize the interview in a written report. The report should also compare and contrast the tribal customs and awareness of tribal heritage of the contemporary American Indians with the experience of Kish um us tubbee. It should conclude by outlining how the Federal Government responds today to issues of concern to contemporary Native Americans.

National Archives Document Citation

U.S. Court of Claims Deposition of Kish um us tubbee, 1837; Entry 270, Choctaw Removal Records; Deposition number 254, U.S. Court of Claims Case number 12742; Evidence File 1837-1838; Records of the Bureau of Indian Affairs, Record Group 75; National Archives Building, Washington, DC.

Article Citation

Blondo, Richard A., Wynell Burroughs Schamel, and Jaqueline A. Matte. "U.S. Court of Claims Deposition of Kish um us tubbee." *Social Education* 58, 1 (January 1994): 51-56.

General Orders Pertaining to Removal of the Cherokees, 1838

In late December 1835, a small group of Cherokee leaders who favored moving to land west of the Mississippi River and representatives of the United States government met in New Echota, the capital of the Cherokee Nation, located in northwest Georgia. The result of their meeting was a treaty, signed on December 29, which required the eastern Cherokee to exchange their lands for land in the Indian Territory, in what is today eastern Oklahoma. The Senate ratified the treaty by a margin of one vote on May 17, 1836 and President Andrew Jackson signed it into law on May 23. The Cherokee were to complete their removal to Indian Territory within two years.

There was a great deal of opposition to the treaty. New Englanders, religious groups, and missionaries who objected to the policy of removal flooded Congress and the President with petitions and memorials. Ralph Waldo Emerson addressed an open letter to President Van Buren in April 1838. Referring to the treaty, he stated, "The soul of man, the justice, the mercy that is the heart's heart in all men, from Maine to Georgia, does abhor this business." Members of the Cherokee tribe who insisted that the treaty was a fraud also petitioned Congress. Most notable among these petitioners was Chief John Ross, who claimed that the individuals who had represented the tribe at the treaty negotiations did not have the authority to do so. He submitted to Congress a petition containing signatures of more than 15,000 Cherokee who opposed the treaty. Supporters of the treaty were quick to claim that there were hardly 15,000 Cherokee in the east, and half of them were children.

Congress responded to the opposition by tabling the petitions and memorials. One such action was recorded in the Senate Journal on March 1, 1837.

"Mr. Southard presented a memorial and petition of a delegation of the Cherokee Nation in relation to the treaty of December 29, 1835, praying that the execution of the same may be suspended. A motion was made by Mr. Southard that the memorial and the accompanying papers be printed and on that motion by Mr. Tipton, ordered, that this motion lie on the table."

Just as Congress chose to ignore petitions and memorials by laying them aside, all but about 2,000 Cherokee ignored the treaty and refused to move to the West or begin making preparations for removal. This reaction was encouraged by Chief John Ross and continued for nearly two years. As a result, on April 6, 1838, General of the Army Alexander McComb ordered Maj. Gen. Winfield Scott to the Cherokee Agency on the Hiwassee River near Calhoun, Tennessee, to ensure compliance with the treaty. Scott was given a large force of regulars (approximately 3,000 troops), and the authority to raise additional state militia and volunteer troops from Tennessee, Georgia, Alabama, and North Carolina to force removal if necessary. Nine days after his arrival at the Cherokee Agency, Scott issued General Order 25, which is featured with this article. In it, he named the members of his staff, established three military districts to expedite "collection" of the Indians, and urged his troops to treat the Indians in a humane fashion.

On May 26, removal operations began in Georgia. In barely three weeks, General Charles Floyd, who commanded the Georgia Militia, reported that no Cherokee remained in the state. In late June, removal operations began in Tennessee, North Carolina, and Alabama. From each of the four states, Indians were rounded up and taken to collecting points. One was located at the Cherokee Agency on the Hiwassee River. The other two were at Ross's Landing in Tennessee and at Gunter's Landing on the Tennessee River in Alabama. From these points, the Cherokee were to be escorted under the direction of General Nathaniel Smith, Superintendent of Emigration for the Bureau of Indian Affairs. A letter sent by Smith to General Scott indicating his preparedness and his plans is also included with this article.

As indicated in Smith's letter, the Army's plan

was to transport the Cherokee to the West primarily via a water route. The Army believed it would take less time, be less expensive, and be less exhausting than a land route. From the collection points, the Indians would travel by boats down the Tennessee River to the Ohio River, down the Ohio to the Mississippi River, down the Mississippi to the Arkansas River, and upstream to Indian Territory. After three contingents of roughly 1,000 Indians each left for the West (accompanied by a military officer, his assistants, and two physicians), the Cherokee Council pleaded with Army leaders to postpone further movement until autumn. The heat and drought of the summer was contributing to illness and death among the Indians both en route and at the collection centers. Illnesses that included fever, measles, diarrhea, dysentery, whooping cough, worms, gonorrhea, cholera, and pneumonia were compounded by the refusal of many of the Indians to accept medicine from the physicians.

One group of Cherokee being held at Ross's Landing submitted a petition to Colonel Lindsay, commander of the Middle District,

'We ask that you will not send us down the river at this time of the year. If you do we shall die, or our wives will die, or our children will die—for our hearts are heavy, very heavy. We want you to keep us in this country [until] the sickly time is over, so that when we get to the West we may be able to work to make boards to cover our families.'

This message and the pleas submitted by other groups had the desired effect: General Scott halted the operations and indicated that removal would resume in the fall.

During the summer, the Cherokee leaders were able to convince General Scott that the Cherokee themselves should take over removal operations and decided that the route for removal would be land-based. Under the terms of the contract negotiated between General Scott and Chief John Ross, for each Cherokee removed, Ross would be paid $66.24. This included an expenditure for soap which had not been provided when the army was in charge. This amount per person was based on an estimate of eighty days of travel time.

Early in the fall of 1838, the Cherokee—divided into 13 contingents of about 1,000 each—began the overland march on foot or on horseback to Indian Territory unaccompanied by a military escort. Supplies, equipment, and clothing were carried in 645 wagons, each pulled by a double span of oxen, or by mules, or horses. Some groups left as early as August, others waited until December. Although John Ross had decided that all would travel by land, the Indians took various routes. Most crossed the Tennessee River at the mouth of the Hiwassee, at Blythe's ferry. Next they journeyed to McMinnville and to Nashville. After crossing the river there, they went to Hopkinsville, Kentucky, and crossed the Ohio River at Golconda, Illinois. They proceeded through southern Illinois to Green's ferry on the Mississippi. Crossing the Mississippi took days, considering the number of people, and horses, and wagons, and livestock. After crossing, they traveled through southern Missouri by way of Springfield and from there to Indian Territory. Three years to the month following the fateful meeting at New Echota, President Van Buren announced to Congress, "It affords me great pleasure to apprise the Congress of the entire removal of the Cherokee Nation of Indians to their new homes west of the Mississippi."

Although more than 12,000 Cherokee, intermarried whites, and slaves left the east significantly fewer actually arrived in Indian Territory. Estimates of the number who died en route range from 500 to 2,000. The actual travel time for each contingent far exceeded the 80-day estimate, averaging 153 days instead. This meant that many traveled during the cold winter months. The extended time also meant, as negotiated in the contract with General Scott, that Ross received additional pay. In total, John Ross received $1,263,338.38 from the federal government for the removal. This amount was deducted from the sum the Cherokee Nation received for their lands in the east under the terms of the Treaty of New Echota. Due to the cold, the distance, the illnesses, the loss of life, the removal from their land, and the general ill-treatment from state and federal officials, the journey of the Cherokee became known as the "Trail of Tears."

Documents featured in this article include General Scott's General Order 25 dated May 17, 1838, and a letter written by Gen. Nathaniel Smith to General Scott on May 18, 1838. Both documents are contained in the Records of the U.S. Army Continental Commands, 1821-1920, Record Group 393, National Archives and Records Administration, Washington, DC. Both are available with other documents related to Cherokee removal on National Archives microfilm publication M1475 "Correspondence of the Eastern Division Pertaining to Cherokee Removal, April-December 1838." Copies of National Archives microfilm publications are available in federal depository libraries and may be ordered by calling 1-800-234-8861.

Digital images of additional documents related to Cherokee Removal are available online from the National Archives in the NAIL database at http://www.archives.gov/research_room/nail/. The documents include the Treaty of New Echota (Control No: NWCTB-11-INTRY-PI159E17-RIT199), a memorial written in both the English and Cherokee languages (Control No: NWL-233-PETITION-HR21AH11-1), a physician's monthly report of emigrating Cherokee's at Chadata in August 183 (Control No: NWCTB-75-PI163E98 SF249(CHADATA), and documents related to John Ross's financial accounts (Control No: NWCTB-217-2AUD-AIE525-6289A).

TEACHING ACTIVITIES

1. As an introductory activity, ask students whether any of them have moved. Ask them what they brought with them, how much time they had to prepare for their move, and if family members visited their new home before relocating. Instruct students to write a paragraph sharing how they might feel if they were told to move, that they were only allowed to take a few items with them, and that no one in their family had been to their new home yet. Encourage volunteers to share their paragraphs with the class.

2. Provide each student with a photocopy of each of the featured documents, and make a transparency with the following questions: What types of documents are they? What are the dates of the documents? Who wrote the documents? What are the purposes of the documents? What information in the documents helps you understand why they were written? What additional questions do the documents prompt? Ask one student to read the documents aloud as the others read silently. Lead the class in oral responses to the questions.

3. Distribute atlases and blank maps of the United States to students. Instruct them to analyze the letter written by General Smith and locate in the atlas the places he mentioned. Ask them to label the places on their maps and connect the points tracing the Army's intended route. Next, read aloud to students the section of the article that describes the land route traveled by most of the Indians. Instruct students again to locate the places using the atlases and label them on their maps and connect the points.

4. Divide the class into two groups. Instruct one group to list the advantages and disadvantages of following the Army's route. Instruct the other group to list the advantages and disadvantages of following the Cherokee' route. Pair students (one from each group) and ask them to compare the advantages and disadvantages of the two routes.

5. Ask students to list the issues and problems anticipated by General Scott in his Orders of May 17, 1838. Direct students to use library resources to determine which of Scott's concerns materialized and how they were addressed.

6. Locate and share with students the painting entitled "The Trail of Tears," by Robert Lindneux. The original is at the Woolaroc Museum in Bartlesville, Oklahoma. Ask students to describe the mood of the painting. Use the following questions: Why did the artist choose to paint the sky gray? What do the expressions on the Indians' faces and their posture suggest about how they feel? What details in the painting jump out at you?

7. Instruct students to conduct additional research into the Treaty of New Echota and the controversy surrounding it. Divide students into groups to research and represent the position of:

    a. the federal government,

    b. one of the states involved,

    c. the Cherokee who supported the treaty,

ORDERS. No. 25
Head Quarters, Eastern Division.
Cherokee Agency, Ten. May 17, 1838.

MAJOR GENERAL SCOTT, of the United States' Army, announces to the troops assembled and assembling in this country, that, with them, he has been charged by the President to cause the Cherokee Indians yet remaining in North Carolina, Georgia, Tennessee and Alabama, to remove to the West, according to the terms of the Treaty of 1835. His Staff will be as follows:

LIEUTENANT COLONEL W. J. WORTH, acting Adjutant General, Chief of the Staff.

MAJOR M. M. PAYNE, acting Inspector General.

LIEUTENANTS R. ANDERSON, & E. D. KEYES, regular Aids-de-camp.

COLONEL A. H. KENAN & LIEUTENANT H. B. SHAW, volunteer Aids-de-camp.

Any order given orally, or in writing, by either of those officers, in the name of the Major General, will be respected and obeyed as if given by himself.

The Chiefs of Ordnance, of the Quarter-Master's Department and of the Commissariat, as also the Medical Director of this Army, will, as soon as they can be ascertained, be announced in orders.

To carry out the general object with the greatest promptitude and certainty, and with the least possible distress to the Indians, the country they are to evacuate is divided into three principal Military Districts, under as many officers of high rank, to command the troops serving therein, subject to the instructions of the Major General.

Eastern District, to be commanded by BRIGADIER GENERAL EUSTIS, of the United States' Army, or the highest officer in rank, serving therein:—North Carolina, the part of Tennessee lying north of Gilmer county, Georgia, and the counties of Gilmer, Union, and Lampkin, in Georgia. Head Quarters, in the first instance, say, at Fort Butler.

Western District, to be commanded by COLONEL LINDSAY, of the United States' Army, or the highest officer in rank serving therein:—Alabama, the residue of Tennessee and Dade county, in Georgia. Head quarters, in the first instance, say, at Ross' Landing.

Middle District, to be commanded by BRIGADIER GENERAL ARMISTEAD of the United States' Army, or the highest officer in rank, serving therein:—All that part of the Cherokee country, lying within the State of Georgia, and which is not comprised in the two other districts. Head Quarters, in the first instance, say, at New Echota.

It is not intended that the foregoing boundaries between the principal commanders shall be strictly observed. Either, when carried near the district of another, will not hesitate to extend his operations, according to the necessities of the case, but with all practicable harmony, into the adjoining district. And, among his principal objects, in case of actual or apprehended hostilities, will be that of affording adequate protection to our white people in and around the Cherokee country.

The senior officer actually present in each district will receive instructions from the Major General as to the time of commencing the removal, and every thing that may occur interesting to the service, in the district, will be promptly reported to the same source. The Major General will endeavour to visit in a short time all parts of the Cherokee country occupied by the troops.

The duties devolved on the army, through the orders of the Major General & those of the commanders of districts, under him, are of a highly important and critical nature.

The Cherokees, by the advances which they have made in christianity and civilization, are by far the most interesting tribe of Indians in the territorial limits of the United States. Of the 15,000 of those people who are now to be removed—(and the time within which a voluntary emigration was stipulated, will expire on the 23rd instant—) it is understood that about four fifths are opposed, or have become averse to a distant emigration; and altho' none are in actual hostilities with the United States, or threaten a resistance by arms, yet the troops will probably be obliged to cover the whole country they inhabit, in order to make prisoners and to march or to transport the prisoners, by families, either to this place, to Ross' Landing or Gunter's Landing, where they are to be finally delivered over to the Superintendant of Cherokee Emigration.

Considering the number and temper of the mass to be removed, together with the extent and fastnesses of the country occupied, it will readily occur, that simple indiscretions—acts of harshness and cruelty, on the part of our troops, may lead, step by step, to delays, to impatience and exasperation, and in the end, to a general war and carnage—a result, in the case of those particular Indians, utterly abhorrent to the generous sympathies of the whole American people. Every possible kindness, compatible with the necessity of removal, must, therefore, be shown by the troops, and, if, in the ranks, a despicable individual should be found, capable of inflicting a wanton injury or insult on any Cherokee man, woman or child, it is hereby made the special duty of the nearest good officer or man, instantly to interpose, and to seize and consign the guilty wretch to the severest penalty of the laws. The Major General is fully persuaded that this injunction will not be neglected by the brave men under his command, who cannot be otherwise than jealous of their own honor and that of their country.

By early and persevering acts of kindness and humanity, it is impossible to doubt that the Indians may soon be induced to confide in the Army, and instead of fleeing to mountains and forests, flock to us for food and clothing. If, however, through false apprehensions, individuals, or a party, here and there, should seek to hide themselves, they must be pursued and invited to surrender, but not fired upon unless they should make a stand to resist. Even in such cases, mild remedies may sometimes better succeed than violence; and it cannot be doubted that if we get possession of the women and children first, or first capture the men, that, in either case, the outstanding members of the same families will readily come in on the assurance of forgiveness and kind treatment.

Every captured man, as well as all who surrender themselves, must be disarmed, with the assurance that their weapons will be carefully preserved and restored at, or beyond the Mississippi. In either case, the men will be guarded and escorted, except it may be, where their women and children are safely secured as hostages; but, in general, families, in our possession, will not be separated, unless it be to send men, as runners, to invite others to come in.

It may happen that Indians will be found too sick, in the opinion of the nearest Surgeon, to be removed to one of the depots indicated above. In every such case, one or more of the family, or the friends of the sick person, will be left in attendance, with ample subsistence and remedies, and the remainder of the family removed by the troops. Infants, superannuated persons, lunatics and women in a helpless condition, will all, in the removal, require peculiar attention, which the brave and humane will seek to adapt to the necessities of the several cases.

All strong men, women, boys & girls, will be made to march under proper escorts. For the feeble, Indian horses and ponies will furnish a ready resource, as well as for bedding and light cooking utensils—all of which, as intimated in the Treaty, will be necessary to the emigrants both in going to, and after arrival at, their new homes. Such, and all other light articles of property, the Indians will be allowed to collect and to take with them, as also their slaves, who will be treated in like manner with the Indians themselves.

If the horses and ponies be not adequate to the above purposes, wagons must be supplied.

Corn, oats, fodder and other forage, also beef cattle, belonging to the Indians to be removed, will be taken possession of by the proper departments of the Staff, as wanted, for the regular consumption of the Army, and certificates given to the owners, specifying in every case, the amount of forage and the weight of beef, so taken, in order that the owners may be paid for the same on their arrival at one of the depots mentioned above.

All other moveable or personal property, left or abandoned by the Indians, will be collected by agents appointed for the purpose, by the Superintendant of Cherokee Emigration, under a system of accountability, for the benefit of the Indian owners, which he will devise. The Army will give to those agents, in their operations, all reasonable countenance, aid and support.

White men and widows, citizens of the United States, who are, or have been intermarried with Indians, and thence commonly termed, *Indian countrymen*; also such Indians as have been made denizens of particular States by special legislation, together with the families and property of all such persons, will not be molested or removed by the troops until a decision, on the principles involved, can be obtained from the War Department.

A like indulgence, but only for a limited time, and until further orders, is extended to the families and property of certain Chiefs and head-men of the two great Indian parties, (on the subject of emigration) now understood to be absent in the direction of Washington on the business of their respective parties.

This order will be carefully read at the head of every company in the Army.

By Command:

Document 1.10a General Winfield Scott's General Order 25, May 17, 1838. [National Archives]

Cherokee Agency East,
18th May 1838.

Maj. Genl. Winfield Scott
Comdg. Army Ch. Nation
			Sir,

I have the honor to inform you that I am now prepared to receive and transport to their new homes Two thousand Cherokees every twenty days, and have for their Subsistence upwards of 600.000 Rations contracted for, about 300000 of which are already delivered at this Post, Ross' Landing, Paduca, Kentucky, and Little Rock, Arkansas.

The plan adopted for the removal of the Cherokees is, to send them down this River in Boats while the water remains at a Stage Sufficient to admit, and afterwards send them in Waggons by way of Ross' Landing, Jasper Tenn:, Bellefonte, Huntsville, and Athens to Waterloo, Alabama, where the Steamer 'Smelter', and as many other Boats as may be necessary, will always be in readiness to receive the Emigrants

			Very Respectfully
			Yr. Mo. Obt. Sert,
			Nat Smith
			Supt. Ch. Removal

Document 1.10b Letter by General Nathaniel Smith to General Scott, May 18, 1838. [National Archives]

d. the Cherokee who did not support the treaty, and

   e. dissenting Senators or others who publicly opposed the treaty.

   Ask students within each group to develop arguments to support the group's position. Then, divide students into new groups with at least one representative from the each of the previous groups. Direct students to negotiate a treaty or other federal policy regarding the Cherokee.

8. Remind students that although the First Amendment to the Constitution guarantees the right to petition the government for a redress of grievances, Congress may choose to table petitions received, as in the case of Cherokee Removal. Direct students to conduct additional research into this Congressional procedure. Ask students to find out what other issues have prompted the tabling of petitions. Encourage students to write a letter (or send a petition) to an elected official expressing their opinion on this practice.

9. Assign students to research what happened to the cherokee land in Oklahoma and to find out how much of this land remains in the possession of the Cherokee Nation today. This activity can be further extended by examining what happened in the removal of several other eastern tribes to Indian Territory beyond the Mississippi.

National Archives Document Citation

General Winfield Scott's General Order 25, May 17, 1838; (National Archives Microfilm Publication M1475); Correspondence of the Eastern Division Pertaining to Cherokee Removal, April-Dec., 1838; Records of U.S. Army Continental Commands, 1821-1920; Record Group 393; National Archives Building, Washington, DC.

Letter by Gen. Nathaniel Smith to Gen. Scott, May 18, 1838; (National Archives Microfilm Publication M1475); Correspondence of the Eastern Division Pertaining to Cherokee Removal, April-Dec., 1838; Records of U.S. Army Continental Commands, 1821-1920; Record Group 393; National Archives Building, Washington, DC.

Article Citation

Potter, Lee Ann and Wynell Schamel. "General Orders Pertaining to Removal of The Cherokee." *Social Education* 63, 1 (January/February 1999): 32-38.

A Ship's Manifest, 1847

Between 1820 and 1874, the captains or masters of all vessels arriving in United States ports from foreign countries were required to submit a list of passengers, known as the *manifest*, to the Collector of Customs in the district in which the ship arrived. These reports included information regarding the age, sex, occupation, nationality, and destination of the aliens. The District Collector of Customs sent quarterly reports with copies of the manifests to the Secretary of State, who submitted this information to Congress. By 1874, only statistical reports to the Treasury Department were required of the customs collectors. In 1891, the Office of Superintendent of Immigration was created under the Treasury Department to further centralize control over immigration.

The ship's manifest presented here is the first page of the passenger list of the brig *Acadian* for May 14, 1847, the year in which 234,968 alien passengers arrived at ports in the United States. Irish immigration peaked between 1841 and 1850, with 49% of the aliens entering the United States coming from Ireland.

This manifest is part of the records of the Bureau of Customs (Record Group 36). The complete manifest is available on microfilm at the National Archives, or through your nearest regional Archives. The microfilm number is M277, roll 22.

TEACHING ACTIVITIES

Duplicate copies of the manifest for your class to use in small groups or individually. Review the arrangement of the manifest with the class, and make note of the column headings. These headings will be essential to the students' understanding of the document.

1. What kinds of information about the passengers can be found in the manifest? Consider the following:
   a. What is the nationality of most passengers?
   b. What are the occupations of the passengers?
   c. What are the final destinations of the passengers?
   d. Note that some of the passengers have the same surnames. What might this tell you about them?
   e. Why would the government want or need to collect information about these passengers?

2. Describe in writing four passengers, or groups of passengers, on the *Acadian*. For example: Ann Brogin was a 20-year-old servant from Ireland traveling to the United States. (This exercise is designed to help students begin to identify and organize the information found in the document. It is necessary for students to be able to do this before they begin to deal with matters of interpretation.)

3. Make a list of possible reasons why you think many of the passengers might be traveling to North America. (Consider the date of the manifest and relevant European events.)

4. What conclusions, if any, about immigration might be drawn from this manifest? (Make sure your conclusions are based on information found within the document.)

5. How might this document, and others like it, be used in a family history project? (Consider the ethnic population of Boston today.)

National Archives Document Citation
Passenger list of Brig Acadian, p. 1, May 14, 1847; (National Archives Microfilm Publication M277, roll 22); Records of the United States Customs Service, Record Group 36; National Archives Building, Washington, DC.

Article Citation
"A Ship's Manifest, 1847." *Social Education* 41, 6 (October 1977): 540-541.

COPY of Report and List of the Passengers taken on board the *Brig Acadian* of *Boston*, whereof *Thos. P. Wood* is Master, burthen *157* tons, and 95ths of a ton, bound from the Port of *Halifax* for *Boston*.

NAMES.	AGE.	SEX.	Occupation, Trade, or Profession.	Country to which they severally belong.	Country of which they intend to become inhabitants.	Remarks relative to any who may have died or left the vessel during the voyage.
Mrs Susan McLane	30	female		Nova Scotia	Nova Scotia	
Miss Isabella M. Tremlett	18	"		New Foundland	"	
" Louisa A. Tremlett	14	"		"	"	
Mr B. C. Brehm	36	Male	Merchant	Nova Scotia	"	
Wm Mowat	25	"	Carpenter	Scotland	Canada	
Revd Peter Ross	38	"		U States	U States	
Cath McAntosh	20	female		Nova Scotia	"	
Mary Herne	40	"	Servant	"	"	
Mary Herne	19	"		"	"	
Cath Welsh	21	"	Dress Maker	"	"	
Mary Ann Fuzzle	17	"	"	"	"	
Ellen Flynn	32	"	"	Ireland	"	
Mary Mackie	53	"	Servant	"	"	
Sarah McGlinch	45	"	"	"	"	
Mary McGlinch	13	"	"	"	"	
Bridget McGlinch	7	"	"	"	"	
Ann McGlinch	10	"	"	"	"	
Amy Brosin	20	"	Servant	"	"	
Catharine Dolin	24	"	"	"	"	
Mary Dolin	14 Mo			"	"	
Paty Murphy	30	Male	Trader	"	"	
John Buckly	30	"	Mechanic	"	"	
Danl McLeod	40	"	Farmer	"	"	
Edward O'Conor	40	"	Lawyer	"	"	
Michael Elward	32	"	Labourer	"	"	

Document 1.11 Passenger list of *Brig Acadian*, p. 1, May 14, 1847. [National Archives]

1.12

Lincoln's Spot Resolutions, 1848

Tension has existed between the legislative and the executive branches of the U.S. government over war powers since the Constitution simultaneously vested Congress with the power to declare war and the president with the power of commander in chief.

Although Jefferson insisted on congressional approval before sending troops into combat, later presidents have not felt bound by this precedent. Their alternate view was boosted by the Supreme Court in 1827 in the case *Martin v. Mott*. The Court ruled that it was constitutional for Congress to vest the president with the discretionary authority to decide whether an emergency had arisen and to raise a militia to meet such a threat of invasion or civil insurrection. Nonetheless, in the winter of 1845-46, as relations between the United States and Mexico deteriorated, there was no express delineation of powers between the two branches.

Prior to Texas's independence, the Neuces River was recognized as the northern boundary of Mexico. Spain had fixed the Neuces as a border in 1816, and the United States ratified it in the 1819 treaty by which the United States had purchased Florida and renounced claims to Texas.

Even following Mexico's independence from Spain, American and European cartographers fixed the Texas border at the Neuces. When Texas declared its independence, however, it claimed as its territory an additional 150 miles of land, to the Rio Grande. With the annexation of Texas in 1845, the United States adopted Texas's position and claimed the Rio Grande as the border.

Mexico broke diplomatic relations with the United States and refused to recognize either the Texas annexation or the Rio Grande border. President James Polk sent a special envoy, John L. Slidell, to propose cancellation of Mexico's debt to United States citizens who had incurred damages during the Mexican Revolution, provided Mexico would formally recognize the Rio Grande boundary. Slidell was also authorized to offer the Mexican government up to $30 million for California and New Mexico.

Between Slidell's arrival on December 6, 1845, and his departure in March 1846, the regime of President Jose Herrara was overthrown and a fervently nationalistic government under General Mariano Paredes seized power. Neither leader would speak to Slidell. When Paredes publicly reaffirmed Mexico's claim to all of Texas, Slidell left in a temper, convinced that Mexico should be "chastised."

Zachary Taylor

The agent for chastisement was already in place. On January 13, 1846, more than 3,500 troops commanded by General Zachary Taylor moved south under President Polk's order, from Corpus Christi on the Neuces River to a location on the north bank of the Rio Grande. Advancing on March 8 to Point Isabel, the U.S. troops found that the settlement had been burned by fleeing Mexicans. By March 28, the troops were near the mouth of the Rio Grande across from the Mexican town of Matamoros.

Polk claimed the move was a defensive measure, and expansionists and Democratic newspapers in the United States applauded his action. Whig newspapers said that the movement was an invasion of Mexico rather than a defense of Texas. While newspapers in Mexico called for war, General Pedro de Ampudia warned, "If you insist in remaining upon the soil of the department of Tamaulipas, it will clearly result that arms, and arms alone, must decide the question."

General Ampudia's prediction came true on April 25 when Mexican cavalry crossed the Rio Grande and attacked a mounted American patrol, killing five, wounding eleven, and capturing forty-seven.

President Polk

In Washington, President Polk, although unaware of the developments, had drafted a message asking Congress to declare war on Mexico on the basis of Mexico's failure to pay U.S. damage claims and refusal to meet with Slidell. At a cabinet meet-

Resolved by the House of Representatives, that the President of the United States, be respectfully requested to inform this House—

First: Whether the spot of soil on which the blood of our citizens was shed, as in his messages declared, was, or was not, within the territories of Spain, at least from the treaty of 1819 until the Mexican revolution.

Second: Whether that spot is, or is not, within the territory which was wrested from Spain, by the Mexican revolution.—

Third: Whether that spot is, or is not, within a settlement of people, which settlement had existed ever since long before the Texas revolution, until its inhabitants fled from the approach of the U.S. Army.—

Fourth: Whether that settlement is, or is not, isolated from any and all other settlements, by the Gulf of Mexico, and the Rio Grande, on the South and West, and by wide uninhabited regions on the North and East.—

Fifth: Whether the People of that settlement, or a majority of them, or any of them, had ever, previous to the bloodshed, mentioned in his messages, submitted themselves to the government or laws of Texas, or of the United States, by consent, or by compulsion, either by accepting office, or voting at elections, or paying taxes, or serving on juries, or having process served upon them, or in any other way.—

Sixth: Whether the People of that settlement, did, or did not, flee from the approach of the United States Army, leaving unprotected their homes and their growing crops, before

Document 1.12a1 Lincoln's "Spot Resolutions," 1848. [National Archives]

the blood was shed, as in his messages stated; and whether the first blood so shed, was, or was not shed, within the inclosure of the People, or some of them, who had thus fled from it—

Seventh: Whether our *citizens*, whose blood was shed, as in his messages declared, were, or were not, at that time, *armed* officers, and *soldiers*, sent into that settlement, by the military order of the President through the Secretary of War— and

Eighth: Whether the military force of the United States, including those *citizens*, was, or was not, so sent into that settlement, after Genl. Taylor had, more than once, intimated to the War Department that, in his opinion, no such movement was necessary to the defence or protection of Texas—

Document 1.12a2 Lincoln's "Spot Resolutions," 1848. [National Archives]

ing on May 9, he notified his cabinet that he would ask for war in a few days. Only Secretary of the Navy George Bancroft counseled for delay, waiting for a Mexican attack.

On that evening, Polk received Taylor's account of the April 25 skirmish. Polk revised his war message, then sent it to Congress on May 11 asserting, "Mexico has passed the boundary of the United States, has invaded our territory and shed American blood upon America's soil." On May 13, Congress declared war, with a vote of 40-2 in the Senate and 174-14 in the House.

Although Congress had declared war, it was not without reservation. An amendment was proposed, although defeated, to indicate that Congress did not approve of Polk's order to move troops into disputed territory. Sixty-seven Whig representatives voted against mobilization and appropriations for a war.

Ohio Senator Tom Corwin accused Polk of involving the United States in a war of aggression. Senator John C. Calhoun of South Carolina abstained from voting, correctly foreseeing that the war would aggravate sectional strife. Massachusetts Senator Daniel Webster voiced doubts about the constitutionality of Polk's actions, believing that Polk had failed to consult adequately with Congress. As the war deepened, "Conscience" Whigs denied Polk had tried to avoid war.

A freshman Whig congressman from Illinois, Abraham Lincoln, questioned whether the "spot" where blood had been shed was really U.S. soil. On December 22, 1847, he introduced the "Spot Resolutions," of which the second and third pages of Lincoln's handwritten copy are shown. One of several congressional resolutions opposing the war, it was never acted upon by the full Congress. Lincoln's action temporarily earned him a derisive nickname, "spotty Lincoln," coined by one Illinois newspaper.

Other citizens shared their legislators' concern, particularly those in the Northeast who saw the war as a ploy to extend slavery. The most celebrated was Henry David Thoreau, who refused to pay his $1 Massachusetts poll tax because he believed the war an immoral advancement of slavery.

Acerbic former president John Quincy Adams described the war as a southern expedition to find "bigger pens to cram with slaves." Regional writer James R. Lowell, author of the *Biglow Papers*, had his Yankee farmer Hosea Biglow scorn fighting to bring in new slave states. Charles Sumner, a noted abolitionist, also condemned the war from pacifist principles. Philadelphian Joseph Sill's diary records widespread public disapproval for the war by October 1847. The Massachusetts state legislature resolved the war an unconstitutional action because it was initiated by order of the president with the "triple object of extending slavery, of strengthening the slave power and of obtaining the control of the free states."

Concern that Taylor's order sending troops into the disputed territory provoked the clash was foremost in an October 1847 article in one Whig newspaper, *The American Review:* "The Constitution contemplates that before deliberate hostilities shall be undertaken in any case, a declaration of war shall be made; but in this case a hostile aggressive move was made under the personal orders of the President."

Ironically, when Lincoln became president, he extended the war powers of the executive, action he had criticized as a congressman. Following the firing on Fort Sumter, he declared a naval blockade on his own authority. The capture and condemnation of four runners led to a case that went to the Supreme Court. In 1863 the Court affirmed Lincoln's actions in the *Prize Cases*, 2 Black 635.

The "Spot Resolutions" are kept in the Records of the U.S. House of Representatives, RG 233, HR 30 A-B 3. A reproduction of the first page of the resolutions is available upon request from the Education Staff, NWE, National Archives, Washington, DC 20408.

TEACHING ACTIVITIES

Interpreting the Document

1. Students should review information in their textbooks about the U.S. entry into the Mexican War and opposition to that war. Supplement the text with information from the note to the teacher.

2. Ask students to locate on a map or in an atlas the following geographical features: the Neuces River, the Rio Grande, Corpus Christi, Point Isabel, Matamoros.

3. Ask students to read the document, either aloud as a class or silently. Then ask them

to summarize each of the eight resolutions in their own words.

   a. Using the text and teacher's note, ask students to answer each of Lincoln's points.

   b. Using Polk's war message, ask students to answer each of the points.

   c. Ask students to compile a list of secondary sources where they might find information to resolve the discrepancies between the two versions of the events.

   d. Ask students to compile a list of primary sources that they could examine to resolve the discrepancies between the two versions.

Public Opinion

4. Most students are aware that television influences public opinion from politics to fashion, but they are less sensitive to the impact of other forms of communication. As a class, discuss the following questions.

   a. Apart from television, how do they get information about current events?

   b. Apart from television, what sources do they turn to for information upon which to base an opinion? (For example, consumer, book, movie, record, or fashion reviews, and editorials?)

   c. Can they tell what side of an issue their local newspaper favors? Opposes? How?

   d. Apart from articles on the editorial page, what other decisions made by newspaper editors influence public opinion and knowledge?

   e. What impact would political party newspapers have had in the 1840s, an era before television or radio?

5. Antiwar protesters did not just appear with the Vietnam War, as some students believe. Time permitting, you may wish to assign students to read Thoreau's essay "Civil Disobedience," or the play based on his incarceration, *The Night Thoreau Spent in Jail*, or James R. Lowell's *Biglow Papers*, or other examples of opposition to the Mexican War. Students should report to the class the issues raised and tactics used by these earlier protesters.

6. Direct students to look into earlier and later antiwar material, from Aristophanes' *Lysistrata* to Holly Near's songs about the conflict in Central America. Ask students to conduct research and prepare written or oral reports or to write an editorial on one of the following topics:

   a. Protesters of conscience against wars other than the Mexican War,

   b. Moral issues raised by conscientious objectors at different periods in history,

   c. Tactics used by antiwar protesters over time and how these tactics have changed.

National Archives Document Citation

Lincoln's "Spot Resolutions," 1848; Spot Resolutions, pp. 2-3; (HR30A-B3); 30th Congress; Records of the United States House of Representatives, Record Group 233; National Archives Building, Washington, DC.

Article Citation

Mueller, Jean West and Wynell B. Schamel. "Lincoln's Spot Resolutions." *Social Education* 52, 6 (October 1988): 455-457, 466.

Lincoln's Letter to Siam, 1861

HISTORICAL BACKGROUND

(Note: Siam became Thailand in 1939.)

Very early in our nation's history, foreign nations began to offer gifts to the President and other high-ranking officials. Article 1, section 9, of the Constitution clearly sets forth the United States government's position on gift offers from heads of foreign governments to federal officials. The specific clause reads: "No Person holding any Office of Profit or Trust under them [the United States], shall, without the Consent of Congress, accept of any present, Emolument, Office, or Title, of any kind whatever, from any King, Prince, or foreign State." When consulted, however, Congress has often allowed United States diplomats to accept relatively inexpensive foreign gifts, especially when refusal of a token gift might be construed as an insult.

Most Presidents accepted gifts only on behalf of the American people, and they deposited them in governmental archives. Usually the State Department received these gifts in the President's name and Congress assumed responsibility for their ultimate disposition. Congress formalized this policy in 1881. But, as the actions of subsequent administrations indicated, the 1881 gift law did not sufficiently address a number of significant questions: Could the President keep gifts personally intended for him as opposed to those officially tendered to him as head of his government? Could the State Department turn over gifts it had received during his term to the President when he left office? Could official gifts be housed somewhere other than with State Department archives–for example, in a Presidential Library? Since 1881, various interpretations of these questions have prompted Congress to draft additional legislation to clarify its position toward foreign gifts.

Lincoln's Response to a Royal Proffer

From 1851 to 1868, Maha Mongkut (Rama IV) ruled Siam. Like the kings that preceded him, King Rama IV wished to resist Western imperialist designs upon Siam, but, unlike them, he so admired certain Western practices, particularly in education, that he sought contacts in the West. His unique melding of Eastern and Western ways has been fancifully characterized in the movie "The King and I." His letters to the United States Presidents of his day are among the treasures of the National Archives.

The two letters to which Lincoln replied demonstrate King Rama IV's knowledge of the United States, or at least its government. One letter recognized that the President could accept royal gifts only as "the common property of the Nation"; the other noted the United States military experiment to introduce camels into the American Southwest and suggested that, in the same spirit, elephants be imported from Siam to perform heavy labor.

In his reply to this offer by King Rama IV, Lincoln graciously accepts three gifts–a daguerreotype portrait of King Rama IV and his favorite daughter (right), a sword, and elephant tusks. However, he courteously declines the proffered elephants.

FURTHER DETAILS

- The Salutation "Great and Good Friend" used in the President's letter to the King was commonly used for addressing members of royalty.
- Several words in the document appear to substitute an "f" character for the first of two consecutive "s"s. Actually, the "f" is what is called a "long s" and was a common writing practice in the 17th and 18th centuries.

Great and Good Friend:

I have received Your Majesty's two letters of the date of February 14th, 1861.

I have also received in good condition the royal gifts which accompanied those letters, — namely, a sword of costly materials and exquisite workmanship; a photographic likeness of Your Majesty and of Your Majesty's beloved daughter; and also two elephants' tusks of length and magnitude such as indicate that they could have belonged only to an animal which was a native of Siam.

Your Majesty's letters show an understanding that our laws forbid the President from receiving these rich presents as personal treasures. They are therefore accepted in accordance with Your Majesty's desire as tokens of your good will and friendship for the American People. Congress being now in session at this capital, I have had great pleasure in making known to them this manifestation of Your Majesty's munificence and kind consideration.

Under their direction the gifts will be placed among the archives of the Government, where they will remain perpetually as tokens of mutual esteem and pacific dispositions more honorable to both nations than any trophies of conquest could be.

I appreciate most highly Your Majesty's tender of good offices in forwarding to this Government a stock from which a supply of elephants might be raised on our own soil. This Government would not hesitate to avail itself of so generous an offer if the object were one which could be made practically useful in the present condition of the United States.

Our political jurisdiction, however, does not reach a latitude so low as to favor the multiplication of the elephant, and steam on land, as well as on water, has been our best and most efficient agent of transportation in internal commerce.

Document 1.13a1 Lincoln's Letter to Siam, 1861. [National Archives]

I shall have occasion at no distant day to transmit to Your Majesty some token of indication of the high sense which this Government entertains of Your Majesty's friendship.

Meantime, wishing for Your Majesty a long and happy life, and for the generous and emulous People of Siam the highest possible prosperity, I commend both to the blessing of Almighty God.

Your Good Friend,
Abraham Lincoln.

Washington, February 3, 1862.
By the President:
William H. Seward,
Secretary of State.

Abraham Lincoln,
President of the United States of America.

To Her Majesty Doña Isabel II,
By the Grace of God and the Constitution of the Spanish Monarchy, Queen of Spain,
&c., &c.

Great and Good Friend:

I have received the letter which Your Majesty was pleased to address to me on the 28th of October, last, announcing that Her Royal Highness the Infanta Doña Maria Christina, spouse of His Royal Highness the Infante Don Sebastian Gabriel, had on the 20th of the preceding August safely given birth to a Prince upon whom, at the baptismal font has been bestowed the names of Francisco Maria Isabel Gabriel Pedro.

I participate in the satisfaction which this happy event has afforded to Your Majesty's Royal Family, and offer my sincere

Document 1.13a2 Lincoln's Letter to Siam, 1861. [National Archives]

- The letter reproduced here is from Volume 3 (1856-1864) of the "Communications to Foreign Sovereigns and Heads of States" Series, General Records of the Department of State, Record Group 59. It is in a clerk's hand, not that of President Lincoln.

TEACHING ACTIVITIES

The following suggestions are ideas for class discussions or for independent student projects. They are organized by course subject.

For Geography classes

1. The gifts offered to President Lincoln by the King of Siam reflect some of the natural resources and cultural values of Siam. Direct students to do research on one country and to select several products or items that might be representative gifts from that country. The following are suggested countries: Belgium, Colombia, Sierra Leone, Pakistan, and New Zealand. Place a map of the world on a bulletin board and ask students to locate their countries and explain to the class the reasons for selecting these particular gifts.

For American History and Government classes

2. American Presidents are prohibited from accepting gifts from foreign governments without Congressional permission. Discuss this policy with students. Consider these issues: What motivates a head of state to send expensive gifts to the leader of another country? Does the value of a gift affect whether it should be accepted?

For World History classes

3. What gifts do you think would have been appropriate for the President to have sent to the King? Would the same gifts be appropriate today? What was the nature of the relationship between the United States and Siam in 1861? What is that relationship today?

For American Studies classes

4. King Rama IV is characterized in the novel Anna and the King of Siam (and later in the movie, "The King and I"). Many other fictionalized books are based on historical incidents. Assign students to read one of these works and to describe to the class how it reflects the historical period: The Confessions of Nat Turner, The Red Badge of Courage, In Cold Blood, Northwest Passage, and The Winds of War.

5. Here is a simple puzzle designed to stimulate interest in the document. We suggest that you post the document on the bulletin board and reproduce copies of the puzzle for interested students.

ANSWER KEY
1 TROPHIES; 2 SEWARD; 3 PACIFIC; 4 ARCHIVES; 5 YEAR
6 SWORD, 7 STEAM, 8 CONGRESS, 9 SIAM

National Archives Document Citation

Lincoln's Letter to Siam, 1861; Volume III; Communications to Foreign Sovereigns and States, 1829-1877; General Records of the Department of State, Record Group 59; National Archives at College Park, College Park, MD.

Article Citation

Alexander, Mary and Marilyn Childress. "Lincoln's Letter to Siam." *Social Education* 44, 7 (November/December 1980): 606-610.

WORD PUZZLE

Student directions: To solve the puzzle, use information from the document to fill in the horizontal spaces. When the puzzle is completed, the word that will appear in the vertical ruled box is one that is significant to the document.

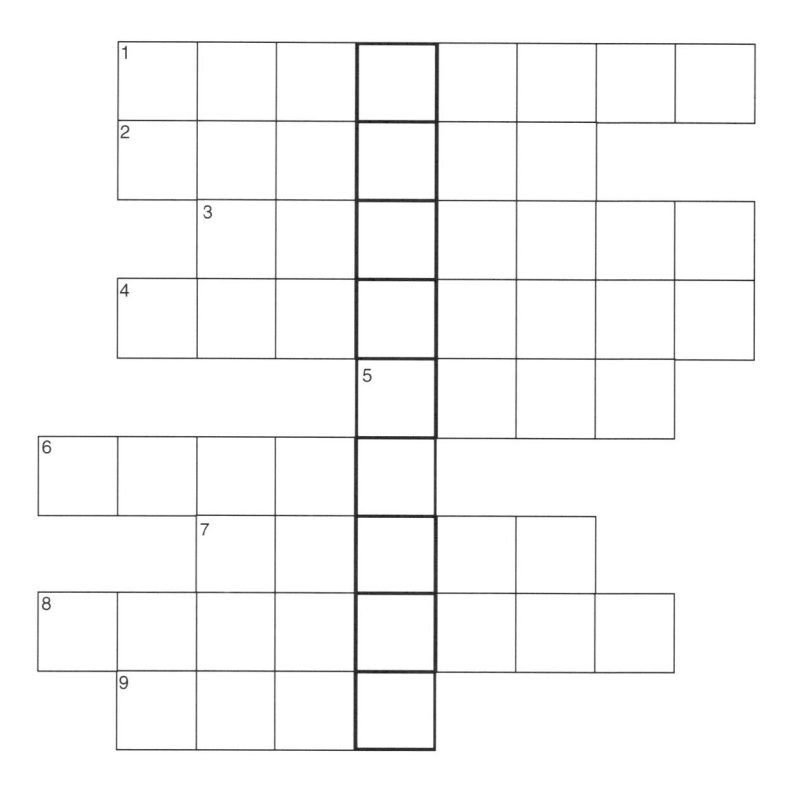

Clues:

1. According to Lincoln, gifts offered in peace are more honorable than _____ of war.

2. Last name of the Secretary of State in 1862.

3. Lincoln considered the Siamese gifts as tokens of peace. What word in the documents means peaceful?

4. The U.S. government would place the King's gifts here.

5. Approximate length of time between the date of the King's letters and the date of Lincoln's reply.

6. One of the gifts from Siam was a _____ of fine quality.

7. The most efficient energy form for land and water transportation in the 1860s.

8. Lincoln informed this legislative group about the Siamese gifts.

9. The name of this country today is Thailand.

Teaching With Documents 57 THE COLONIAL PERIOD TO 1879

Robert E. Lee's Resignation from the U.S. Army, 1861

Duty. Honor. Country. These three words appear on the crest of the United States Military Academy and frame the ideals of conduct by which many of its graduates strive to live. Robert E. Lee, West Point class of 1829, was a man driven by honor and duty. His resignation from the U.S. Army in 1861 was a tragedy for the United States and a personal one for Lee himself.

Today's highly mobile Americans, having grown up reciting the Pledge of Allegiance and singing the "Star Spangled Banner," find it difficult to comprehend such passionate loyalty to a state or region. But in 1861, the concept of the United States as a nation remained abstract to many Americans. The ratification of the Constitution was still a memorable milestone for elders who recalled the event and the debates over that voluntary association. It was not a stretch of the imagination to wonder if states that had voluntarily combined to form a national union could withdraw without harsh penalty. Distance and slow communications made Washington, DC, physically remote and created a rift more profound than the current cultural gap between those "inside and outside the Beltway." Even in the mid-19th century, Government officials were viewed with doubt and accused of a fondness for red tape. When differences over the issues of slavery and states rights deepened, the new, fragile bond of loyalty to the Union was broken by millions of its citizens.

Robert E. Lee's dilemma was not strictly a political one. The Lee family was inextricably bound with the creation of both the United States of America and the Commonwealth of Virginia. Lee's cousin, Richard Henry Lee, was a delegate to the Second Continental Congress and introduced the resolution for independence that led to the Declaration of Independence. He served in the Virginia legislature and later in the Confederation Congress. Richard Henry Lee opposed ratification of the Constitution in 1787 because it lacked a bill of rights and because he feared that a strong Federal Government would become too centralized. Nonetheless, he later served in the U.S. Senate.

Lee's father, Henry "Light Horse Harry" Lee, fought under Gen. George Washington as a cavalry officer during the American Revolution. He subsequently served in the Virginia legislature and Confederation Congress. Unlike his cousin, Richard, he supported the Constitution and voted for its ratification as a representative to the Virginia convention. He was a three-term governor of the State and also served in the Federal Government as a member of the U.S. House of Representatives. Washington called upon Lee to put down the Whisky Rebellion in 1794.

Robert E. Lee's own relationship with the United States was one of intense commitment and service. For nearly 35 years, he served in the U.S. Army with honor and distinction. Early in his career. he worked in the Mississippi River region and along the Atlantic coast defenses as an engineer. During the Mexican War (1846-48) he distinguished himself in reconnaissance and command of artillery. He served as superintendent of West Point for three years. Lee returned to active duty with the cavalry on the Texas frontier. From 1857 onward, family obligations forced him to request extended leaves of absence from military duty, but in 1859 he led the forces that captured abolitionist John Brown at Harper's Ferry.

As the Nation moved inexorably towards Civil War, Lee passed through his own personal crisis. He had written that "secession is nothing but revolution." Although a slave owner, he stated that even if he owned every slave in the South, he would free them all to save the Union. He rejected the idea that "our people will destroy a government inaugurated by the blood and wisdom of our patriot fathers, that has given us peace and prosperity at home, power and security abroad, and under which we have acquired a colossal strength unequaled in the history of mankind." He professed his love for the United States by saying, "I feel as if I could easily lay down my life for its safety." Yet, his assertions were based on the vain hope that Virginia could either avoid the struggle ahead or remain neutral. Unfortunately for Lee and the Nation, that was not possible.

Arlington, Washington City P.O.
20 April 1861

Hon.ble Simon Cameron
  Sec.t of War

    Sir
        I have the honour to tender the resignation of my Commission as Colonel of the 1st Reg.t of Cavalry
            Very resp.t your obt.svt
                R E Lee
                Col 1st Cav.y

Document 1.14 Robert E. Lee's Resignation from the U.S. Army, April 20, 1861. [National Archives]

In February of 1861, prior to returning east from Texas, he confided to another officer, "I shall never bear arms against the Union, but it may be necessary for me to carry a musket in defense of my native state, Virginia, in which case I shall not prove recreant to my duty." When Lee reported to Winfield Scott, General in Chief of the Army, in early March, he offered to resign at once. Because there had been much more talk of reconciliation by Lincoln's Cabinet members, Scott encouraged Lee to remain. Lee warned, "If a disruption takes place, I shall go back to my people and share the misery of my native state, and save in her defense, there will be one soldier less in the world." Nonetheless, on March 16, 1861, Scott promoted Lee to the rank of colonel in the 1st U.S. Cavalry.

On April 18, 1861, the day after Virginia voted for secession, President Lincoln sent an unofficial representative, Francis P. Blair, Sr., to ask Robert E. Lee to take command of the United States Army. At this meeting, Lee spoke of his devotion to the Union and then asked to speak to fellow Virginian Winfield Scott. Lee told Scott that he would resign. The old Mexican War hero replied, "Lee, you have made the greatest mistake of your life." (Later, when a delegation of Virginians invited Scott to join their army, he would rebuff them sharply saying, "I have served my country, under the flag of the Union, for more than 50 years, and so long as God permits me to live, I will defend that flag with my sword, even if my own native state assails it.")

Lee returned to his home in Arlington, VA, located directly across the Potomac River from Washington, DC. In a letter to his sister, Anne Marshall, he explained, "I have not been able to make up my mind to raise my hand against my relatives, my children, my home. I have therefore resigned my commission in the Army, and save in defense of my native State, with the sincere hope that my poor services may never be needed, I hope I may never be called on to draw my sword." His wife reported to a friend Lee's emotional turmoil over the decision. She wrote, "You can scarcely conceive the struggle it has cost Robert to resign to contend against the flag he has so long honored disapproving, as we both do, the course of the North & South, yet our fate is now linked with the latter & may the prayers of the faithful for the restoration of peace be heard."

Two days later, a delegation of Virginians invited Robert E. Lee to become "commander of the military and naval forces of Virginia." He accepted without hesitation and was appointed to the position on April 23, 1861. Once he committed himself to the cause of Virginia, and subsequently to that of the Confederacy, Lee committed himself fully. He fought with skill and shrewdness, inflicting terrifying casualties upon the men of the U.S. Army.

Yet, during his surrender at Appomattox in April 1865–through his act of submission to Grant, his demeanor during the surrender, and his words to the Confederate troops–Lee may have performed the greatest service of his lifetime to the Union he had renounced 4 years earlier. It would have been easy for the American Civil War to have continued as a guerrilla war, with generation upon generation revisiting past hatreds and renewing violent animosities. Indeed, given the scars of this war, it is almost miraculous that the United States did not become another Lebanon, Ireland, or Bosnia. Robert E. Lee deserves much of the credit for the peace. Toward the conclusion of the war, he rebuked a lieutenant who had urged him to allow about 8,000 armed soldiers to slip off into the hills of Virginia and continue the war, saying he was "too old to go bushwhacking."

In August of 1865 he wrote of his native State, Virginia, "The interests of the State are therefore the same as those of the United States. Its prosperity will rise or fall with the welfare of the country. The duty of its citizens then appears to me too plain to admit of doubt. All should unite in honest efforts to obliterate the effects of war, and to restore the blessings of peace. They should remain if possible in the country; promote harmony and good feeling; qualify themselves to vote; and elect to the State and General Legislatures wise and patriotic men who will devote their abilities to the interests of the country, and the healing of all dissensions." He followed his own advice, setting an example for his fellow Virginians by applying for amnesty and pardon.

On October 12, 1870, Lee died. His farewell words to his troops at Appomattox could as well have applied to him: "You will take with you the satisfaction that proceeds from the consciousness of duty faithfully performed."

Lee's letter of resignation from the U.S. Army is found in the Records of the Adjutant General's Office, 1780's-1917, Record Group 94.

TEACHING ACTIVITIES

Retrieving Information

1. Ask students to answer the following questions:
   a. Who wrote the document?
   b. Who received the document?
   c. What is the date of the document?
   d. What distinguishing marks do you find on the document?
   e. What action is the writer taking in this document?

Class Discussion

2. Poll students for a reply to the question, "What is your citizenship?" You may choose to do this aloud or on a ballot with the following headings: [Name of state], United States of America, [Name of another nation], United Nations. Tally the results for the class, and discuss the outcome. Ask students to account for the likely result that most of them identify with a nation. Explain to students that all U.S. citizens are citizens not only of the United States, but also of the state in which they reside.

3. Survey students to determine if they know the name of:
   a. The Governor of their state
   b. The Lieutenant Governor of their state
   c. The state senator for their district
   d. The state representative in the house for their district
   e. The President of the United States
   f. The Vice President of the United States
   g. The two state senators in the U.S. Senate
   h. The representative in the U.S. House for their district
   i. The Secretary General of the United Nations
   j. The U.S. representative to the United Nations

Tally the results, and discuss with the class why they are more familiar with figures in the U.S. Government (as is most likely) than in their state government or the United Nations. Ask students to consider what contact they have with the state government. You may need to remind them that school attendance requirements are the state's domain. Investigate together what contact your students have had with international organizations such as the United Nations, the International Olympic Committee, Amnesty International, or UNICEF.

Research

4. Ask students to research and report to the class other Federal officers who resigned their commissions and offered their services to the Confederacy, such as Samuel Cooper, Joseph E. Johnston, Albert Sidney Johnston, James Longstreet, Jeb Stuart, or Pierre Gustave Toutant Beauregard.

Writing Activity

5. Ask students to assume the identity of Robert E. Lee and write a journal entry describing one of the following:
   a. The pros and cons of refusing command of the U.S. Army
   b. The pros and cons of resigning his commission from the U.S. Army
   c. How he felt about fighting against classmates and students from West Point and men with whom he had served in the Mexican War
   d. How he felt about giving his word of honor and oath to support the Constitution of the United States and the Union in 1865

National Archives Document Citation

Robert E. Lee's Resignation from the U.S. Army, April 20, 1861; L-60, AGO 1861; (National Archives Microfilm Publication M619, roll 34); Letter Received by the Office of the Adjutant General (Main Series), 1861-1870; Records of the Adjutant General's Office, 1780's-1917, Record Group 94; National Archives Building, Washington, DC.

Article Citation

West, Jean M. and Wynell Schamel. "Robert E. Lee's Resignation from the U.S. Army." *Social Education* 61, 2 (February 1997): 108-111.

1.15

Letter to Giuseppe Garibaldi, 1861

BACKGROUND

During the early years of the Civil War, the Union Army solicited the aid of experienced foreign officers to lead the untrained, newly recruited troops. The intent was to have these men play much the same role that General Lafayette played during the American Revolution. One such man whom the Union sought was Giuseppe Garibaldi of Italy.

Garibaldi was born July 4, 1807, in Nice, Italy (now a part of France). At a young age he joined the revolutionary forces to fight for the unification of the Italian states and their freedom from Austria. Garibaldi quickly proved himself to be a capable, charismatic leader.

In 1850, after suffering defeat at the hands of the French, Garibaldi fled to America. He was hailed by some Americans as the "Washington of Italy." He returned to Italy in 1854 and rejoined the fight for Italian independence in 1859.

Because of Garibaldi's ability and persistence as a leader, Secretary of State William H. Seward offered him command of a Union force in 1861. An American diplomat assured Garibaldi that "thousands" of Italian and Hungarian immigrants would be willing to serve under him. In fact, only 17,157 Italians and 3,737 Hungarians lived in the United States at the time. Garibaldi refused the Union offer at first because he thought his military expertise would be needed soon at home. However, the King of Italy, Victor Emmanuel II, gave him permission to go to America if he chose. Garibaldi indicated that he would join the Union Army if he were named Commander in Chief and if the Union would adopt the abolition of slavery as a war goal. The United States would not comply; Lincoln was still hopeful that the Union might be reunited without abolishing slavery. Garibaldi, therefore, refused the offer of a commission.

Garibaldi lived to see Italy united and freed from Austrian rule. He joined the French in their fight against the Prussians in 1870. He retired to his home on the Island of Caprera, in the Tyrrhenian Sea, where he died on June 2, 1882.

TEACHING ACTIVITIES

These activities are varied according to ability levels. Activity 1 is designed for use with students of average to below average reading abilities. It would also be suitable for some junior high students. The worksheet in Activity 1 will help these students achieve success in gathering factual information from a document. Activities 2, 3, and 4 are alternative teaching strategies for students with average to above average reading ability. Any of these activities can be used to build upon Activity 1.

Activity 1: Garibaldi Letter and Worksheet
(Information gathering, reading skills, and copying skills)

1. Make copies of the document (or a transparency for an overhead projector) and of the worksheet, "Letter to Garibaldi," for each student.

2. Provide each student with a copy of the document or project the transparency.

3. Ask a student volunteer to read the letter to the class while other students follow silently.

4. Give each student a copy of the worksheet to complete by using the information in the document. Provide a copy of the document for each student as an exercise in near-point (close) copying, or use a transparency on the overhead projector to practice far-point (distance) copying skills.

Activity 2: Garibaldi's Job Description
(Oral and written communication skills, creative expression)

1. Tell students to imagine themselves in the following situation:

    You are Lincoln's Secretary of State, William H. Seward, and you have offered

Teaching With Documents — THE COLONIAL PERIOD TO 1879

Antwerp, June 8th 1861.

General Garibaldi:

The papers report that you are going to the United States, to join the army of the North in the conflict of my country. If you do, the name of <u>LaFayette</u> will not surpass yours. There are thousands of Italians and Hungarians who will rush to your ranks, and there thousands and tens of thousands of American citizens who will glory to be under the command of the "Washington of Italy."

I would thank you to let me know if this is really your intention. If it be, I will resign my position here as Consul and join you in the support of a Government formed by such names as Washington, Franklin, Jefferson, and their compatriots, whose names it

Document 1.15a1 Letter to General Giuseppe Garibaldi from J.W. Quiggle, June 8, 1861. [National Archives]

is not necessary for me to mention to you.

I sincerely regret the death of Cavour. He was a great statesman. But you were right in demanding for your officers and soldiers what you did; for they had fought bravely under your command and deserved your highest thought.

With assurances of my profound regard,

Yours &c.

(Signed) J. W. Quiggle.

To Gen. Garibaldi,
Caprera, Italy.

WORKSHEET FOR ACTIVITY 1

Letter to Garibaldi

¹_____ June 8th, ²____.

General ³_____:

    The papers report that you are going to the ⁴_____ to join the ⁵_____ of the ⁶_____ in the conflict of my country. If you do, the name of ⁷_____ will not surpass yours. There are thousands of ⁸_____ and ⁹_____ who will rush to your ranks, and there [are] thousands and tens of thoursands of American citizens who will glory to be under the command of the ¹⁰ "_____."

    I would thank you to let me know if this is really your intention. If it be, I will ¹¹_____ my position here as ¹²_____ and join you in the support of a ¹³_____ formed by such men as ¹⁴_____, ¹⁵_____, ¹⁶_____, and their compatriots whose names it is not necessary for me to mention to you.

    I sincerely regret the death of ¹⁷_____. He was a great ¹⁸_____. But you were right in demanding for your officers and soldiers what you did, for they had fought bravely under your command and deserved your highest thought.

    With assurances of my profound regard.

        Yours yet,

            (Signed) ¹⁹_____

            To General ²⁰_____

                Caprera ²¹_____.

Garibaldi a position of leadership with the Union Army. Garibaldi informs you by letter that he is giving serious consideration to the offer. Before making his decision, however, he requests a detailed job description of his duties.

2. Write a job description for Garibaldi. Encourage students to be creative in their job descriptions and to include as many details as they can. You may wish to have your class work in pairs or small groups.

Activity 3: You Were There
(Comparing and contrasting points of view)

1. Begin this activity by discussing with the class the following questions: Would all Union leaders want the aid of an Italian military leader in the Civil War? What factors might shape their points of view?

2. Place the following names on the board: Abraham Lincoln, President of the United States; General George McClellan, Commander of the Union Army; Antonio Enrico, 21-year-old Italian-American draftee.

3. Ask the class to imagine that the year is 1861 and the war has just begun. Ask each student to assume the role of one of the above personalities. Then direct the students to list three reasons why they would or would not support a Union policy of enlisting the aid of foreign leaders in the cause of the North. Later, ask students to compare and contrast the viewpoints of each person on this issue.

Activity 4: Garibaldi's Motivation
(Critical thinking)

1. Use the following list to begin a discussion of factors that might have motivated Garibaldi or some other important foreign leader to support the Union cause. (As an alternative approach, ask students to develop their own list of motivations.)

    a. To enhance the leader's glory.
    b. To aid an ally in need.
    c. To enhance the glory of his or her country in the world's eyes.
    d. To increase personal wealth.
    e. To gain support from a country that could help the leader's country if assistance were needed at a future time.
    f. To help eliminate oppression within another country.
    g. To gain land or colonies as a reward.
    h. To support emigrants from the leader's country who have settled in the warring country.
    i. To increase the leader's influence in his own country.
    j. To gain military experience.

2. Ask the class to rank the reasons in order of the importance they may have had in Garibaldi's decision on whether to enter the Union cause. Encourage students to justify the order of choices, keeping in mind Garibaldi's various roles as a national leader, a military leader, and an individual. You may want to raise these additional questions: Is there enough evidence available to analyze Garibaldi's motivations? What other information would be helpful in making a careful assessment?

The letter reproduced here is enclosed in Despatch 20, Quiggle to Secretary of State, July 5, 1861, Despatches from United States Consuls in Antwerp, 1802-1906, Volume 5, General Records of the Department of State, Record Group 59.

National Archives Document Citation
Letter to Gen. Giuseppe Garibaldi from J.W. Quiggle, June 8, 1861; Volume 5, July 5, 1861, Dispatch 20; Dispatches from United States Consuls in Antwerp, 1802-1906; General Records of the Department of State, Record Group 59; National Archives at College Park, College Park, MD.

Article Citation
Gent, Kathryn. "A letter to Giuseppe Garibaldi." *Social Education* 43, 7 (November/December 1979): 604-606.

Circular from the Surgeon General's Office, 1862

When news of the outbreak of the Civil War reached Dorothea Dix, she immediately headed for Washington to volunteer her services. Miss Dix was already well known for her efforts to secure humane treatment for the mentally ill, and Secretary of War Simon Cameron gladly accepted her offer to organize women nurses for the Union cause.

In her rented quarters, Miss Dix became a one-woman bureaucracy, organizing and dispatching nurses as the tides of battle changed. On June 10, 1861, she was officially commissioned the nation's first Superintendent of Women Nurses.

In the early days of the war, confusion reigned. Lack of coordinated action and shortages of supplies, along with an abundance of willing but untrained volunteers, presented enormous challenges. Some way was needed to select volunteers who could withstand the rigors of wartime nursing. Miss Dix wanted particularly to discourage women whom she suspected of wishing only to be near husbands or sweethearts on the battlefield.

The featured document, Circular Order No. 8 of July 14, 1862, was intended as much to limit volunteers as to recruit them. It reflected Miss Dix's own preference for simplicity, and stoutheartedness. It emphasized plain looks, plain manner, and maturity. Ability to care for the wounded was one desirable qualification, but, strangely, not the foremost one. In the early 1860s, nursing was not yet a profession for which women formally trained.

All inquiries about nursing service and all women seeking to volunteer were referred by the Surgeon General's Office to Dorothea Dix.

The letter books of the Surgeon General at the National Archives contain handwritten copies of these letters as well as requests that Miss Dix locate and dispatch supplies and nurses immediately to new scenes of action. Some women who failed to pass her scrutiny sneaked aboard troop trains and served gallantly on the front lines. Others, like Clara Barton, acted on their own.

One of Miss Dix's best-known nursing recruits was Louisa May Alcott, later the famous author of *Little Women*. Miss Alcott had only served briefly in a converted Washington hotel when she became seriously ill. Dorothea Dix helped nurse her back to health, and Miss Alcott thanked her in "Hospital Sketches," a series of newspaper articles describing her Civil War experience, later published in book form.

Ironically, Dorothea Dix could not have met the standards she outlined in her circular order. At the start of the Civil War she was already 60 years old. Born in 1802, she had grown up in Massachusetts, taught school, and written a number of popular books for children. Despite chronic ill health, she had then spent two decades traveling all over the country visiting the mentally ill, publicizing their plight, and persuading state legislatures to furnish money to build clean, modern, restful institutions for the insane.

A major figure in the period of antebellum reform, she is credited with prompting the establishment of more than 20 state hospitals. Although she had strong views on the other reform issues of her day–temperance, slavery, and votes for women–she did not speak on them publicly for fear of distracting attention from the cause of better care for the mentally ill.

The Civil War presented Dorothea Dix with a new opportunity for service, as it did for many women. Although she lacked nursing experience or training, she knew a great deal about hospitals and had high standards for patient care. She found it hard to adjust those standards to the difficult conditions of wartime and was often frustrated by inevitable delays and inefficiency. She clashed with doctors who resented her interference and her surprise inspections. By the war's end she retained her title but little of her once absolute authority over women nurses.

With characteristic dedication, she had labored for years without a day off. She remained in Washington after the war to secure a suitable memorial for Union soldiers buried in the National Cemetery at Fort Monroe, Virginia. She refused all honors and compensation, asking only for the flag of the nation she had served so long.

Secretary of War Edwin Stanton responded with a set of flags and a letter praising her work. Among her bequests, Miss Dix left the flags to Harvard College and $100 to Hampton Institute, located near the site of the Union soldiers' memorial.

The featured document is found in the Records of the Surgeon General's Office, Record Group 112, Volume 1, Circulars and circular letters, 1861-85.

TEACHING ACTIVITIES

1. Ask your students to discuss what qualifications are necessary for a nurse today. How do these compare with the requirements set out by Dorothea Dix in Circular Order No. 8? Consider what factors might account for the differences.

2. Women writing to the Surgeon General about service as a nursing volunteer were advised to contact Miss Dorothea Dix at 505 12th Street, Washington, D.C. Today's volunteers for emergency services (firefighting, nursing service, rescue squad) must be prepared to convince professionals of their suitability for service. Ask your students to draft a letter either to Miss Dix or a contemporary figure, describing their qualifications and reasons for wanting to serve.

3. Dorothea Dix interviewed all women who came to Washington to volunteer before approving them for service as nurses for the Union army. Volunteers for emergency services today must also go through interviews. Ask students to dramatize such an interview, either in a contemporary situation or between Miss Dix and an eager nursing recruit (using the information provided in the article and in the circular).

4. Ask students to locate evidence to support or to disprove the following statement: The Civil War was the bloodiest war in American history because the technology to kill was on the threshold of the 20th century while medicine was still in the Middle Ages.

5. Following the Civil War, Dorothea Dix raised money to complete a memorial to Union soldiers who had died in the conflict. She personally selected items for a time capsule sealed in the base of the monument at Fort Monroe, including Civil War mementos, pictures of U.S. presidents, coins, maps, a Bible, and a copy of the Constitution. Discuss with your class what they would put in a time capsule today.

Compile a list of items or gather together things in a two-foot square box to be used as a time capsule to show what is noteworthy about American life in the late 1980s.

National Archives Document Citation

Circular No. 8 from the Surgeon General's Office, July 14, 1862; Volume I; Circular and Circular Letters, 1861-1885; Records of the Office of the Surgeon General (Army), Record Group 112; National Archives at College Park, College Park, MD.

Article Citation

Burroughs, Wynell, Jean Mueller and Jean Preer. "Surgeon General's Office." *Social Education* 52, 1 (January 1988): 66-68.

Circular No. 8.

WASHINGTON, D. C., *July* 14, 1862,

No candidate for service in the Women's Department for nursing in the Military Hospitals of the United States, will be received below the age of thirty-five years, nor above fifty.

Only women of strong health, not subjects of chronic disease, nor liable to sudden illnesses, need apply. The duties of the station make large and continued demands on strength.

Matronly persons of experience, good conduct, or superior education and serious disposition, will always have preference; habits of neatness, order, sobriety, and industry, are prerequisites.

All applicants must present certificates of qualification and good character from at least two persons of trust, testifying to morality, integrity, seriousness, and capacity for care of the sick.

Obedience to rules of the service, and conformity to special regulations, will be required and enforced.

Compensation, as regulated by act of Congress, forty cents a day and subsistence. Transportation furnished to and from the place of service.

Amount of luggage limited within small compass.

Dress plain, (colors brown, grey, or black,) and while connected with the service without ornaments of any sort.

No applicants accepted for less than three months' service; those for longer periods always have preference.

D. L. DIX.

Approved,
 WILLIAM A. HAMMOND,
  Surgeon General.

Document 1.16 Circular No. 8 from the Surgeon General's Office, July 14, 1862. [National Archives]

The Fight for Equal Rights:
A Recruiting Poster for Black Soldiers in the Civil War, ca. 1862

"Once let the black man get upon his person the brass letter, U.S., let him get an eagle on his button, and a musket on his shoulder and bullets in his pocket, there is no power on earth that can deny that he has earned the right to citizenship."

Frederick Douglass

The issues of emancipation and military service were intertwined from the onset of the Civil War. News from Fort Sumter set off a rush by free black men to enlist in U.S. military units. They were turned away, however, because a Federal law dating from 1792 barred Negroes from bearing arms for the U.S. army (although they had served in the American Revolution and in the War of 1812). In Boston disappointed would-be volunteers met and passed a resolution requesting that the Government modify its laws to permit their enlistment.

The Lincoln administration wrestled with the idea of authorizing the recruitment of black troops, concerned that such a move would prompt the border states to secede. When Gen. John C. Frémont in Missouri and Gen. David Hunter in South Carolina issued proclamations that emancipated slaves in their military regions and permitted them to enlist, their superiors sternly revoked their orders. By mid-1862, however, the escalating number of former slaves (contrabands), the declining number of white volunteers, and the increasingly pressing personnel needs of the Union Army pushed the Government into reconsidering the ban.

As a result, on July 17, 1862, Congress passed the Second Confiscation and Militia Act, freeing slaves who had masters in the Confederate Army. Two days later, slavery was abolished in the territories of the United States, and on July 22 President Lincoln presented the preliminary draft of the Emancipation Proclamation to his Cabinet. After the Union Army turned back Lee's first invasion of the North at Antietam, MD, and the Emancipation Proclamation was subsequently announced, black recruitment was pursued in earnest. Volunteers from South Carolina, Tennessee, and Massachusetts filled the first authorized black regiments. Recruitment was slow until black leaders such as Frederick Douglass encouraged black men to become soldiers to ensure eventual full citizenship. (Two of Douglass's own sons contributed to the war effort.) Volunteers began to respond, and in May 1863 the Government established the Bureau of Colored Troops to manage the burgeoning numbers of black soldiers.

By the end of the Civil War, roughly 179,000 black men (10% of the Union Army) served as soldiers in the U.S. Army and another 19,000 served in the Navy. Nearly 40,000 black soldiers died over the course of the war—30,000 of infection or disease. Black soldiers served in artillery and infantry and performed all noncombat support functions that sustain an army, as well. Black carpenters, chaplains, cooks, guards, laborers, nurses, scouts, spies, steamboat pilots, surgeons, and teamsters also contributed to the war cause. There were nearly 80 black commissioned officers. Black women, who could not formally join the Army, nonetheless served as nurses, spies, and scouts, the most famous being Harriet Tubman, who scouted for the 2nd South Carolina Volunteers.

Because of prejudice against them, black units were not used in combat as extensively as they might have been. Nevertheless, the soldiers served with distinction in a number of battles. Black infantrymen fought gallantly at Milliken's Bend, LA; Port Hudson, LA; Petersburg, VA; and Nashville, TN. The July 1863 assault on Fort Wagner, SC, in which the 54th Regiment of Massachusetts Volunteers lost two-thirds of their officers and half of their troops, was memorably dramatized in the film *Glory*. By war's end, 16 black soldiers had been awarded the Medal of Honor for their valor.

In addition to the perils of war faced by all Civil War soldiers, black soldiers faced additional problems stemming from racial prejudice. Racial discrimination was prevalent even in the North, and discriminatory practices permeated the U.S. military. Segregated units were formed with black enlisted men and typically commanded by white officers and black noncommissioned officers. The 54th Massachusetts was commanded by Robert Shaw and the 1st South Carolina by Thomas Wentworth Higginson–both white. Black soldiers were initially paid $10 per month from which $3 was automatically deducted for clothing, resulting in a net pay of $7. In contrast, white soldiers received $13 per month from which no clothing allowance was drawn. In June 1864 Congress granted equal pay to the U.S. Colored Troops and made the action retroactive. Black soldiers received the same rations and supplies. In addition, they received comparable medical care.

The black troops, however, faced greater peril than white troops when captured by the Confederate Army. In 1863 the Confederate Congress threatened to punish severely officers of black troops and to enslave black soldiers. As a result, President Lincoln issued General Order 233, threatening reprisal on Confederate prisoners of war (POWs) for any mistreatment of black troops. Although the threat generally restrained the Confederates, black captives were typically treated more harshly than white captives. In perhaps the most heinous known example of abuse, Confederate General Nathan B. Forrest shot to death black Union soldiers captured at the Fort Pillow, TN, engagement of 1864.

The document featured with this article is a recruiting poster directed at black men during the Civil War. It refers to efforts by the Lincoln administration to provide equal pay for black soldiers and equal protection for black POWs. The original poster is located in the Records of the Adjutant General's Office, 1780's-1917, Record Group 94.

TEACHING ACTIVITIES

Analyzing the Document

1. Make a copy of the featured document for students, and direct them to read the poster and answer the following questions:

    a. Who do you think is the intended audience for the poster?

    b. What does the Government hope the audience will do?

    c. What references to pay do you find in this document?

    d. What references to treatment of prisoners of war do you find in this document?

    e. What evidence of discrimination during the Civil War do you find in this document?

    f. What evidence of Government efforts to improve conditions for black soldiers do you find in this document?

    g. What purpose(s) of the Government is/are served by this poster?

    h. How is the design of this poster different from contemporary military recruitment posters?

    After the students have completed the assignment, review it and answer any questions they might raise. Then discuss more generally the contribution and status of black soldiers in the Civil War. Ask students to read the additional documents provided with this article to encourage further discussion.

Creative Writing Activities

2. Share with students the information in the introductory note; then assign them to draw on information from the note and the document to write one of the following:

    - a journal entry of a member of the U.S. Colored Troops

    - a letter from a U.S. Colored Troops soldier to a son who wants to enlist

    - an account of the role of black soldiers for either an abolitionist or Confederate newspaper

- an interior monologue of the wife of a soldier in the U.S. Colored Troops reflecting on the circumstances of her family during his absence.

Oral Reports

3. President Harry S. Truman's Executive Order 9981, issued in 1948, marked the transition of the black military experience from a period of segregated troops to one of integrated forces. The order provided for "equal treatment and opportunity for all persons in the armed services" and commanded the desegregation of the military "as rapidly as possible."

   Divide the class into six groups: Civil War, Indian wars, World War I, World War II, Korea and Vietnam, and Persian Gulf War. Assign each group the task of locating information about black troops engaged in these conflicts and presenting the information they discover in an oral report. Encourage imaginative presentations.
   Students should collect information about pay, equipment, service assignments, promotion potential, treatment of black prisoners of war, and the relation of combat service to the struggle for equal rights in each instance. Each group should attempt to locate statistical information about the numbers of black soldiers in arms for their assigned conflict and the numbers of black casualties, decorations, and commissioned officers. Outstanding individual or unit contributions in engagements should be described as well.

For Further Research

4. Select one of the following activities as a follow-up:

   a. Arrange with the school or public library to set up a reserved reading shelf for your students on the topic of the black Civil War experience.

   b. Assign students to read a copy of Robert Lowell's poem "Colonel Shaw and the Massachusetts' 54th," alternately titled, "For the Union Dead." (The poem can be located in the Norton Anthology of American Literature.) Ask students to consider the following questions:

   - Why does Lowell say "their monument sticks like a fishbone in the city's throat"?
   - Why do you think Shaw's father wanted no monument "except the ditch, where his son's body was thrown"?
   - What is Lowell's attitude toward the "stone statues of the abstract Union Soldier"?
   - Lowell altered the inscription on the Shaw Memorial that reads "Omnia Reliquit Servare Rem Publicam" ("He leaves all behind to serve the Republic") to his epigraph "Relinquunt Omnia Servare Rem Publicam" ("They give up everything to serve the Republic"). How is the inscription typical of attitudes in 1897, when the memorial was dedicated? How is the epigraph, written in 1960, different, and what does that say about Lowell's attitude toward these soldiers?

   The Web site of the National Gallery of Art provides valuable information about the Shaw memorial.

   c. Ask for volunteers to watch the film *Glory*, a fictional account of the 54th Massachusetts, then the American Experience documentary, *The 54th Colored Infantry*. (If that tape is not available, you might use the segments on black units in Ken Burns's series *Civil War*.) Students should then review *Glory* for historical accuracy.

TO COLORED MEN!

FREEDOM,
Protection, Pay, and a Call to Military Duty!

On the 1st day of January, 1863, the President of the United States proclaimed FREEDOM to over THREE MILLIONS OF SLAVES. This decree is to be enforced by all the power of the Nation. On the 21st of July last he issued the following order:

PROTECTION OF COLORED TROOPS.

"WAR DEPARTMENT, ADJUTANT GENERAL'S OFFICE,
WASHINGTON, July 21.

"*General Order, No. 233.*

"The following order of the President is published for the information and government of all concerned:—

EXECUTIVE MANSION, WASHINGTON, July 30.

"'It is the duty of every Government to give protection to its citizens, of whatever class, color, or condition, and especially to those who are duly organized as soldiers in the public service. The law of nations, and the usages and customs of war, as carried on by civilized powers, permit no distinction as to color in the treatment of prisoners of war as public enemies. To sell or enslave any captured person on account of his color, is a relapse into barbarism, and a crime against the civilization of the age.

"'The Government of the United States will give the same protection to all its soldiers, and if the enemy shall sell or enslave any one because of his color, the offense shall be punished by retaliation upon the enemy's prisoners in our possession. It is, therefore, ordered, for every soldier of the United States, killed in violation of the laws of war, a rebel soldier shall be executed; and for every one enslaved by the enemy, or sold into slavery, a rebel soldier shall be placed at hard labor on the public works, and continued at such labor until the other shall be released and receive the treatment due to prisoners of war.

"'ABRAHAM LINCOLN.'"

"'By order of the Secretary of War.
"'E. D. TOWNSEND, Assistant Adjutant General.'"

That the President is in earnest the rebels soon began to find out, as witness the following order from his Secretary of War:

"WAR DEPARTMENT, WASHINGTON CITY, August 8, 1863.

"SIR: Your letter of the 3d inst., calling the attention of this Department to the cases of Orin H. Brown, William H. Johnston, and Wm. Wilson, three colored men captured on the gunboat Isaac Smith, has received consideration. This Department has directed that three rebel prisoners of South Carolina, if there be any such in our possession, and if not, three others, be confined in close custody and held as hostages for Brown, Johnston and Wilson, and that the fact be communicated to the rebel authorities at Richmond.

"Very respectfully your obedient servant,
"EDWIN M. STANTON, Secretary of War.

"The Hon. GIDEON WELLES, Secretary of the Navy."

And retaliation will be our practice now—man for man—to the bitter end.

LETTER OF CHARLES SUMNER,
Written with reference to the Convention held at Poughkeepsie, July 15th and 16th, 1863, to promote Colored Enlistments.

BOSTON, July 13th, 1863.

"I doubt if, in times past, our country could have expected from colored men any patriotic service. Such service is the return for protection. But now that protection has begun, the service should begin also. Nor should relative rights and duties be weighed with nicety. It is enough that our country, aroused at last to a sense of justice, seeks to enrol colored men among its defenders.

"If my counsels should reach such persons, I would say: enlist at once. Now is the day and now is the hour. Help to overcome your cruel enemies now battling against your country, and in this way you will surely overcome those other enemies hardly less cruel, here at home, who will still seek to degrade you. This is not the time to hesitate or to higgle. Do your duty to our country, and you will set an example of generous self-sacrifice which will conquer prejudice and open all hearts.

"Very faithfully yours,
"CHARLES SUMNER."

Document 1.17 Circular: "To Colored Men! Freedom…" A recruiting poster for black soldiers in the Civil War, ca. 1862. [National Archives]

National Archives Document Citation

Circular: "To Colored Men! Freedom…" A recruiting poster for black soldiers in the Civil War, ca. 1862; D-135, 1863; Colored Troops Division, Letter Received; Records of the Adjutant General's Office, 1780's-1917, Record Group 94; National Archives Building, Washington, DC.

Article Citation

Freeman, Elsie, Wynell Burroughs Schamel, and Jean West. "The Fight for Equal Rights: A Recruiting Poster for Black Soldiers in the Civil War." *Social Education* 56, 2 (February 1992): 118-120. [Revised and updated in 1999 by Budge Weidmann.]

The Homestead Act of 1862, 1862

On January 1, 1863, Daniel Freeman, a scout for the Union Army, was scheduled to leave Gage County, Nebraska Territory, for St. Louis to report for duty. Fortunately for him, while attending a New Year's Eve party in a hotel in Brownsville, Nebraska, he spoke with some Land Office officials. He was able to convince one of the clerks to open the office shortly after midnight, so that he could file a land claim before his departure. In doing so, Freeman became one of the first to seize the opportunity made possible by the Homestead Act, a law signed by President Abraham Lincoln on May 20, 1862.

The Homestead Act provided that any U.S. citizen, or intended citizen, who had never borne arms against the U.S. government could claim 160 acres of surveyed government land. Claimants were required to "improve" the plot by building a dwelling measuring at least 12 by 14 and cultivating the land. After five years on the land, the original filer was entitled to the property, free and clear–except for a small registration fee. Title could also be acquired after only a six-month residency and trivial improvements, provided the claimant paid the government $1.25 per acre. After the Civil War, Union soldiers could deduct the time they served from the residency requirements.

Although this act was included in the Republican party platform of 1860, support for it began decades earlier. Even under the Articles of Confederation before 1787, the distribution of government lands generated much interest and discussion. These early discussions focused on land measurement and price.

A congressional committee decided to end the chaos experienced by settlers and government officials in Kentucky in 1779 by resolving the issue of measurement. Under the existing Virginia System, plots were generally guided by natural landmarks. A Kentuckian could simply step off whatever land he wanted (regardless of shape), survey, and register it. This system led to confusion and a number of overlapping claims. The federal solution was the creation of a system of land surveys to be completed prior to settlement. These surveys were based on a defined unit of measurement called a township. Each township was a six-mile square, divided into 36 sections, measuring 1 square mile or 640 acres each. Astronomical observations determined the starting points of the measurements. As the country acquired vast new territory throughout the first half of the 1800s, this system of measurement continued.

The early government's prevailing belief that public land was best used as a source for revenue, rather than as a cheap inducement to settlement, influenced early decisions about price and distribution. In the 1780s, the minimum price for public land was set at $1 per acre, and the minimum amount to be sold to an individual was 640 acres (one section). The cost was prohibitive and the amount of land was simply too much for most would-be settlers, as much of it was wooded and required labor intensive clearing to serve as agricultural land. Consequently, provisions were made by 1800 that halved the minimum amount to 320 acres and allowed settlers to pay in four installments.

In the 1830s and 1840s, as the price of corn, wheat, and cotton rose, well-financed, large farms–particularly the plantations of the South–forced small farmers to sell out and move further west to lands they could afford to develop. All public land during these years sold for $1.25 an acre regardless of condition. Superior plots sold easily, inferior ones did not. To induce settlement to these less desirable areas, Senator Thomas Hart Benton of Missouri led a long battle to graduate land prices according to desirability. He even suggested that land be given away if it had not been purchased within a certain time period, in order to bring it into minimal cultivation. The policies of graduating prices and giving away public land were not adopted until later, but their suggestion fueled the growing belief that public land should not be sold simply to raise revenue, but to furnish homesteads and encourage settlement.

Prior to the war with Mexico (1846-1848), people settling in the West demanded "pre-emption"–an individual's right to settle land first and pay later. Essentially, they wanted an early form of credit.

Application No. 1.

Homestead Land Office
Brownville N.T. January 1st 1863

I Daniel Freeman of Gage County Nebraska Territory Do hereby apply to Enter under the Provisions of the act of Congress aproved May 20th 1862 Entitled, an act to Secure Homesteads to actual Settlers on the Public Domain The South half of N.W¼ & NE¼ of NW¼ & SW¼ of NE¼ Sec. 26. in Township (4) N in Range Five East, containing 160 acres Having filed my Pre Emption Decleration thereto on the Eighth day of September 1862

Daniel Freeman

Land office at;
Brownville N.T. January 1st 1863

I Richard F Barret Register of the Land office do Hereby Certify that the above application is For Surveyed Lands of the Class which the applicant is legally Entitled to Enter under the Homestead act of May 20th 1862 and that there is No Prior valid adverse Right to the Same

Richard F Barret
Register

Document 1.18a Homestead Application No. 1 from Daniel Freeman of Gage County, January 1, 1863. [National Archives]

HOMESTEAD.

Land Office at Brownville Neb January 20th 1868.

CERTIFICATE, No. 1

APPLICATION, No. 1

It is hereby certified, That pursuant to the provisions of the act of Congress, approved May 20, 1862, entitled "An act to secure homesteads to actual settlers on the public domain," Daniel Freeman has made payment in full for E½ of NW¼ and W½ of NW¼ and SW¼ of NE¼ of Section Twenty-Six (26) in Township Four (4) N of Range Five (5) E containing 160 acres.

Now, therefore, be it known, That on presentation of this Certificate to the COMMISSIONER OF THE GENERAL LAND OFFICE, the said Daniel Freeman shall be entitled to a Patent for the Tract of Land above described.

Henry M. Atkinson, Register.

Document 1.18b Homestead Certificate No. 1 issued to Daniel Freeman, January 20, 1868. [National Archives]

PROOF REQUIRED UNDER HOMESTEAD ACTS MAY 20, 1862, AND JUNE 21, 1866.

WE, *Joseph Graff* & *Samuel Kilpatrick* do solemnly swear that we have known *Daniel Freeman* for over five years last past; that he is the head of a family consisting of wife and two children and is — a citizen of the United States; that he is an inhabitant of the S½ of NW¼ & NE of NW¼ & SW¼ of NE¼ of section No. 26 in Township No. 4 N of Range No. 5 E and that no other person resided upon the said land entitled to the right of Homestead or Pre-emption.

That the said *Daniel Freeman* entered upon and made settlement on said land on the 1st day of January, 1863, and has built a house thereon part log & part frame 14 by 20 feet one story, with two doors two windows, Shingle roof, board floors and is a comfortable house to live in

and has lived in the said house and made it his exclusive home from the 1st day of January, 1863, to the present time, and that he has since said settlement ploughed, fenced, and cultivated about 35 acres of said land, and has made the following improvements thereon, to wit: built a Stable, a Sheep Shed 100 feet long Corn Crib, and has 40 apple and about 400 peach trees set out

Joseph Graff
Samuel Kilpatrick

I, *Henry M. Atkinson Register* do hereby certify that the above affidavit was taken and subscribed before me this 20th day of January, 1868.

Henry M. Atkinson
Register

WE CERTIFY that *Joseph Graff* & *Samuel Kilpatrick* whose names are subscribed to the foregoing affidavit, are persons of respectability.

Henry M. Atkinson, Register.
Jno. L. Carson, Receiver.

Document 1.18c Proof Required Under Homestead Acts on behalf of Daniel Freeman, January 20, 1868. [National Archives]

Although Easterners feared that this practice would drain cheap labor from their factories, pre-emption became national policy. This was due to impatient pioneers jumping borders to settle where they wished, as had been done since colonial days, and insufficient funding that caused surveys to lag behind settlement.

Following the war with Mexico, a number of circumstances contributed to the growing support for the homestead movement: unprecedented numbers of immigrants arrived, drawn by the nation's prosperity and cheaper trans-Atlantic crossings; new canals and roadways reduced western dependence on New Orleans; England's repeal of its corn laws opened new markets to American agriculture; and the practice of granting land to railroad companies set precedents for similar land concessions to citizens. Furthermore, more people believed that they could successfully farm non-wooded western lands.

Finally, in 1854, Senator Benton's principle of graduation was used to sell land that had been on the market for 30 years for 12 1/2 cents per acre. In the next couple of years, extraordinary bonuses were extended to veterans and those interested in settling the Oregon Territory.

Three times–in 1852, 1854, and 1859–the House of Representatives passed homestead legislation, but on each occasion the Senate defeated the measure. In 1860, a homestead bill, providing federal land grants to western settlers, was passed by Congress and vetoed by President Buchanan. These failures resulted from sectional concerns about slavery. Southerners believed that making the public domain available in 160-acre plots, free of charge, would fill the West with small farmers opposed to slavery.

After the South seceded from the Union, congressional opposition dwindled and the Homestead Act of 1862 was passed and signed into law. On the first day the law went into effect, Daniel Freeman and 417 others filed claims. Before the law was ultimately repealed in 1934, over 1.6 million homestead applications were processed, which resulted in more than 270 million acres–10 percent of all U.S. lands–being given by the federal government to individuals.

The homestead acquisition process was threefold: filing an application, improving the land, and filing for deed of title. When an individual selected a site, he filed an application with a government land office. For the next five years, the homesteader lived on the land and improved it by building a 12 by 14 dwelling and growing crops. At the end of the 5 years, the homesteader could file for his patent or deed of title to the land. This required submitting proof of residency and improvements to the land office. The paperwork accumulated by the local land office was forwarded to the General Land Office in Washington, DC, along with a final certificate that declared the case file eligible for a patent. The case file was examined, and if found valid, a patent to the land was sent back to the local land office for delivery to the homesteader.

Unfortunately, there was corruption in the system. For example, speculators took advantage of the fact that the law did not specify whether the 12 by 14 dwelling was to be built in feet or inches. Others acquired homestead land by hiring phony claimants or buying up abandoned land. The General Land Office received inadequate funding to provide the number of investigators needed for its widely scattered offices. Those who did conduct investigations were overworked and underpaid and therefore susceptible to bribery.

The conditions the homesteaders faced on the land were even more challenging than the required paperwork. Depending on the location, the challenges could include plagues of grasshoppers and locusts, blizzards, wind, prairie fires, little water, and no wood. The lack of trees for building timbers, particularly in western Kansas and Nebraska and eastern Colorado, prompted the building of homes out of sod. Limited wood also meant limited fuel for cooking and heating, and scarce natural vegetation made it particularly difficult to raise livestock. While 160 acres may have been sufficient for an eastern farmer, it was simply not enough on the dry plains. As a result, in many areas, the original homesteader did not stay on the land long enough to fulfill the claim.

The challenges, however, also led to opportunities for those who stayed. Six months after the Homestead Act was passed, the act providing for a transcontinental railroad was signed. Railroads provided easy transportation for homesteaders (many of whom were new immigrants lured by railroad companies eager to sell off their excess land at inflated prices). The new rail lines also provided a means by which homesteaders could receive manufactured goods. Through catalog houses like Montgomery Ward, homesteaders could order farm tools, plows, windmills, barbed wire, linens, weapons, even houses, and have them delivered via the rails. As homesteaders populated the territories, they filed for statehood, and built prairie schools. In many areas, the schools became the focal points for community life, serving as churches, polling places, and gathering spots for clubs and organizations.

One such school built in 1872, near Beatrice, Nebraska, is today part of the Homestead National Monument. The monument, administered by the National Park Service, includes the land claimed by Daniel Freeman. Although a number of other claimants received applications that indicated that their claim was the first, Freeman capitalized on his. In 1886, he sent Congressman Galusha Grow, author of the Homestead Act, a cane made from wood grown on his property. The Congressman accepted the cane along with Freeman's claim that he was the first entryman, and subsequently referred to Freeman as "the first" in a number of speeches.

The national recognition that Freeman received brought forth a number of other claimants. An investigation conducted for the centennial of the Homestead Act by the Bureau of Land Management and experts at the National Archives determined that William Young of Palmyra, Nebraska; Mahlon Gore, of Vermillion, Dakota Territory; and Daniel Freeman all might have a claim to this national honor. The investigation also found that Orin Holdbrook of Des Moines, Iowa, might also be a contender, because he was the only homesteader to file for his claim on the first day and to file for his final certificate exactly five years later, on January 1, 1868. The Department of the Interior, however, embraced Freeman's claim and established the monument on his homestead in 1936. Today, the site commemorates the lives and accomplishments of all pioneers and the changes to the land and to people brought by the Homestead Act.

Documents featured in this article include a homestead application, certificate, and proof. Freeman's application, certificate, and proof and those of other homesteaders are contained in the Records of the General Land Office, RG 49. For more information about land records, General Information Leaflet Number 67 entitled *Research in the Land Entry Files of the General Land Office*, RG 49, written by Kenneth Hawkins, is available free from the National Archives and Records Administration, NWPS, Washington, DC, 20408.

TEACHING ACTIVITIES

1. Provide each student with a photocopy of each of the featured documents, and make a transparency with the following questions: What types of documents are they? What are the dates of the documents? Who wrote the documents? What is the purpose of the documents? What information in the documents helps you understand why they were written? Ask one student to read the documents aloud as the others read silently. Lead the class in oral responses to the questions.

2. Instruct students to analyze the documents and make a list of the Homestead Act requirements. Ask them to check their answers by referring to the text of the Act, available in Henry Steele Commager's and Milton Cantor, eds., *Documents of American History*, and in the *Westward Expansion: 1842-1912* teaching packet available from the National Archives, as well as some textbooks. Lead a class discussion using some of the following questions:

   - What were settlers' citizenship requirements?
   - What were their age requirements?
   - Why was there a clause pertaining to never having borne arms against the government?
   - How long did a homesteader have to reside on the property?
   - What was a homesteader required to do to improve the land?
   - Whose names appear on the documents?
   - With what office were these documents filed?
   - In order to locate this property on a map, what additional information is necessary?
   - Did Freeman receive a patent for the land?
   - Why are these documents preserved by the federal government?

3. The case file for Virgil Earp, Prescott, Arizona (1870-1905) and the case file for Charles P. Ingalls, father of Laura Ingalls Wilder (1880-1907) are available at <http://www.archives.gov/digital_classroom/history_day/migration_history/migration_history.html>.

   Encourage students to look at these later files and write a paragraph comparing them to the Freeman documents.

4. Divide the class into three groups representing each of the three regions of the country in the 1840s: the North, the South, and the West. Ask each group to research and write their region's position on the homestead issue. Ask representatives from each group to conduct a mock congressional debate on a proposed homestead bill.

5. Invite a local real estate developer, surveyor, or land official to talk to your class about present-day real estate prices and land measurement. Ask them to bring documents describing property locations using section, township, and range. Then ask the students to use local sources to determine the section, township, and range of your school.

6. Locate and read the article entitled "How to Use an Economic Mystery in Your History Course," written by Donald R. Wentworth and Mark C. Schug and published in the January 1994 issue of *Social Education*. Divide the class into six groups and assign each group one of the principles of economic reasoning to consider as they begin to solve the mystery of the Homestead Act of 1862 as proposed in the article. Use the jigsaw method of regrouping for students to share information gathered about all six principles to answer the question: why did so many people fail to take advantage of the Homestead Act?

7. Assign pairs of students different public land states. Inform them that it is 1880, and they have just filed for a homestead in their assigned state. Using information contained in their history books, geography books, and library resources, ask them to determine what crops they will cultivate, if they will raise livestock, how they will obtain water and fuel, and where they will live. Ask them to construct a 12 by 14 (inch) dwelling out of materials that would have been available to them.

8. Divide the class into three groups. Ask one group to determine the population of the Plains states in 1860, 1870, and 1880, and create a large bar graph with their data. Ask another group to determine how many immigrants came to the United States between 1850-1860, 1860-1870, and 1870-1880, and also create a bar graph with their data. Finally, ask the third group to investigate the miles of railroad tracks in the United States built between 1850-1860, 1860-1870, and 1870-1880, and also create a bar graph with their data. Ask each group to present their findings and hold a class discussion on cause and effect. To what extent did acts of the federal government influence these three factors? *Historical Statistics of the United States*, almanacs, and other library sources will be helpful for this activity.

National Archives Document Citation

Homestead Application No. 1 from Daniel Freeman of Gage County, January 1, 1863; Records of the Bureau of Land Management, Record Group 49; National Archives Building, Washington, DC.

Homestead Certificate No. 1 issued to Daniel Freeman, January 20, 1868; Records of the Bureau of Land Management, Record Group 49; National Archives Building, Washington, DC.

Proof Required Under Homestead Acts on behalf of Daniel Freeman, January 20, 1868; Records of the Bureau of Land Management, Record Group 49; National Archives Building, Washington, DC.

Article Citation

Potter, Lee Ann and Wynell Schamel. "The Homestead Act of 1862." *Social Education* 61, 6 (October 1997): 359-364.

Ex parte Milligan Letter, 1864

One of the challenges we face in teaching the U.S. Constitution is in helping our students understand how Supreme Court decisions have come to further shape and define the Constitution. This document concerns an extremely important civil liberties case–*Ex parte Milligan*–in which the Supreme Court decided whether the President has the right, in regions where the civil courts are in operation, to suspend the writ of habeas corpus and to substitute trial by the military. The document is a simple but powerful plea from a man who has been condemned to die. Despite its brevity and simplicity, it raises numerous questions. What crime is Milligan guilty of? Was he really sentenced without evidence, or is this just his opinion? Why does he refer to the Secretary of War as "an old acquaintance and friend?" In short, what is the story behind this piece of history?

Article I, section 9, clause 2 of the Constitution states, "The privilege of the writ of habeas corpus shall not be suspended, unless when in cases of rebellion or invasion the public safety might require it." A writ of habeas corpus is one of the oldest civil liberties in the English-speaking world. Addressed to the jailer of a prisoner by a judge, its literal translation is "Thou (shalt) have the body (in court)"; that is, the jailer must produce the prisoner and explain to the judge why the prisoner is being held. If the judge finds that the prisoner is being unlawfully detained, the judge may order the prisoner's release. Habeas corpus has served over the centuries as a protection for citizens against arbitrary detainment and has allowed the judiciary to intervene to protect individuals from arbitrary use of legislative and executive power.

During the Civil War President Lincoln found it necessary to proclaim, in September of 1862, that "all persons..., guilty of any disloyal practise...shall be subject to martial law and liable to trial and punishment by Courts Martial or Military Commissions." In October 1864, Lambdin P. Milligan and two others were tried in a military court in Indiana and found guilty of conspiring with the Confederate States of America to set up a "Northwestern Confederacy." The military court sentenced all three to hang the following May.

Milligan maintained that he was innocent of the charges and that he had been framed by a political opponent in Indiana. Because he had been tried in a military court where the rules of evidence, procedure, and appeal are different, Milligan's only recourse was to appeal for a Presidential pardon. Two weeks after he was sentenced, Milligan wrote to his old friend Edwin Stanton, who was now Lincoln's Secretary of War, creating the document shown here. In an irony reminiscent of an Ambrose Bierce short story, these two had taken their bar examinations together some thirty years before but were now as much enemies as any two soldiers on the field of battle. As far as we now know, Stanton never replied to this letter.

The war ended in April 1865, bringing an end to the suspension of the writ of habeas corpus. In early May, shortly before Milligan's scheduled execution, his lawyers filed a petition for a writ of habeas corpus at the U.S. circuit court in Indianapolis. The lawyers argued that a military court has no right to try a citizen if a civil court is in operation. Supreme Court Justice Davis, sitting as a member of the circuit court, felt the lawyers' request to be an issue requiring a decision by the Supreme Court. But Milligan and his fellow conspirators were sentenced to hang before any of this could come to pass. Justice Davis wrote a moving letter to President Andrew Johnson asking him to stay the execution until the Supreme Court could hear the case.

President Johnson complied, reluctantly, to Justice Davis's request, first by staving the execution until June and later by commuting the sentence to life in prison. The order to commute the sentence was delivered to Edwin Stanton with instructions not to tell the prisoners until just before their scheduled execution that they were to live. Believing that even the Constitution could not save him, Milligan spent what he thought were his last days arranging his own funeral and writing an address, which he expected to deliver before he was hanged.

In due course the Supreme Court considered the case and ruled in favor of Milligan's contention that a citizen's right to a trial in a civil court could not be revoked even if war produced situations in which the privilege of the writ of habeas corpus might be revoked. Justice Davis, writing for the majority, argued that the case went to the very heart of what it meant to be a free people. He wrote into his decision a reminder that one of the grievances against King George III in the Declaration of Independence was that he had "'rendered the military power independent of and superior to the civil power.'" He went on to say, "No graver question was ever considered by this court, nor one which more clearly concerns the rights of the whole people; for it is the birthright of every American citizen when charged with a crime, to be tried and punished according to the law." On April 12, 1866, Milligan and his fellow prisoners were released from custody by order of the U.S. Supreme Court.

The Civil War was a crisis that stretched the Constitution, but this Supreme Court decision defined just how far it could be stretched by drawing a clear line between the government's need for security and the rights of individual citizens. As Professor Allan Nevins observed, "The heart of this decision is the heart of the difference between the United States of America and Nazi Germany or Communist Russia."

This document is taken from the Records of the Office of the Judge Advocate General (Army), Record Group 153: Court Martial Records; NN3409, Box 1165.

TEACHING ACTIVITIES

Distinguishing Fact from Opinion

1. With students in groups of five, distribute a copy of the document to each student and have them read it carefully. A recorder for the group should make a list of questions that the group members raise after reading the document.

2. Instruct the group members to decide if the questions on their list can be answered with a fact (+) or by a supporting opinion (*). Have them place an appropriate mark next to each question.

3. Instruct the groups to choose their two best fact questions and their two best supporting opinion questions.

4. As the groups report, record their questions on the board in a chart like the one below.

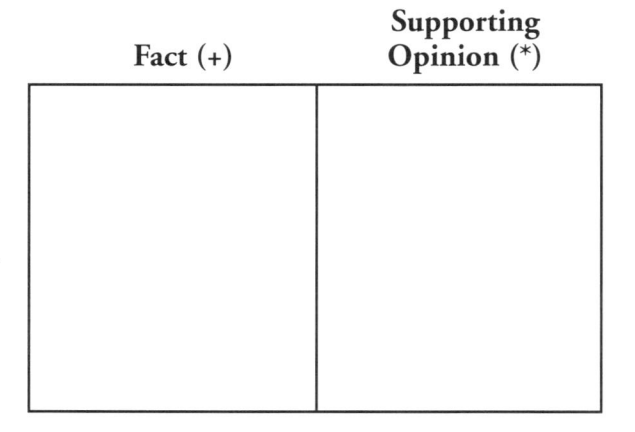

Fact (+)	Supporting Opinion (*)

Moral Dilemma

Although we know little about the extent of the friendship between Milligan and Stanton, the dilemma of a public official's response to a former friend is an interesting one.

5. Have students read the story below and discuss it with their groups.

   The country is involved in a civil war. You are the Secretary of Defense, and the President has had to arrest many people who disagree with him in order to protect the country. There is some question as to whether the President has acted within the Constitution, but you agree that these steps are necessary to protect the government. Much to your surprise, a letter comes across your desk one day from your old friend _____, who has been sentenced to die by a military court. What do you do? Why do you do it?

6. After they have listed and discussed their decision and the reasons for their decision, have them draft a letter to their friend explaining their decision.

> Indianapolis 28 Dec. 1864
>
> Hon. E. M. Stanton Sec. War.
>
> Dear Sir I have been condemned to die without evidence. Please examine the facts and advise the President do this much for an old acquaintance and friend —
>
> Yours very truly
>
> L. P. Milligan

Document 1.19 *Ex parte Milligan* letter, December 28, 1864. [National Archives]

Exploring the Constitution: Civil Liberties Search

Using the copy of the Constitution in their text, students should complete the puzzle below.

1. ___ ___ ___ ___   ___ ___   ___ ___ ___ (○) ___

2. ___ (○) ___   ___ ___ ___ ___   ___ ___ ___ ___ ___

3. ___ (○) ___   ___ ___ ___ ___

4. ___ ___ ___ (○) ___

5. (○) ___ ___ ___

6. ___ ___ (○) ___   ___ ___ ___ ___ ___ ___

7. ___ ___ (○) ___

Clues:

1. Amendments I-X.

2. Article I, sec. 9, cl. 3, prohibits laws that are_____, i.e., retroactive criminal laws that work to the disadvantage of an individual.

3. Amendment IV says a criminal has a right to a trial that is public and _____.

4. Protection from unreasonable search and seizure is in this amendment.

5. Amendment VIII states that this cannot be excessive.

6. Article I, sec. 9, cl. 2, promises the privilege of this writ.

7. Amendment XXVI gives this right to 18-year-olds.

   Hidden clue:
   The circled letters when rearranged spell a Latin phrase which means "on behalf of one side only."

For Further Research

7. Possible topics for further research could focus on

   a. Treason trials in Cincinnati and Indianapolis

   b. Secret societies such as The Sons of Liberty, The Knights of the Golden Circle, and The Union League

   c. Supreme Court cases related to Ex parte Milligan such as Ex parte Merryman, Ex parte McCardle, Ex parte Quirin, and Duncan v. Kahanamoku.

PUZZLE ANSWERS

1. B I L L   O F   R I G H (T) S
2. E (X)   P O S T   F A C T O
3. S (P) E E D Y
4. F O U (R)
5. B (A) I L
6. H A B (E) A S   C O R P U S
7. V O T (E)

Unscrambled Word: **Ex Parte**

National Archives Document Citation
Ex parte Milligan letter, December 28, 1864; NN3409; Court Martial Records; Records of the Office of the Judge Advocate General (Army), Record Group 153; National Archives at College Park, College Park, MD.

Article Citation
Gray, Leslie and Wynell Burroughs. "Constitutional Issues Through Documents: *Ex Parte Milligan.*" *Social Education* 50, 7 (November/December 1986): 549-552.

1.20

Civil Rights Mini-Unit, 1865–1978

During the 1960s and 1970s, a number of Federal and State programs were set up to provide educational opportunities for minorities and women. These included Head Start, special admissions programs to institutions of higher learning, and affirmative action plans. In 1974 Allan Bakke, a white male seeking admission to the University of California Medical School at Davis, challenged as discriminatory the university's special admissions program. Subsequently, the California State Supreme Court ruled in favor of Bakke. The Regents of the University of California challenged this decision before the U.S. Supreme Court. The Court's decision raises questions about the future of affirmative action programs specifically and about the rights of minorities generally. The issues surrounding this case make it a most relevant topic for discussion in the social studies.

This mini-unit provides you with a selection of historical documents that serves as background for studying the recent U.S. Supreme Court decision in the case of the Regents of the University of California v. Bakke. The documents relate to the 14th Amendment: *Plessy v. Ferguson, Brown v. the Board of Education*, and the Bakke case. Accompanying the documents are suggested activities for use in the classroom. The first activity focuses on each document individually, while the second uses all the documents with a data retrieval chart. The mini-unit also contains a time line of major events relating to the history of civil rights in the United States; it will be helpful to you and your students as you work with the documents.

We recommend that you introduce your students to primary sources by examining a selected document for factual information. This examination will underscore the significance of such information in the development of conclusions and generalizations.

In the first activity, students select a single document and review a series of related questions. Two sets of questions are included with each document. The first set of questions requires students to review the document for factual information, thus reinforcing the importance of reading documents with care. Once students have read the document, a second set of questions provides the basis for a broader discussion of the individual documents in their historical context.

In the second activity, students should carefully review all the documents as background for a general discussion of broad issues that relate to all of the documents. The discussion will encourage students to develop their own conclusions and generalizations based on factual information. The data retrieval chart will guide students in extracting factual information from the documents. Once students understand the information, they can discuss at length one or several of the following general issues. These issues are only examples. You may wish to develop your own general topics for discussion.

TIME LINE

This is a selective list of events leading to the present legal and judicial positions on civil rights in the United States. It is intended to be used as background for the documents in this mini-unit, and not as a definitive list.

Vocabulary

amendment
equal protection of the laws
franchise
monopoly
public accommodation
Reconstruction
invalid
stipulation
segregate
doctrine
grandfather clause
disfranchise
executive order
NAACP
discrimination
U.S. Court of Appeals
nullify
stay

Date: 1865
Focus: The Bureau of Refugees, Freedmen, and Abandoned Lands
Action: This Bureau was established in the War Department to help freed slaves adjust to living as free persons and to overcome the disabilities of slavery. It worked also to assist displaced whites and to administer land confiscated from the Confederacy.
Impact: The Bureau represented the Federal Government's first major attempt at social welfare. Perhaps the most important aspect of the Bureau's work was its system of public education.

Date: 1866
Focus: 14th Amendment
Action: This amendment was designed principally to provide citizenship rights to former slaves.
Impact: It guaranteed that all citizens were to receive equal protection before the law.

Date: 1866
Focus: Civil Rights Act of 1866
Action: This act provided that persons born in the United States and not subject to foreign powers were citizens of the United States.
Impact: It gave the Federal Government legal authority to deal with violators of the civil liberties of individuals.

Date: 1870
Focus: 15th Amendment
Action: This amendment was largely designed to give full voting rights to black males. It also reinforced the citizenship guarantees of the 14th Amendment.
Impact: More than 700,000 former slaves registered to vote.

Date: 1872
Focus: Bureau of Refugees, Freedmen, and Abandoned Lands
Action: The Bureau was abolished.
Impact: Blacks found themselves without Federal protection and provisions in former Confederate States unwilling to continue the work begun by the Bureau.

Date: 1873
Focus: United States Supreme Court, *Slaughter House Cases*. The State of Louisiana granted one corporation a 25-year exclusive franchise to conduct all butchering business in three of the state's parishes. The monopoly prompted a lawsuit by rival slaughterhouses, which claimed that 1,000 butchers had been denied the right to earn a living.
Action: The Court held that there were two categories of citizens–national and state–and that the privileges and immunities clause of the 14th Amendment protected only those rights derived from national citizenship.
Impact: This ruling in effect weakened the 14th Amendment because it gave State governments authority over the protection of citizenship rights.

Date: 1875
Focus: Civil Rights Act of 1875
Action: This act prohibited discrimination in places of public accommodation, excluding churches, cemeteries, and public schools.
Impact: It represented the Federal Government's last attempt to secure civil rights for blacks before Reconstruction ended in 1877.

Teaching With Documents   THE COLONIAL PERIOD TO 1879

Date: 1883
Focus: U.S. Supreme Court, Civil Rights Cases
Action: The Court ruled in five separate cases that the 14th Amendment prohibited States, not individuals, from violating civil rights.
Impact: These rulings reversed the Civil Rights Act of 1875 and undermined the effect of the 14th and 15th Amendments.

Date: 1890
Focus: Second Morrill Act (the First Morrill Act, 1862, provided Federal support for higher education in the form of land-grant colleges). These colleges usually concentrated on agricultural and mechanical subjects.
Action: One of the stipulations of the Second Morrill Act provided that annual grants be withheld from States that segregated blacks without providing separate agricultural or mechanical colleges for them.
Impact: Seventeen colleges for blacks were established. These were mainly non-degree-granting agricultural, mechanical, and industrial schools.

Date: 1896
Focus: U.S. Supreme Court, *Plessy v. Ferguson*
Action: The Court upheld a Louisiana law requiring segregated railroad facilities, maintaining that as long as accommodations were equal, blacks were not deprived of equal protection granted under the 14th Amendment.
Impact: This ruling established the doctrine of separate but equal.

Date: 1908
Focus: U.S. Supreme Court, *Berea College v. Kentucky*
Action: The Court upheld a Kentucky law that banned private schools from admitting black and white students to the same campus.
Impact: This case was interpreted to mean that States could outlaw bi-racial contacts.

Date: 1915
Focus: U.S. Supreme Court, *Guinn and Beal v. United States*
Action: The Court declared the Oklahoma "grandfather clause" unconstitutional because it violated the 15th Amendment by disenfranchising blacks.
Impact: The 15th Amendment was used to overturn a State law.

Date: 1938
Focus: U.S. Supreme Court, *Missouri ex rel. Gaines v. Canada*
Action: The Court ruled that Missouri must provide legal education for Lloyd Gaines, a black, within its boundaries.
Impact: The ruling required States to make equal provisions for blacks or admit them to State-supported universities for whites.

Date: 1941
Focus: Executive Order 8802
Action: The Order established the Committee on Fair Employment Practices to investigate complaints of discrimination against companies with Government defense contracts.
Impact: The Order paved the way for blacks to be freely hired in defense plants.

Date: 1946
Focus: Executive Order 9808
Action: The Order created the Presidential Committee on Civil Rights. The Committee issued a major report, *To Secure These Rights,* which condemned racial segregation and the denial of civil rights to blacks.
Impact: The report was seen as a landmark statement of the Federal Government's intentions in the field of civil rights.

Date: 1948
Focus: U.S. Supreme Court, *Sipuel v. Board of Regents of the University of Oklahoma*
Action: The Court ruled that denial of the applicant's admission to the university violated the equal protection clause of the 14th Amendment.
Impact: The NAACP played a major role in the case. This case represented its first real victory in the campaign against segregated facilities.

Date: 1948
Focus: Executive Order 9981
Action: "There shall be equality of treatment and opportunity for all persons in the Armed Services without regard to race...."
Impact: The Order represented the first step toward elimination of segregation in one of the country's largest institutions, the Armed Forces. Executive Orders 9808 and 9981 recognized and began the attack on discriminatory practices.

Date: 1950
Focus: U.S. Supreme Court, *Sweatt v. Painter* (Texas)
Action: The Court held that the black law school at the University of Texas did not provide "a truly equal education in law." It concluded that Sweatt's exclusion from the white law school at the university violated the equal protection clause of the 14th Amendment.
Impact: The decision gave support to the admission of blacks to previously all-white graduate or professional schools.

Date: 1954
Focus: U.S. Supreme Court, *Brown v. Board of Education, Topeka, Kansas*
Action: This case was consolidated with the District of Columbia case of *Boiling v. Sharpe*, the Delaware case of *Gebhart v. Belton*, and the Virginia case of *Davis v. County School Board of Prince Edward County*. The Court decided unanimously in all these cases that school segregation violated the Constitution.
Impact: In May 1955 the Court issued its school desegregation enforcement order to admit, "with all deliberate speed," the parties involved to public schools on a racially non-discriminatory basis. The ruling was widely understood to mean that the concept of separate but equal established in Plessy v. Ferguson was overturned.

Date: 1956
Focus: U.S. Supreme Court, *Gayle v. Browder*
Action: The Court referred to the *Brown v. Board of Education, Topeka, Kansas* case to strike down segregated bus facilities in Montgomery, Alabama.
Impact: In this case, the Court officially declared that segregation, particularly in public facilities, was unconstitutional.

Date: 1957
Focus: Civil Rights Act
Action: This act prohibited interference in the exercise of voting rights; simplified the system for Federal Government involvement in voting rights violations; and established a national Commission on Civil Rights.
Impact: The act increased Federal involvement in ensuring voting rights.

Date: 1958
Focus: U.S. Supreme Court, *Cooper v. Aaron* (Little Rock, Arkansas)
Action: The Court upheld the U.S. Court of Appeals reversal of a stay against integration, saying that "the constitutional rights of children regardless of race can neither be nullified openly and directly by state legislators or state executive officials nor nullified by them by evasive schemes for segregation."
Impact: This action resulted from racial turmoil that erupted in Little Rock, Arkansas, when an attempt at desegregating the schools was made.

Date: 1961
Focus: Executive Order 10925
Action: The Order established the President's Committee on Equal Employment Opportunity.
Impact: The Committee had responsibility for ending discrimination by Government contractors as well as by the Federal Government itself.

Date: 1963
Focus: March on Washington
Action: Over 200,000 people gathered in Washington, D.C., to protest inequality and to ask for a remedy.
Impact: The march demonstrated wide support for the enactment of civil rights legislation.

Date: 1964
Focus: U.S. Supreme Court, *Griffin v. County School Board of Prince Edward County, Va.*
Action: The Court ruled that State aid to white children attending all-white private schools was unconstitutional.
Impact: Such attempts were viewed as blatant efforts to circumvent desegregation. School boards were mandated to develop "workable desegregation plans."

Date: 1964
Focus: Civil Rights Act of 1964
Action: This is the most comprehensive civil rights measure passed by Congress to date. It prohibited discrimination in public accommodations; banned the use of literacy tests as a requirement for voting, unless written tests were given to everyone; provided for Federal assistance in desegregating school systems; and banned discrimination in Federally assisted programs. The Act also provided for equal employment opportunity by declaring

discrimination based on race, color, religion, sex, or national origin an unlawful employment practice. This section was to be implemented over a three-year period. It was for this purpose that the Equal Employment Opportunity Commission was created, with enforcement to be carried out by the Attorney General.
Impact: The Act abolished legal segregation and guaranteed a more favorable climate for later civil rights legislation dealing with such issues as housing discrimination and voting rights.

Date: 1964
Focus: U.S. Supreme Court, *Heart of Atlanta Motel v. United States* and *Katzenbach v. McClung*
Action: In these two cases involving a motel and restaurant, the proprietors based their rights to refuse accommodation to blacks on the grounds that their businesses were intrastate, not interstate. The Court ruled that each of the establishments was involved in interstate business and therefore subject to the conditions of the Civil Rights Act of 1964.
Impact: The interpretation of interstate commerce was expanded to include restaurants, motels, and other privately owned facilities that served the public.

Date: 1965
Focus: Executive Order 11246
Action: This Order was amended by Executive Orders 11375 of October 1967, and 11478 of August 1969. It established the Government's nondiscrimination compliance program. The Order is implemented by Office of Federal Contract Compliance regulations which exist in two parts: (a) obligations of contractors and subcontractors not to discriminate, and (b) contractors' obligations to develop an affirmative action program.
Impact: The Order gives the Federal Government a device for deterring discrimination in employment practices in private institutions.

Date: 1965
Focus: Voting Rights Act of 1965
Action: This act abolished all remaining deterrents to exercising the franchise and authorized Federal supervision of voter registration where necessary.
Impact: This act closed loopholes in the 1964 measure.

Date: 1968
Focus: Civil Rights Act of 1968
Action: This Civil Rights Act, passed one week after the assassination of Dr. Martin Luther King, Jr., focused on eradicating discrimination in housing and on protecting the right of blacks to vote.
Impact: The act provided additional force to the Civil Rights Act of 1964.

Date: 1968
Focus: U.S. Supreme Court, *Jones v. Mayer Co.*
Action: This ruling based on the 1866 Civil Rights Act barred all racial discrimination in the sale or rental of property.
Impact: This ruling closed the loophole in the open housing section of the 1968 Civil Rights Act, which excluded owner-sold single housing and units of four or fewer owner-occupied apartments.

Date: 1972
Focus: Equal Employment Opportunity Act
Action: Public and private education institutions, State and local governments, and employees and unions with eight or more workers were covered by Federal legislation barring discrimination and were brought under the Equal Employment Opportunity Commission (EEOC).
Impact: The Commission was given authority to have its decisions enforced in the courts, but Congress did not provide the Commission with "cease and desist" power.

Data Retrieval Chart

Date	Author(s)	Recipient(s)	Main Subject(s)	For What Purpose Was the Document Written?	Unanswered or Outstanding Questions

Teaching With Documents — THE COLONIAL PERIOD TO 1879

Eight Key Documents on Civil Rights

Document 1: 14th Amendment

Vocabulary: naturalized, jurisdiction, abridge, privileges, immunities, apportioned, electors, insurrection, validity, bounties, emancipation.

Questions for Students

1. Review and discuss the meaning of each section of the amendment.
2. What do the terms "privileges and immunities" and "equal protection" mean?

Discussion Questions

1. Why do you think this amendment to the Constitution was necessary?
2. The 15th Amendment specifically prohibits the disenfranchisement of citizens based on race, color, or previous condition of servitude. If the 14th Amendment protects the privileges and immunities of citizens, why was the 15th Amendment necessary? Consider also why many people feel an equal rights amendment is needed despite the fact that the 14th Amendment appears to guarantee the rights of women.

Document 2: Interstate Commerce Commission Order

Note: When he was denied a seat in a first-class railroad car after paying first-class fare, William H. Councill, principal of the State Colored Normal and Industrial School in Huntsville, Alabama, filed a complaint with the Interstate Commerce Commission (ICC) against the Western and Atlantic Railroad Company. The ICC, created in 1887, the same year in which this case was filed, was charged with protecting the public in matters relating to transportation and commerce between States. Councill alleged that by his removal to the Jim Crow car he was subjected to "unreasonable prejudice and unjust discrimination." He sought from the ICC $25,000 in damages and $1,500 in legal costs.

Vocabulary: petition, complaint, cease and desist.

Questions for Students

1. Review the report of the ICC to ascertain these facts: a. Who is the defendant? b. Who is the complainant? c. Who heard the case? When? d. When was the final decision on this case issued?
2. What was the outcome of the case?

Discussion Questions

1. Discuss the concept of separate but equal. Consider in your discussion the question of inherent inequality.
2. This case was heard before the ICC nine years before *Plessy v. Ferguson*. Discuss the development of precedents and their role in lawmaking.

Document 3: Hale County, Alabama, Resolution

Vocabulary: incumbent, resolution, petitioners.

Questions for Students

1. To whom are the black citizens addressing their petition?
2. What are they requesting?

Discussion Questions

1. What are the duties and privileges of citizenship?
2. Why do you think the petitioners are concerned with military duty? What do you think they are trying to accomplish by their petition? Are their requests realistic or rhetorical? Consider in your discussion the role of blacks in the military.
3. Compare and contrast the sentiments expressed in this resolution with those of the Baptist Ministers' Union Resolution (page ____). How might you explain their differences or similarities?

Note: Truman H. Aldrich was the Congressman from the 9th District of Alabama. This resolution was received by the Committee on the Judiciary on March 1, 1897.

"Beat No. 12" refers to the election precinct or supervisory district of the writers of the resolution.

Document 4: Photograph: "Separate But Equal"

Questions for Students

1. Does it tell you about black educational facilities in Macon, Georgia, in 1936? What questions does this information raise?
2. What are the obvious differences between the two schools as evidenced in the photographs?

Discussion Questions

1. What can you infer from this photograph about the quality of education provided by each school? Consider how you are defining quality and make only those inferences that can safely be drawn.
2. This photograph is part of a file that includes materials from the National Association for the Advancement of Colored People. Why do you think this photo was used by the organization? Why do you think it is in Federal records?

Document 5: Baptist Ministers' Union of Southern California Resolution

Vocabulary: resolution, psychological inferiority, emancipation.

Questions for Students

1. To whom is the resolution addressed? Why?
2. What is the U.S. Supreme Court decision that prompted this resolution, and how did the Court rule?
3. Can you determine the race of the writers from the evidence in the document?
4. Why do you think this resolution was written?
5. The last lines of the resolution read: "And that we urge our people North and South to be obedient to this law, which is in their favor, as much as they have been obedient to laws that have been against them, and their Constitutional rights." Discuss.

Discussion Questions

1. How might such civil rights activists as Martin Luther King, Jr., and Stokely Carmichael have viewed the last sentence of the resolution?
2. Compare and contrast the sentiments expressed in this resolution with those of the Hale County citizens. How might you explain their differences and similarities?

Document 6: North Carolina Resolution

Questions for Students

1. When was the resolution written? What U.S. Supreme Court decision is it in response to?
2. Based on this resolution, what would be the policy of North Carolina toward desegregation?

Discussion Questions

1. What do these reasons reveal about the climate of opinion in North Carolina at the time? What do they tell us about the relation between social customs and the law? How valid do these reasons seem today?
2. Suppose that you are the superintendent of schools for a North Carolina school district. You believe in school integration. How does this resolution affect you as a school administrator? As a citizen of North Carolina?

Document 7: Dawson Letter

Vocabulary: intrastate, interstate, Interstate Commerce Commission, Pilate, 1954 U.S. Supreme Court decision.

Questions for Students

1. Explain the difference between interstate and intrastate.
2. Why do you think the waiting room signs distinguish between white and colored waiting rooms for intrastate passengers?
3. What action does Dawson want taken? By whom?

4. List the reasons Dawson gives for her demands. What do you think of her reasons?

5. Why do you think Dawson refers to the 1954 U.S. Supreme Court decision?

Discussion Questions

1. Why did civil rights groups focus on inequities in bus and train station facilities?

2. Consider the date of this letter and the reasons why, seven years after the Brown case, segregated facilities remained.

3. "Americans seem to want laws expressing high ideals but they seem also to want the convenience of ignoring or violating many of them with impunity." Monroe Berger, *Equality by Statute* (New York, 1968), p. 1. Discuss.

Document 8: Bakke Syllabus

Vocabulary: syllabus, regents, *certiorari*, grade point average, extracurricular, respondent, discretionary, mandatory injunction, declaratory relief, allege, *inter alia*, petitioner, strict-scrutiny standard, affirm, proscribe, violate, inherently, foreclose, chronic, remedial, concur, dissent. *(You may wish to consult a legal dictionary for definitions of some of these terms.)*

Questions for Students

1. Based on the syllabus, develop a chronological outline of the process by which Allan Bakke sought admission to the Medical School of the University of California at Davis.

2. Restate in your own words the final decision of the U.S. Supreme Court in the Bakke case.

Discussion Questions

1. What issues have arisen around the Bakke decision? Why does it appear to have historical importance?

2. What can be inferred from the number of separate opinions filed by the Justices?

3. "Technically, the Court's decision in a case applies only to the particular facts of that case and to the parties to it. But the reasoning outlined by the Court gives lower court judges a basis for deciding similar cases." James E. Clayton, *The Making of Justice* (New York, 1962), p. 85. Discuss.

4. What might be the reactions of the following individuals to the Bakke decision? What justifications might they offer for their opinions?

   a. White male, first-generation American. Your parents immigrated to America from Latvia. You earned your undergraduate degree by attending evening classes.

   b. Black female. You are the first member of your family to pursue an advanced degree.

   c. White female from middle-class professional family.

5. What comments do you have on the Bakke decision?

General Discussion

1. Compare and contrast the situations outlined in the following documents with the guarantees of the 14th Amendment. What can you conclude about the relationship between interpretation of the Constitution and prevailing social attitudes at the time?

2. Discuss the roles of the U.S. Supreme Court and the Federal Government in the regulation of our lives and social customs. Consider such areas of involvement as education, rights of the accused, abortion, death with dignity, voting practices, and privacy.

3. Discuss the nature of the relationship between State and Federal Governments as revealed in the documents. Consider how citizenship has come to be defined.

4. Discuss the role of precedents and landmark cases in lawmaking.

5. Compare and contrast the impact of a constitutional amendment and that of a U.S. Supreme Court decision. Why are women seeking a constitutional amendment to protect their rights?

6. What are the rights of minorities in a nation of immigrants, such as the United States? What have these rights been in the past and how might they evolve in the future? To what extent should minority rights be protected? How do the rights of minorities impinge upon rights of the majority?

7. Discrimination is often built into our institutional practices: for example, Jim Crow laws, vot-

ing restrictions, and housing patterns. What is the role of legislation with respect to institutional discrimination? What is the relationship between institutional discrimination and the practices of individuals toward members of minority groups?

8. Is there such a thing as a bad law? How might you define "bad" in the context of these documents? How do opinions vary among your students on the nature of a bad law? Is civil disobedience justified?

9. What constraints and limitations exist in carrying out constitutional guarantees?

10. What is affirmative action?

11. List several Federal policies directed at minority groups or women that you would classify as affirmative action programs. Consider each program in view of the following:

    a. At what group(s) was the policy directed?
    b. Why was the policy initiated?
    c. What were the goals or objectives of the program?
    d. To what extent were those goals achieved?

12. To obtain a basis for understanding the need for affirmative action programs directly related to education, students might research the history of minority education in the United States and might consider groups such as blacks, American Indians, and Mexican Americans.

13. Review the time line. What does it indicate about the status of blacks from 1865 to the present? Does it seem adequate as an overview of the status of blacks, other minorities, or women? Why, or why not? Does there appear to be repetition in the laws or policies included?

National Archives Document Citation

Fourteenth Amendment to the Constitution, June 16, 1886; Enrolled Acts Part III, 39th Congress; Enrolled Acts and Resolutions of Congress, 1789-1999; General Records of the U.S. Government, Record Group 11; National Archives at College Park, College Park, MD.

Interstate Commerce Commission Order, December 3, 1887; Docket 21; Formal Dockets of the Interstate Commerce Commission; Records of the Interstate Commerce Commission, Record Group 134; National Archives at College Park, College Park, MD.

Hale County, Alabama, Resolution, ca. 1897; Judiciary Committee; (HR54A-H16.8); 54th Congress; Records of the U.S. House of Representatives, Record Group 233; National Archives Building, Washington, DC.

Photograph: "Separate But Equal"; Photographs from "Preface to Peasantry" by Arthur Raper, University of North Carolina Press, 1936: Public School for White Children, Macon County, GA, and Public School for Negro Children, Macon County, GA; Letters to the Secretary of Agriculture re: NAACP; Records of the Office of the Secretary of Agriculture, Record Group 16; National Archives at College Park, College Park, MD.

Baptist Ministers' Union of Southern California Resolution, May 27, 1954; (SEN83A-J11); 83rd Congress; Records of the U.S. Senate, Record Group 46; National Archives Building, Washington, DC.

North Carolina Resolution, December, 30, 1954; File 8/1, NO 55,629, 1954; Records of the Supreme Court of the U.S., Record Group 267; National Archives Building, Washington, DC.

Letter from Osceola Dawson to the Chairman of the Interstate Commerce Commission, April 13, 1961; Accession No. NN-374-146; Folder RDO; General File #1; Records of the Interstate Commerce Commission, Record Group 134; National Archives at College Park, College, MD.

Bakke Syllabus, Argued October 12, 1977, decided June 28, 1978; Available from the U.S. Government Printing Office, Washington, DC.

Article Citation

Alexander, Mary, CeCe Byers and Elsie Freivogel. "Civil Rights Mini Unit." *Social Education* 42, 7 (November/December 1978): 563-581.

Article XIV.

Section 1. All persons born or naturalized in the United States, and subject to the jurisdiction thereof, are citizens of the United States and of the State wherein they reside. No State shall make or enforce any law which shall abridge the privileges or immunities of citizens of the United States; nor shall any State deprive any person of life, liberty, or property, without due process of law; nor deny to any person within its jurisdiction the equal protection of the laws.

Section 2. Representatives shall be apportioned among the several States according to their respective numbers, counting the whole number of persons in each State, excluding Indians not taxed. But when the right to vote at any election for the choice of electors for President and Vice President of the United States, Representatives in Congress, the Executive and Judicial officers of a State, or the members of the Legislature thereof, is denied to any of the male inhabitants of such State, being twenty-one years of age, and citizens of the United States, or in any way abridged, except for participation in rebellion, or other crime, the basis of representation therein shall be reduced in the proportion which the

Document 1.20a1 Fourteenth Amendment to the Constitution, June 16, 1886. [National Archives]

number of such *** citizens shall bear to the whole number of male citizens twenty-one years of age in such State.

Section 3. No person shall be a Senator or Representative in Congress, or elector of President and Vice President, or hold any office, civil or military, under the United States, or under any State, who, having previously taken an oath, as a member of Congress, or as an officer of the United States, or as a member of any State legislature, or as an executive or judicial officer of any State, to support the Constitution of the United States, shall have engaged in insurrection or rebellion against the same, or given aid or comfort to the enemies thereof. But Congress may by a vote of two-thirds of each House, remove such disability.

Section 4. The validity of the public debt of the United States, authorized by law, including debts incurred for payment of pensions and bounties for services in suppressing insurrection or rebellion, shall not be questioned. But neither the United States nor any State shall assume or pay any debt or obligation incurred in aid of insurrection or rebellion against the United States, or any claim for the loss or emancipation of any slave; but all such debts, obligations and claims shall be held illegal and void.

Section 5. The Congress shall have power to enforce, by appropriate legislation, the provisions of this article.

Attest.

Edw. McPherson.
Clerk of the House of Representatives.

J. W. Forney
Secretary of the Senate.

Schuyler Colfax
Speaker of the House of Representatives.

La Fayette S. Foster,
President of the Senate pro tempore.

Document 1.20a2 Fourteenth Amendment to the Constitution, June 16, 1886. [National Archives]

At a general session of the INTERSTATE COMMERCE COMMISSION, held at its office in Washington on the *third* day of *December*, A. D. 1887:

Present:
Hon. THOMAS M. COOLEY, *Chairman*,
Hon. WILLIAM R. MORRISON,
Hon. AUGUSTUS SCHOONMAKER, } *Commissioners.*
Hon. ALDACE F. WALKER,
Hon. WALTER L. BRAGG,

IN THE MATTER OF THE PETITION OF

William H. Councill

against

The Western & Atlantic Railroad Company.

This case being at issue upon complaint and answer on file, and having been duly assigned for hearing on the *23rd* day of *July*, 188*7*, and a hearing having been had upon the pleadings, proofs, and arguments of counsel, and the Report and Opinion of the Commission having been made and filed; *wherein it is found upon such investigation, so made, that the defendant has the legal right to separate its white and colored passengers paying the same fare, by providing separate cars for each which are equally safe and comfortable, that this separation may be carried out*

Document 1.20b1 Interstate Commerce Commission Order, December 3, 1887. [National Archives]

on railroad trains without unjust preference or undue prejudice and disadvantage to either race, provided it be done on fair and reasonable terms. And it is further found, upon said investigation, that in denying to complainant equal accommodations furnished the other passengers, paying the same fare, the defendant railroad company subjected him to undue prejudice and unreasonable disadvantage in violation of the provisions of the Act of Congress entitled an "Act to regulate Commerce", approved February 4th, 1887.

Now it is ordered and adjudged that the defendant, The Western and Atlantic Railroad Company, be and it hereby is notified and required to cease and desist from subjecting colored persons to undue and unreasonable prejudice and disadvantage in violation of section three of the Act to regulate Commerce, and from furnishing to colored persons purchasing first-class tickets on its road accommodations which are not equally safe and comfortable with those furnished other first-class passengers.

And it is further ORDERED that a notice embodying this order be forthwith sent to the defendant corporation, together with a copy of the Report and Opinion of the Commission herein, in conformity with the provisions of the fifteenth section of the act to regulate Commerce.

                                  Secretary.

Document 1.20b2 Interstate Commerce Commission Order, December 3, 1887. [National Archives]

Hon. T. H. Aldrich

Washington

D.C.

Sir:—

Our rights as citizens of the United States being practicably denied us, we the undersigned colored citizens of Beat No 12 Hale County, Alabama, respectfully ask that the Congress of the United States relieve us of all the duties incumbent upon us as citizens of the United States. We think is unjust to us to require of us the duties of a citizen of the United States without granting to us all the privileges of citizenship and without guaranteeing us all the rights of a citizen. We ask that a law be passed relieving us of all military duty in case of a war with any foreign country.

And your petitioners will ever pray.

	P. H. Green		1	Daniel Banks	27
	T. G. Green		2	Haywood Wilson	28
	Isaac Owens		3	John McConico	29
	M. G. Green		4	Mathew Silver	30
	Watson Bell		5	Joseph Bell	31
	Arthur Jones		6	Cious Gray	32
	Bolton Jones		7	Elex Gray	33
	H. C. White		8	William Dobbins	34
	F. C. Owens		9	William Turner	35
	J. H. Green		10	Daniel Bester	36
	William Anderson		11	Sam Bester	37
	Handy Amos		12	Lewis Peters	38
	Austin Silver		13	Silver Bell	39
	S. S. Smith		14	W. M. Bowden	40
	Robt. Hardaway		15	Ed. Clemons	41
	George Patton		16	S. C. Carleton	42
	Judge Williams		17	Lewis Allen	43
	Lewis Shorter		18	Charl. Allen	44
	Holman James		19	Jacob Owens	45
	Abraham James		20	Joseph Richard	46
	Alfred James		21	Willis Kenedy	47
	Paul James		22	Simon Witherspoon	48
	William Thomas		23	Green Sample	49
	John McCrackin		24	H. C. Brown	50
	Andrew Lavoughan		25	A. W. Brown	51
	Steven Turner		26	Jack Evins	52

Document 1.20c Hale County, Alabama, Resolution, ca. 1897. [National Archives]

Document 1.20d1 Public School for White Children, Macon County, Georgia, 1936. [National Archives]

Teaching With Documents — 103 — THE COLONIAL PERIOD TO 1879

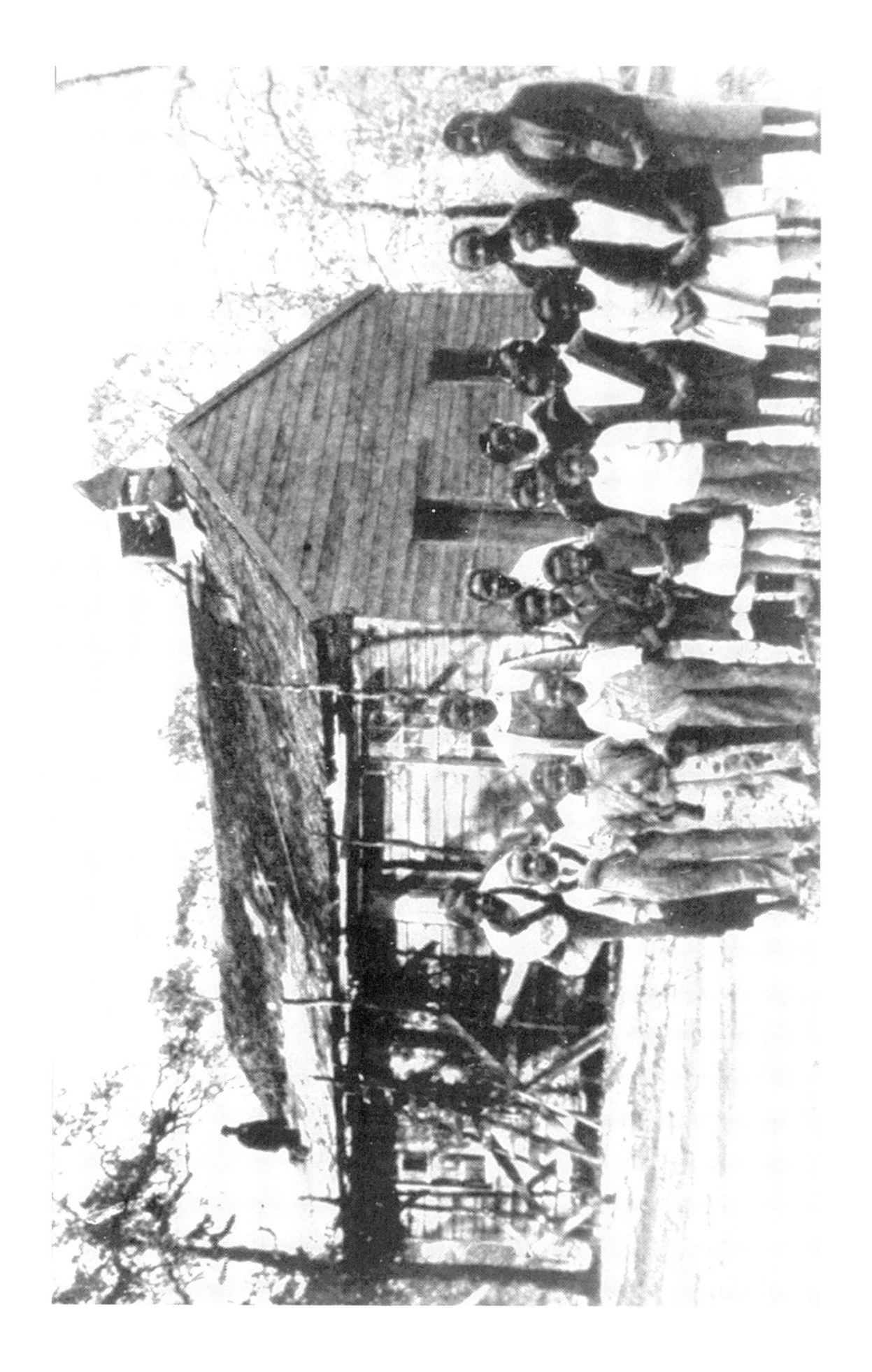

Document 1.20d2 Public School for Negro Children, Macon County, Georgia, 1936. [National Archives]

The Baptist Ministers' Union of Southern California

Box.115. Duarte.California
May.27th.1954.

To his ~~Honor Richard Nixon~~
~~V. President of the U.S.~~
Washington.D.C.

Dear Sir:
The enclosed Resolution was submitted to the Baptist Ministers Union of Southern California,at its last meeting held on Tuesday.May.25th.1954. by Dr:A.Wendell Ross.

.... RESOLUTION............

WHEREAS, The Supreme Court of the United States of America,under the leadership of Cheif Justice.Earl Warren,in its recent ruling against segregation in the American Schools,is an outstanding contribution to the full citizenship of all peoples of our nation; as well as a continuation of Americanism in the world.

WHEREAS,this decision is a vital blow to Communism,and the toll of the bell to second class citizenship of Negro peoples of America North and South;moving in a legal way to blot out physical psychological inferiority customs and laws against the most loyal group of citizens in the nation.

WHEREAS,this constitutional and God given right has come after 85 years since the emancipation of slavery by President Abraham Lincoln.

WHEREAS,This educational liberty along with the emancipation are worth-while Spiritual advances,which after all are the only true values that are eternal;which were enunciated by our Lord and Saviour Jesus Christ.

THEREFORE BE IT RESOLVED,that the Baptist Ministers Union of Southern California,send this Resolution as a vote of thanks and appreciation representing the true leadership of the Negro Race,and the Preachers of the Gospel of Jesus Christ,to the Supreme Court of the United States.The Hon:Earl Warren.Cheif Justice of the Supreme Court.To His Excellency.Dwight D.Eisenhower.President of the United States,and to other leading diplomats in the RepublicanParty.
And that we urge our people North and South to be obedient to this law;which is in their favor,as much as they have been obedient to laws that have been against them,and their Constitutional rights.

Rev: B.B.Charles. President.
Rev: John A.Davis.Secretary.

Document 1.20e Baptist Ministers' Union of Southern California Resolution, May 27, 1954. [National Archives]

Nos. 1-5 / 54

A JOINT RESOLUTION STATING THE POLICY OF THE STATE OF NORTH CAROLINA WITH REFERENCE TO THE MIXING OF THE CHILDREN OF DIFFERENT RACES IN THE PUBLIC SCHOOLS OF THE STATE, AND CREATING AN ADVISORY COMMITTEE ON EDUCATION.

WHEREAS, Governor William B. Umstead, shortly before his death, appointed a Special Advisory Committee on Education, composed of outstanding citizens of our State of both races, to study the difficult and far reaching problems presented by the May 17, 1954, decision of the Supreme Court of the United States on the question of segregation in the public schools, and our present Governor, Honorable Luther H. Hodges, recommissioned that Committee soon after assuming the duties of Governor of North Carolina, and said Committee filed its report with the Governor on December 30, 1954, which report stated, among other things, the following:

> "The mixing of the races forthwith in the public schools throughout the state cannot be accomplished and should not be attempted. The schools of our state are so intimately related to the customs and feelings of the people of each community that their effective operation is impossible except in conformity with community attitudes. The Committee feels that the compulsory mixing of the races in our schools, on a state-wide basis and without regard to local conditions and assignment factors other than race, would alienate public support of the schools to such an extent that they could not be operated successfully." and

WHEREAS, his Excellency, the Governor of North Carolina, has transmitted the report of this Special Committee to this General Assembly recommending it as the policy for this State to follow, and

WHEREAS, the Attorney General of the State of North Carolina has filed a brief with the Supreme Court of the United States in the pending segregation cases before said court, which brief states, among other things, the following:

Document 1.20f1 North Carolina Resolution, December 30, 1954. [National Archives]

"The people of North Carolina know the value of the public school. They also know the value of a social structure in which two distinct races can live together as separate groups, each proud of its own contribution to that society and recognizing its dependence upon the other group. They are determined, if possible, to educate all of the children of the State. They are also determined to maintain their society as it now exists with separate and distinct racial groups in the North Carolina community.

"The people of North Carolina firmly believe that the record of North Carolina in the field of education demonstrates the practicability of education of separate races in separate schools. They also believe that the achievements of the Negro people of North Carolina demonstrate that such an educational system has not instilled in them any sense of inferiority which handicaps them in their efforts to make lasting and substantial contributions to their state."

NOW, THEREFORE,

Be it resolved by the House of Representatives, the Senate concurring:

Section 1. That the report of the Governor's Special Advisory Committee on Education and the brief of the Attorney General of North Carolina, filed in the Supreme Court of the United States in the pending segregation cases, are hereby approved as a declaration of the policy of the State of North Carolina with respect to the serious problems in public education created by the opinion of the Supreme Court of the United States handed down on May 17, 1954.

Sec. 2. That the mixing of the races in the public schools within the State cannot be accomplished and if attempted would alienate public support of the schools to such an extent that they could not be operated successfully.

Document 1.20f2 North Carolina Resolution, December 30, 1954. [National Archives]

-3-

Sec. 3. (a) In order to provide for a continuing study of the problems which may arise as a result of the decision of the United States Supreme Court on May 17, 1954, and to provide counsel and advice to the Governor, the General Assembly, the State Board of Education and the county and local school boards throughout the State, there is hereby created a committee to be known as The Advisory Committee on Education.

(b) The Committee shall consist of seven members to be appointed by the Governor for terms of two years, or until their successors are appointed. Two members of the Committee shall be appointed from the membership of the Senate, two from the membership of the House of Representatives, and three from the public at large. The Governor shall designate one member of the Committee to be its Chairman.

(c) The Committee shall be authorized to employ an executive secretary and such other assistants as it may from time to time, with the approval of the Governor, find necessary. The salaries of the executive secretary and of all other assistants employed by the Committee shall be fixed by the Committee, with the approval of the Governor, and shall be paid, together with all other necessary and proper expenses of the Committee, from the Contingency and Emergency Fund.

(d) The Committee shall make a continuing study of the problems which exist and may arise in this State directly or indirectly from the decision of the Supreme Court of the United States on May 17, 1954, in the matter of separate schools

Document 1.20f3 North Carolina Resolution, December 30, 1954. [National Archives]

for the races. The Committee shall from time to time report to the Governor its findings and recommendations, and shall, so far as it may find practicable, provide counsel, information and advice to the General Assembly, the State Board of Education and the county and local school boards when requested by them to do so.

(e) The Committee is authorized to call upon the Attorney General for such legal advice as it shall deem necessary.

Sec. 4. This resolution shall be in full force and effect from and after its adoption.

WEST KENTUCKY VOCATIONAL SCHOOL
1400 Thompson Avenue
Paducah, Kentucky

April 13, 1961

Chairman
Interstate Commerce Commission
Washington 25, D. C.

Dear Sir:

On traveling through the states of Louisiana, Mississippi, Tennessee, one observes signs on the waiting rooms as follows:

   Colored Waiting Rooms Intrastate Passengers

   White Waiting Rooms Intrastate Passengers

According to the signs, there is no waiting room (either White or Negro) for Interstate Passengers.

These signs are more ridiculous and more confusing than the original "White and Colored Room" signs. The intention of such foolish signs is quite obvious. They are intended to do just what they are doing, confuse the issue and evade the law. The whole thing boils down to segregated waiting rooms, which is contrary to your ruling. It seems to me if the Interstate Commerce Commission or other agencies of the Federal Government concerned with the problem really wanted to do the right thing, it (or they) would force all ethnic signs removed, partitions torn away and only the sign "Waiting Room."

Too, I do not see how morally or legally your department can continue to permit segregated lunch counters at bus and railway terminals under the guise that they are operated by private companies. How can anything so public as a lunch counter in a bus station be a private concern?

It has now been approximately seven years since the 1954 Supreme Court Decision, and I honestly think that there has been ample time for the discountinuance of all indecent undemocratic practices such as I have memtioned in this letter. I see no reason why the proper agency of the Federal Government would not now be justified in enforcing its own law just as the appropriate Federal Agency does the Income Tax Law. If the payment of Income Tax were left to the conscience and discretion of individuals, I am sure the Government would soon become bankrupt. It

Document 1.20g1 Letter from Osceola Dawson to the Chairman of the Interstate Commerce Commission, April 13, 1961. [National Archives]

Chairman   -2-   April 13, 1961

is the same way with other areas. As long as the Federal Government remains spineless and continues to leave racial matters to the conscience and discretion of individuals and localities, injustices will continue to prevail and the United States will continue to be ridiculed as a big hypocrite among nations.

I hope the Interstate Commerce Commission and all other agencies combined will start and effect a real revolution not merely to do something in name or for the purpose of saving face or impressing the Russians or some one else, but to bring about real Democracy. I think tearing down White and Negro signs, tearing out partitions in bus and train stations will be an effective beginning.

I trust this letter will be considered seriously, because far too long have we played the hypocrite. Far too long has the Federal Government been too lax in these matters, acting like the spineless, infamous Pilate. I hope Attorney General Kennedy will probed into discriminatory practices as deeply and as vigorously as he has probed into the very bottom of price fixing by the big corporations.

Sin and mal-practices should be fought in all areas. If we are to ever be the Democracy we profess to be, we must practice true Democratic Principles.

Respectfully yours,

(Miss) Osceola A. Dawson

OAD/jaw
CC
  Mr. Clarence Mitchel
  President Kennedy
  Attorney General Kennedy
  Courier Journal
  Louisville Defender
  Sun Democrat
  Senator John Cooper
  Attorney Dearing
  Mr. Roy Wilkins
  Civil Rights Commission

Document 1.20g2 Letter from Osceola Dawson to the Chairman of the Interstate Commerce Commission, April 13, 1961. [National Archives]

DOCUMENT 8: *BAKKE SYLLABUS*

NOTE: Where it is feasible, a syllabus (headnote) will be released, as is being done in connection with this case, at the time the opinion is issued. The syllabus constitutes no part of the opinion of the Court but has been prepared by the Reporter of Decisions for the convenience of the reader. See *United States v. Detroit Lumber Co.*, 200 U.S. 321, 337.

SUPREME COURT OF THE UNITED STATES

Syllabus

REGENTS OF THE UNIVERSITY OF CALIFORNIA *v.* BAKKE

CERTIORARI TO THE SUPREME COURT OF CALIFORNIA

No. 76-811. Argued October 12, 1977—Decided June 28, 1978

The Medical School of the University of California at Davis (hereinafter Davis) had two admissions programs for the entering class of 100 students—the regular admissions program and the special admissions program. Under the regular procedure, candidates whose overall undergraduate grade point averages fell below 2.5 on a scale of 4.0 were summarily rejected. About one out of six applicants was then given an interview, following which he was rated on a scale of 1 to 100 by each of the committee members (five in 1973 and six in 1974), his rating being based on the interviewers' summaries, his overall grade point average, his science courses grade point average, and his Medical College Admissions Test (MCAT) scores, letters of recommendation, extracurricular activities, and other biographical data, all of which resulted in a total "benchmark score." The full admissions committee then made offers of admission on the basis of their review of the applicant's file and his score, considering and acting upon applications as they were received. The committee chairman was responsible for placing names on the waiting list and had discretion to include persons with "special skills." A separate committee, a majority of whom were members of minority groups, operated the special admissions program. The 1973 and 1974 application forms, respectively, asked candidates whether they wished to be considered as "economically and/or educationally disadvantaged" applicants and members of a "minority group" (blacks, Chicanos, Asians, American Indians). If an applicant of a minority group was found to be "disadvantaged," he would be rated in a manner similar to the one employed by the general admissions committee. Special candidates, however, did not have to meet the 2.5 grade point cut-off and were not ranked against candidates in the general admissions process. About one-fifth of the special applicants were invited for interviews in 1973 and 1974, following which they were given benchmark scores, and the top choices were then given to the general admissions committee, which could reject special candidates for failure to meet course requirements or other specific deficiencies. The special committee continued to recommend candidates until 16 special admission selections had been made. During a four-year period 63 minority students were admitted to Davis under the special program and 44 under the general program. No disadvantaged whites were admitted under the special program, though many applied. Respondent, a white male, applied to Davis in 1973 and 1974, in both years being considered only under the general admissions program. Though he had a 468 out of 500 score in 1973, he was rejected since no general applicants with scores less than 470 were being accepted after respondent's application, which was filed late in the year, had been processed and completed. At that time four special admission slots were still unfilled. In 1974 respondent applied early, and though he had a total score of 549 out of 600, he was again rejected. In neither year was his name placed on the discretionary waiting list. In both years special applicants were admitted with significantly lower scores than respondent's. After his second rejection, respondent filed this action in state court for mandatory injunctive and declaratory relief to compel his admission to Davis, alleging that the special admissions program operated to exclude him on the basis of his race in violation of the Equal Protection Clause of the Fourteenth Amendment, a provision of the California Constitution, and

§ 601 of Title VI of the Civil Rights Act of 1964, which provides, *inter alia*, that no person shall on the ground of race or color be excluded from participating in any program receiving federal financial assistance. Petitioner cross-claimed for a declaration that its special admissions program was lawful. The trial court found that the special program operated as a racial quota, because minority applicants in that program were rated only against one another, and 16 places in the class of 100 were reserved for them. Declaring that petitioner could not take race into account in making admissions decisions, the program was held to violate the Federal and State Constitutions and Title VI. Respondent's admission was not ordered, however, for lack of proof that he would have been admitted but for the special program. The California Supreme Court, applying a strict-scrutiny standard, concluded that the special admissions program was not the least intrusive means of achieving the goals of the admittedly compelling state interests of integrating the medical profession and increasing the number of doctors willing to serve minority patients. Without passing on the state constitutional or federal statutory grounds the court held that petitioner's special admissions program violated the Equal Protection Clause. Since petitioner could not satisfy its burden of demonstrating that respondent, absent the special program, would not have been admitted, the court ordered his admission to Davis.

Held: The judgment below is affirmed insofar as it orders respondent's admission to Davis and invalidates petitioner's special admissions program, but is reversed insofar as it prohibits petitioner from taking race into account as a factor in its future admissions decisions.

18 Cal. 3d 34, 553 P. 2d 1152, affirmed in part and reversed in part.

Mr. Justice Powell concluded:

1. Title VI proscribes only those racial classifications that would violate the Equal Protection Clause if employed by a State or its agencies. Pp. 12-18.

2. Racial and ethnic classifications of any sort are inherently suspect and call for the most exacting judicial scrutiny. While the goal of achieving a diverse student body is sufficiently compelling to justify consideration of race in admissions decisions under some circumstances, petitioner's special admissions program, which forecloses consideration to persons like respondent, is unnecessary to the achievement of this compelling goal and therefore invalid under the Equal Protection Clause. Pp. 18-49.

3. Since petitioner could not satisfy its burden of proving that respondent would not have been admitted even if there had been no special admissions program, he must be admitted. P. 49.

Mr. Justice Brennan, Mr. Justice White, Mr. Justice Marshall, and Mr. Justice Blackmun concluded:

1. Title VI proscribes only those racial classifications that would violate the Equal Protection Clause if employed by a State or its agencies. Pp. 4-31.

2. Racial classifications call for strict judicial scrutiny. Nonetheless, the purpose of overcoming substantial, chronic minority underrepresentation in the medical profession is sufficiently important to justify petitioner's remedial use of race. Thus, the judgment below must be reversed in that it prohibits race from being used as a factor in university admissions. Pp. 31-55.

Mr. Justice Stevens, joined by The Chief Justice, Mr. Justice Stewart, and Mr. Justice Rehnquist, being of the view that whether race can ever be a factor in an admissions policy is not an issue here; that Title VI applies; and that respondent was excluded from Davis in violation of Title VI, concurs in the Court's judgment insofar as it affirms the judgment of the court below ordering respondent admitted to Davis. Pp. 1-14.

Powell, J., announced the Court's judgment and filed an opinion expressing his views of the case, in Parts I, III-A, and V-C of which White, J., joined; and in Parts I and V-C of which Brennan, Marshall, and Blackmun, JJ., joined. Brennan, White, Marshall, and Blackmun, JJ., filed an opinion concurring in the judgment in part and dissenting in part. White, Marshall, and Blackmun, JJ., filed separate opinions. Stevens, J., filed an opinion concurring in the judgment in part and dissenting in part, in which Burger, C. J., and Stewart and Rehnquist, JJ., joined.

Document 1.20h Bakke Syllabus, Argued October 12, 1977, decided June 28, 1978. [U.S. Government Printing Office]

Reconstruction, the Fourteenth Amendment, and Personal Liberties, 1866 and 1874

Following the Civil War, Congress submitted to the states three amendments as part of its Reconstruction program to guarantee equal civil and legal rights to black citizens. On June 16, 1866, the House Joint Resolution proposing the 14th Amendment to the Constitution (the first featured document) was submitted to the states. On July 28, 1868, the 14th Amendment was declared ratified and became part of the supreme law of the land.

Congressman John A. Bingham of Ohio, the primary author of the first section of the 14th Amendment, intended that the amendment also nationalize the federal Bill of Rights by making it binding upon the states. Senator Jacob Howard of Michigan, introducing the amendment, specifically stated that the privileges and immunities clause would extend to the states "the personal rights guaranteed and secured by the first eight amendments." He was, however, alone in this assertion. Most senators argued that the privileges and immunities clause did not bind the states to the federal Bill of Rights.

Not only did the 14th Amendment fail to extend the Bill of Rights to the states, it also failed to protect the rights of black citizens. One legacy of Reconstruction was the determined struggle of black and white citizens to make the promise of the 14th Amendment a reality. Citizens petitioned and initiated court cases, Congress enacted legislation, and the executive branch attempted to enforce measures that would guard all citizens' rights. While these citizens did not succeed in empowering the 14th Amendment during Reconstruction, they effectively articulated arguments and offered dissenting opinions that would be the basis for change in the 20th century.

The first case to test the impact of the 14th Amendment on the Bill of Rights began in 1870 when the Butchers Benevolent Association of New Orleans filed a lawsuit against a monopoly granted by the Louisiana legislature to the Crescent City Livestock Landing and Slaughter House Company. The butchers claimed that the state had interfered with "life, liberty, [and] the pursuit of Honorable and just means for promoting happiness and obtaining comfort," in violation of the 14th Amendment's guarantee of privileges and immunities of U.S. citizens. On April 14, 1873, in a five to four decision, the Supreme Court ruled that the privileges and immunities clause of the 14th Amendment was not binding and that protection of ordinary civil liberties was a power reserved to the states. It was not until *Gitlow v. New York* in 1925 that, through the due process clause of the 14th Amendment, the Bill of Rights would begin to be nationalized.

The second featured document is the articulate plea of the "colored citizens of Cleveland & vicinity, Tenn.," petitioning Congress to pass legislation to enforce the 14th Amendment more effectively. On January 19, 1874, the petition was referred to the House Committee of the Judiciary where it languished. State legislation had already begun to construct the system of segregation that would remain legal until 1954.

The House Joint Resolution proposing the 14th Amendment to the Constitution, June 16, 1866, is found in the General Records of the U.S. Government, Record Group 11. The petition for the enforcement of the 14th Amendment, January 19, 1874, is found in the Records of the U.S. House of Representatives, Record Group 233.

TEACHING ACTIVITIES

1. Ask students to review what their textbooks say about the Civil War amendments and share with them the background information on the 14th Amendment from the note to the teacher. Ask the class to "brainstorm" on what they consider to be their privileges and immunities as U.S. citizens. List their ideas on the chalkboard.

2. Duplicate a set of the two documents and prepare a worksheet for each student from the questions below. Direct students to study the documents and the U.S. Constitution and complete the worksheet as homework.

Article XIV.

Section 1. All persons born or naturalized in the United States, and subject to the jurisdiction thereof, are citizens of the United States and of the State wherein they reside. No State shall make or enforce any law which shall abridge the privileges or immunities of citizens of the United States; nor shall any State deprive any person of life, liberty, or property, without due process of law; nor deny to any person within its jurisdiction the equal protection of the laws.

Section 2. Representatives shall be apportioned among the several States according to their respective numbers, counting the whole number of persons in each State, excluding Indians not taxed. But when the right to vote at any election for the choice of electors for President and Vice President of the United States, Representatives in Congress, the Executive and Judicial officers of a State, or the members of the Legislature thereof, is denied to any of the male inhabitants of such State, being twenty-one years of age, and citizens of the United States, or in any way abridged, except for participation in rebellion, or other crime, the basis of representation therein shall be reduced in the proportion which the

Document 1.21a1 Fourteenth Amendment to the Constitution, June 16, 1886. [National Archives]

number of such male citizens shall bear to the whole number of male citizens twenty-one years of age in such State.

Section 3. No person shall be a Senator or Representative in Congress, or elector of President and Vice President, or hold any office, civil or military, under the United States, or under any State, who, having previously taken an oath, as a member of Congress, or as an officer of the United States, or as a member of any State legislature, or as an executive or judicial officer of any State, to support the Constitution of the United States, shall have engaged in insurrection or rebellion against the same, or given aid or comfort to the enemies thereof. But Congress may by a vote of two-thirds of each House, remove such disability.

Section 4. The validity of the public debt of the United States, authorized by law, including debts incurred for payment of pensions and bounties for services in suppressing insurrection or rebellion, shall not be questioned. But neither the United States nor any State shall assume or pay any debt or obligation incurred in aid of insurrection or rebellion against the United States, or any claim for the loss or emancipation of any slave; but all such debts, obligations and claims shall be held illegal and void.

Section 5. The Congress shall have power to enforce, by appropriate legislation, the provisions of this article.

Attest.

Edw. McPherson
Clerk of the House of Representatives.

J. W. Forney
Secretary of the Senate.

Schuyler Colfax
Speaker of the House of Representatives.

La Fayette S. Foster
President of the Senate pro tempore.

Document 1.21a2 Fourteenth Amendment to the Constitution, June 16, 1886. [National Archives]

To the Senate and House of Representatives of the United States in Congress assembled—

Your Petitioners Colored Citizens of Cleveland & vicinity, Tenn. humbly pray that the Fourteenth Amendment to the Constitution of the United States, be so enforced by appropriate legislation that no State be, hereafter, permitted to make or enforce any law abridging our privileges or immunities as citizens of the United States.

As reasons for presenting this Petition we urge the following,—

1. Without such enforcement the first section of said Amendment is for the Colored People, virtually, a dead letter. In our own State a colored man though eligible to the office of Governor or President, is not allowed to travel in a first-class R. Road car or send his children to the same school with his white neighbors. Tennessee has never had a Common School nor can she have one till the evil of which we complain be abated.

2. The deprivation of these, and others of our rights as Citizens is a contempt to our race, a great injury to us individually, and at the same time a damage to the white race as well. To instance only one item— not a few of the public white schools about us have been continued this year only two and one-half months.— If the Public School Fund in these sparsely populated States, must, to gratify a slavery-engendered prejudice, be divided, it will follow with unfailing certainty, that the illiteracy of whites as well as blacks will increase continually.

3. We petition not for any favor but for the undisturbed enjoyment of our chartered rights. The organic law of our whole land knows nothing of white citizens or black citizens, as such

Document 1.21b1 Petition for the enforcement of the Fourteenth Amendment, January 19, 1874. [National Archives]

but decrees that all born or naturalized in the land are equal before the law. If a State be tolerated in shutting the colored man out of the public schools it might with equal reason be allowed to deny to him the right to testify or vote.

4. We would remind our Rulers that in those dark days when a gigantic Rebellion threatened the national life, the colored men of Tennessee, so loved liberty, that while yet slaves and with no _promise_ even of personal freedom for their race, they rushed by thousands into the Federal armies. We do not complain that the disabilities of the men we then fought, are removed, but we confess ourselves unable to understand on what principle of equity or expediency it is that our own disabilities are allowed to remain. We do not question the policy of the General Government being magnanimous to its _enemies_, but we must doubt the wisdom of its tolerating States in visiting insult and injury upon its _friends_.

5. We urge our Petition with the more of assurance since all we claim was pledged us in both of the Party Platforms of 1872 — platforms voted upon by more than six millions of American freemen. We ask respectfully but with earnestness, and persistently, that the pledge thus solemnly given by the nation be redeemed.

Names

Anthony Carter
Geo. T. Warson
Major Brown
Cage Parks
Geo. Calaway
Scott Perstin
Geo Christmas

Names

Document 1.21b2 Petition for the enforcement of the Fourteenth Amendment, January 19, 1874. [National Archives]

3. When the students have completed the worksheet, discuss questions they may have. Then ask the class to consider the two documents together and to discuss the following questions:
   a. What privileges and immunities of citizens were of paramount interest to the creators of these documents over one hundred years ago? How are they similar or different from the list brain stormed by the class?
   b. Ours is a nation of laws that people may disagree with and work to change, but may not disobey with impunity. What do these documents reveal about the legal avenues available to people of the Reconstruction era for pursuing an extension of the privileges and immunities of citizens? What do these documents reveal about the methods of those who opposed the extension of such privileges?
   c. It is sometimes said that we stand on the shoulders of those who have gone before us. Citizens of the Reconstruction era failed in their efforts to extend Bill of Rights protections against state acts. Were their efforts futile, or did later personal liberties advocates or civil rights movements benefit from the efforts of these earlier citizens?
4. Use one or both of the activities below for further research:
   a. Assign one or two good students to find out what political parties have said about citizens' rights in their party platforms in a particular election and report their findings to the class. For example, they may wish to locate the black civil rights planks of the 1872 Republican and Democratic platforms alluded to in the Cleveland, TN, petition. Most major library systems should have the two-volume National Party Platforms: 1840-1984, and may have recent Republican Party official convention proceedings. Democratic state committees have the party's most recent platforms. Or, students may wish to contact the Democratic National Committee's research office or the Republican National Committee's archives office in Washington, DC.
   b. Assign a student to check the current constitution of your state to see what rights are guaranteed to citizens of the state and to share the information with the class. In the report, the student should compare and contrast state privileges and immunities with those of U.S. citizens and compare and contrast the protection provided in the state by the class in activity one.

This lesson has been adapted from an exercise included in *The Bill of Rights: Evolution of Personal Liberties* developed and published by the National Archives and Records Administration and ABC-CLIO.

National Archives Document Citation

The Fourteenth Amendment to the Constitution, June 16, 1886; Enrolled Acts Part III, 39th Congress; Enrolled Acts and Resolutions of Congress, 1789-1999; General Records of the U.S. Government, Record Group 11; National Archives at College Park, College Park, MD.

Petition for the enforcement of the Fourteenth Amendment, January 19, 1874; Committee on the Judiciary; Petitions and Memorials on Civil Rights Legislation (HR43A-H8.3); 43rd Congress; Records of the U.S. House of Representatives, Record Group 233; National Archives Building, Washington, DC.

Article Citation

Mueller, Jean West and Wynell Burroughs Schamel. "Reconstruction, the Fourteenth Amendment, and Personal Liberties." *Organization of American Historians* (OAH) *Magazine of History* 4, 1 (Winter 1989).

Reconstruction, the 14th Amendment, and Personal Liberties Worksheet

Directions: Use the information contained in documents one and two and Article V of the U.S. Constitution to complete the worksheet.

Document One: The 14th Amendment

1. What branch of the government initiates a constitutional amendment?

2. How much of a majority is required in each house of Congress for the proposed amendment to advance?

3. How much of a majority in the state legislatures is required for ratification of an amendment?

4. According to Section 1, you are a citizen of what two jurisdictions?

5. What branch of the government is responsible for enabling a ratified amendment to be enforced, according to Section 5?

Document Two: Petition

1. What means did these citizens of Cleveland, TN, use to try to improve their living conditions?

2. What types of state laws were abridging black citizens' rights in Tennessee in 1874?

3. According to the petition, how were such laws hurting white citizens as well?

4. What evidence do the petitioners offer to substantiate their claim that black Union veterans have fewer rights than white Confederate veterans?

5. Why do you believe the petitioners mentioned the 1872 party platforms and elections?

6. What other methods to push enforcement of the 14th Amendment were available to these citizens at this time?

7. Underline the adjectives used in the petition.

    a. What pattern emerges?

    b. What is the tone assumed toward the Federal Government?

    c. What words, in the main body of the petition, were underlined by the writers? Why do you think they underlined them?

    d. List emotionally charged words or expressions that the petitioners used to try to persuade Congress to pass enforcing legislation.

1869 Petition:
The Appeal for Woman Suffrage, 1869

Between 1848, when a resolution calling for woman suffrage was first adopted in New York, and 1920, when the 19th Amendment was ratified, women repeatedly petitioned both the state and Federal Governments for the right to vote. During the course of this two-generation contest, women devoted their careers, sacrificed their time and energy, and on several occasions, risked their lives in their campaign to obtain the most basic right in a democracy–the right to vote. An increased appreciation and awareness of this momentous struggle and the labor it required is crucial for a thorough understanding of the evolution of women's rights in the history of the United States.

History of the Early Suffrage Movement

The legal status of American women in the mid-19th century was defined by English common law, which was largely uncodified and based on custom and traditional court decisions. According to the law, unmarried women were considered the property of their fathers, while married women belonged to their husbands. Neither group of women enjoyed many individual rights. Women could not vote, own land, make a will, sign a contract, serve on a jury, testify in court, or be sued. Even a woman's wages legally belonged to her husband or father. If her husband died without a will, a woman could inherit neither the house they lived in nor more than one-third of their mutual property. If she were widowed or divorced, she had no rights to her own children. What control a woman had over her own life was largely determined by the amount of influence she exerted over men and children through her role as nurturer and instiller of family values.

Despite their few legal or political rights, women found a powerful voice for addressing individual and societal grievances in their First Amendment right to petition the Government. Although many of the earliest of women's petitions to Congress are pension requests from the widows of Revolutionary War soldiers, by 1830 petitioning had become an important means for relating public grievances to the Government. Traveling door to door to collect signatures, many women joined the abolitionist movement in petitioning Congress for an end to the institution of slavery. The belief in equality that led women to champion the rights of slaves also led some women to question the denial of their own political rights. Women of the antislavery movement began laying the ideological foundations for the subsequent movement for women's equality. From their exposure to the tactics of the abolitionists, women learned valuable organizational and political skills, which would later benefit them in their drive for suffrage. The featured document, an appeal and petition from the Records of the U.S. House of Representatives, Record Group 233, illustrates the increasing sophistication with which women voiced their cause.

The Roots of Suffrage

The roots of suffrage took hold when Lucretia Mott, an accomplished and confident abolitionist speaker, traveled to London in 1840 for the World Anti-Slavery Convention. Although male delegates denied her a voice at the international convention, Mott resolved to publicly confront the issue of women's rights in society. In 1848 Mott and Elizabeth Cady Stanton, a reform-minded woman with a clear memory of the cruel and unjust treatment of women in her father's courtroom, organized the first women's rights convention at Seneca Falls, NY. The convention was the earliest organized effort for social equality for women.

The climactic event of the convention came when Stanton presented to the assembly the Declaration of Sentiments, modeled after the Declaration of Independence. She stated, "We hold these truths to be self evident: that all men and women are created equal," then listed 15 grievances and 12 resolutions, including demands for public speaking rights and increased educational opportunities for women.

The delegates voted unanimously for every resolution except the ninth, the right to vote. Many of the women, including Mott, felt that the demand for "elective franchise" might be too controversial and prejudice their cause. Only when the famous black abolitionist Frederick Douglass spoke in favor of women's right to vote did the resolution finally pass. At the close of the convention, 68 female and 32 male delegates, among a curious crowd of almost 300 citizens who attended the meeting, signed the Declaration of Sentiments, which included a demand for the right to vote. Although mostly a local audience attended the meeting, word of the Seneca Falls convention and the women's movement began to spread. While the early movement received much ridicule and condemnation in the established press, reform-minded organizations like the abolitionist movement were more sympathetic, and it was from these ranks that support continued to grow.

Many women around the country began discussing the issues of women's social and political rights. Lucy Stone, after graduating from Oberlin College in Ohio in 1847, began organizing and helping women to mobilize politically for the right to vote. When Stone married Henry Blackwell, she kept, against the custom of the day, her maiden name. Other women who followed suit became known as "Lucy Stoners." In 1850 Lucy Stone, by then an experienced and dynamic abolitionist lecturer, helped to organize the first national convention on women's rights in Worcester, MA.

Another momentous event in the history of women's rights occurred in 1851 when Elizabeth Cady Stanton befriended temperance reformer Susan B. Anthony. These two like-minded woman began a 50-year partnership to promote the cause of equal rights between the sexes. Working together, Stanton, Anthony, and Stone led the women's rights movement, using and honing their speaking, campaigning, and organizing skills in the process. All three women contributed their talents and energy both to the National Women's Rights Convention–which was held every year from 1850 to the Civil War, except in 1857 when funds were insufficient–and to the increasingly popular abolitionist movement.

Suffrage Derailed

The outbreak of the Civil War interrupted the momentum of the equal rights movement because many of the women reformers, mostly Northerners and abolitionists, dedicated their valuable time and efforts to helping the Union war effort. The enormous number of men going to fight in the war forced women to take over many traditionally male-dominated jobs. Beyond helping to feed and clothe the soldiers, women, for the first time, officially served as nurses for the U.S. Army and, in a few cases, even fought in the war. Experienced in nursing family members at home, women contributed vital medical skills to a deficient and previously male-dominated nursing corps. Stanton and most of the leaders of the women's rights movement believed that their hard work and loyalty to the Union during the war would be rewarded with the vote.

Even though many of the women's rights organizers anticipated that a grateful Congress would grant both women and freed blacks suffrage after the war, their expectations quickly faded. Surprisingly, they found that former advocates of woman suffrage shifted their support solely to obtaining rights for freed black men. A further setback came when the ratification of the 14th Amendment in 1868, which penalized states that prohibited black males from voting, resulted in the insertion of the word "male" into the Constitution for the first time. After lobbying to get women and blacks enfranchised together in the proposed 15th Amendment, Stanton, Anthony, and their supporters vowed to campaign against any version of the amendment that denied women the vote. This insistence that the rights of women could not take second place to the rights of black men caused many former abolitionists, male and female, to side against them, producing a breech in the women's movement. In February 1869 the 15th Amendment to the Constitution was proposed, guaranteeing blacks, but not women, the right to vote.

The ideological and strategic differences that grew among suffrage leaders during and immediately after the Civil War formally split the women's movement into two rival associations. Stanton and Anthony, after accusing abolitionist and Republican supporters of emphasizing the civil rights of blacks at the expense of women's rights, formed the National Woman Suffrage Association (NWSA) in

AN APPEAL.

TO THE MEN AND WOMEN OF AMERICA.

DO WOMEN WISH TO VOTE? ARE MEN WILLING THEY SHOULD VOTE?

We are often told that, if women really wanted to vote, it would not be very long before they could do so. We give below a form of petition just sent out by the New England Woman's Suffrage Association. A similar one was issued by the American Equal Rights Association, at the anniversary in May last; subsequently, also, by the Washington Universal Franchise Association, and by Mrs. Stanton.

Thus early have these friends of equal human rights resorted to the one means at their command to secure justice for woman. If it be faithfully used, our object will be accomplished. It is probable that during the next session of Congress a law or constitutional amendment will be passed extending suffrage. If women are not included in this extension, it should be by no fault of theirs.

Let every woman who reads this article cut out the petition, attach it to a large sheet of paper, sign it, and get every man or woman to sign it who is not satisfied while women, idiots, felons and lunatics, and men guilty of bribery are the only classes excluded from the exercise of the right of suffrage.

Let the great army of working-women, who wish to secure a fair day's wages for a fair day's work, SIGN IT.

Let the widow, living on her "life-use" of the pitiful "thirds," and "allowed to remain forty days without paying rent in the house of her deceased husband," SIGN IT.

Let the wife, from whom the law takes the right to what she earns and the power to make a will without her husband's consent, SIGN IT.

Let the mother, who has no legal right to her own children, SIGN IT.

Let the young man, just gone out from the home where his best friend and counselor has been his mother, SIGN IT.

Let the father, whose little daughter looks trustingly to him for every good, SIGN IT.

Let the soldier, returned from battle sounder in health and stronger of limb because of the woman's hand who dressed his wounds and ministered to his wants in sickness, SIGN IT.

Let every man who regards his own right to the ballot as sacred SIGN IT.

And, when the longest possible list of names has been secured, let the petition be returned to Mary E. Gage, secretary of the American Equal Rights Association, care of the *Anti-Slavery Standard*, 39 Nassau street, New York.

We will join them in one long roll, and send them to brave Ben Wade, whom all the world knows as the avowed friend of Impartial Suffrage for women as well as men.

Then, if _____ a petition before them, presented by such a man, our senators and representatives can afford to place a ballot in the hands of the late rebels, and refuse it to the loyal mothers of this country, women can afford to wait until the American people learn that the path of justice is the only path of peace and safety. LUCY STONE.

PETITION.

To the Senate and House of Representatives of the United States in Congress assembled:

The undersigned citizens of the United States pray your honorable bodies that in any proposed amendment to the Constitution which may come before you in regard to suffrage, and in any law affecting Suffrage in the District of Columbia, or any territory, the right of voting may be given to women on the same terms as to men.

Document 1.22 Petition: The Appeal for Woman Suffrage, January 29, 1869. [National Archives]

May 1869. Beyond campaigning for a Federal woman suffrage amendment, the NWSA broadened its platform to confront other issues such as the unionization of women workers and the reformation of labor and divorce law. In contrast, the American Woman Suffrage Association (AWSA), founded six months later by Lucy Stone, Julia Ward Howe, and Thomas Wentworth Higginson, protested the confrontational tactics of the NWSA and tied itself closely to the Republican Party while concentrating solely on securing woman suffrage state by state. Stone and other members of the AWSA accused Stanton and Anthony of distracting attention from the suffrage movement by adopting a broader social reform agenda. Unlike the NWSA, Stone's association endorsed the 15th Amendment and accepted men into its ranks.

Although political differences between these rival associations faded over the next two decades, this split in the woman suffrage movement lasted until 1890, when the two merged into the National American Woman Suffrage Association, a merger due in a large part to the efforts of Lucy Stone's daughter, Alice Stone Blackwell. Despite this reconciliation, 30 years would pass and three more constitutional amendments would be ratified before women gained the right to vote in 1920 with the 19th Amendment.

TEACHING ACTIVITIES

Close Reading of Document

1. Distribute a copy of the featured document to each student. After reading through the text with them, ask students the following questions: What kind of document is this? When do you think the document was created? What evidence in the text supports your conclusions about the date of the document? Who wrote the appeal for this petition? Where did the signers live? Did many men sign the petition?

Persuasive Writing

2. Share with students the background information on the suffrage movement. On the chalkboard, list the rights and privileges denied to women as mentioned in the appeal. Ask students to suggest reasons the author might have for mentioning these restrictions in a petition asking for the vote for women. Ask students to list in a second column rights and privileges they believe women are still denied today. Divide students into groups of three each. Assign each group to either defend or refute the following statement: Today women have equal rights that are guaranteed to them under the Constitution of the United States. After 15 minutes, record the strongest arguments for and against the statement on an overhead projector while students make copies of the arguments. For homework, assign students to write a well-developed persuasive paragraph on the topic. Remind students to anticipate and dismantle the opposing argument in their writing.

Comparing Citizens' Voices

3. Discuss with your students some of the differences in communication between 1869, when the appeal was created, and now. Ask students how they think Lucy Stone expected to distribute her petitions for people to sign freely and how many signers they think she could have expected to respond to this effort. In a show of hands, ask the students how many of them have signed a petition. Ask them what tactics people use today to influence the views of their senators and representatives. Direct the students to contact the local office of their U.S. representative or senators to collect data about tactics contemporary constituents use to be heard. Students may want to inquire how the staff keeps track of telephone and e-mail inquiries to determine if paper petitions are considered more seriously.

Biographical Writing

4. Assign students to write an obituary or an epitaph for Lucy Stone, making sure to mention her greatest achievements and the most significant events in her life. In prepa-

ration for the writing, students should answer the following questions: What was unique about Lucy Stone's marriage to Henry Blackwell? What kind of education did Stone have? Who were some of the other famous women and men that she knew and worked with? (It may be helpful for students to read some obituaries and epitaphs to get an idea of the style and the types of information they include.)

Creating a Time Line

5. Assign small groups of students to research segments of the history of voting rights, including passage of the 14th, 19th, and 26th Amendments. Attach a long piece of butcher paper to one wall of the classroom, draw and divide a line into 10-year blocks, and direct students to place significant events in voting rights history on this time line. Lead a class discussion about the landmark events and the historical context for each of them.

Staging a Play

6. Divide the class into five teams. Ask each team to research, write, and stage one act of a television play about the events and personalities in the struggle for woman suffrage after the Civil War. The acts might focus on Susan B. Anthony's arrest in 1872; woman suffrage victories in the West; the work of Sojourner Truth, Mary Church Terrell, and the suffrage movement among black women; the great march on Washington, DC, led by Alice Paul in 1913; the picketing of the White House in 1917; the final vote on the 19th Amendment taken in the Senate on June 4, 1919; or the final battle for ratification of the amendment in the Nashville statehouse in August 1920. Schedule a media specialist to videotape the final production.

National Archives Document Citation
Petition: The Appeal for Woman Suffrage, 1869; "January 29, 1869"; Committee on the Judiciary; (SEN40A-H10.3); 40th Congress; Records of the U.S Senate, Record Group 46; National Archives Building, Washington, DC.

Article Citation
Schamel, Wynell, Beth Haverkamp, Lucinda Robb, and John Harper. "1869 Petition: The Appeal for Woman Suffrage." *Social Education* 59, 5 (September 1995): 299.

A Bill to Relieve Certain Legal Disabilities of Women, 1872

In February 1878, by a vote of 169 to 87 in the House of Representatives, and twelve months later, by a vote of 39 to 20 in the Senate, Congress approved a "Bill to relieve certain legal disabilities of women." On February 15, 1879, President Rutherford B. Hayes signed it into law. Sixteen days later, the Supreme Court's minute book included an entry that read, "It is ordered that Belva A. Lockwood, of Washington City, District of Columbia, be admitted to practice as an attorney and consellor [sic] of this court and she was sworn in accordingly." Thus, Lockwood became the first woman admitted to the bar of the Supreme Court. Her admission, however, came after a long struggle.

She was born Belva Ann Bennett in Royalton, NY, in 1830. She began teaching school there when she was 15, earning half the salary that her male colleagues earned. She married at 18, became a mother at 20, and was widowed at 22. At 24 in 1854 she enrolled in Genessee College, leaving her daughter with her parents. Following her graduation in 1857, she taught at a seminary and later became a school principal. After the Civil War, in 1866, she moved herself and her 16 year old daughter to Washington, DC, where she opened the first coeducational school in the city, became involved in the suffrage and temperance movements, and began to study law. In 1868 she married Dr. Ezekiel Lockwood, a dentist and Baptist minister; he died in 1877.

In 1870 at the age of forty, she entered the National University Law School (it later became George Washington University) and completed her course work three years later. She was refused her diploma, however, on the basis of her gender. Without the diploma she was not admitted to the District of Columbia Bar and could not practice law. So she promptly wrote a letter to President Ulysses S. Grant, ex-officio President of the school, and demanded it. Grant did not respond to her letter, but two weeks later the university's chancellor presented Lockwood with her diploma. Soon after, she was admitted to the District of Columbia Bar, becoming the second woman attorney in the nation's capital (following Charlotte E. Ray, who had been admitted in 1872) and one of the very few who were licensed to practice law anywhere in the country.

As a practicing attorney, Lockwood developed a specialization in pension and land claims. The staff of her law office processed thousands of Civil War veterans' pension claims between the early 1870s and the 1890s. She also represented other clients and it was in this capacity that her admission to the Supreme Court Bar became necessary.

In 1874 Charlotte Van Cort hired Lockwood to file a case against the government for use and infringement of a patent. Lockwood anticipated the need to argue the case before the U.S. Court of Claims, and in April 1874 she asked Washington attorney A.A. Hosmer to move for her admission to the Claims Court Bar. Surprisingly, given her status as a practicing attorney in the District, her admission was refused. The basis for the denial was her gender; had she been male the motion for her admission would have been granted. In the denial, Court of Claims Judge Charles Nott indicated that "admission to the bar constitutes an office . . . It is an artificial employment, created not to give idle persons occupation, nor needy persons subsistence, but to aid in the administration of public justice." He concluded by saying, "if we err, the Supreme Court can review our error and give relief to the applicant by mandamus."

Immediately Lockwood turned to Congress, lobbying for legislation that would address the discrimination against women in the federal courts. Neither house took action, though, other than referring her petition to committee where it sat for two years. She also considered asking the Supreme Court for relief.

Lockwood knew that the Rules of the Supreme Court permitted an attorney to apply for permission to practice at that court after successfully practicing in a state, territory, or District of Columbia Supreme Court for 3 years. By the fall of 1876, she

45TH CONGRESS, } **S. 476.**
2D SESSION.

IN THE SENATE OF THE UNITED STATES.

JANUARY 10, 1878.

Mr. SARGENT asked and, by unanimous consent, obtained leave to bring in the following bill; which was read twice and referred to the Committee on the Judiciary.

A BILL

To relieve certain legal disabilities of women.

1 *Be it enacted by the Senate and House of Representa-*
2 *tives of the United States of America in Congress assembled,*
3 That any woman who shall have been a member of the
4 bar of the highest court of any State or Territory or of the
5 supreme court of the District of Columbia for the space of
6 three years, and shall have maintained a good standing before
7 such court, and who shall be a person of good moral charac-
8 ter, shall, on motion, and the production of such record, be
9 admitted to practice before the Supreme Court of the United
10 States.

Document 1.23 "A Bill to Relieve Certain Legal Disabilities of Women," February 1878. [National Archives]

had met that requirement and her admission to the Supreme Court's Bar was moved by local attorney, supporter of women's rights, and former Ohio congressman, Albert G. Riddle.

Riddle's motion, however, was denied. In explaining the denial, Chief Justice Morrison R. Waite announced, "By uniform practice of the court from its origin to the present time and by the fair construction of its rules, none but men are permitted to practice before it as attorneys and counselors. This is in accordance with immemorial usage in England, and the law and practice in all the States, until within a recent period, and that the Court does not feel called upon to make a change until such a change is required by statute or a more extended practice in the higher courts of the States."

Waite's announcement confirmed Lockwood's belief that legislation was her only option. So she returned to Capitol Hill for the next two years, stubbornly pleading the case for women attorneys' right to equal treatment. In a four-page brief that she submitted to members of Congress in early 1878, she refuted each item in both Judge Charles Nott's and Chief Justice Waite's denials. She referred members of Congress to the inalienable rights guaranteed in the Declaration of Independence, to Article Four of the Constitution, and to the 14th Amendment. She offered instances in which women had practiced law in England and gave other examples of women holding government offices, including pension agents and notary publics.

Many of the same arguments Lockwood made were also presented by California Senator Aaron Sargent on the floor of the Senate prior to its vote. He stated, "Men have not the right, in contradiction to the intentions, the wishes, the ambition, of women, to say that their sphere shall be circumscribed, that bounds shall be set which they cannot pass. The enjoyment of liberty, the pursuit of happiness in her own way, is as much a birthright of woman as of man." His arguments also made it clear that passage of the bill would not only allow women admission to the bar, but also would secure for all citizens the right to select his or her own counsel.

The Senate followed the House's lead and voted to approve the bill, which is featured in this article. Within days of the President's signing it, Belva Lockwood became the first woman admitted to the Bar of the Supreme Court and to the Bar of the U.S. Claims Court. She later moved for the admission of Samuel R. Lowery, the first Southern African-American attorney to the Bar of the Supreme Court, and became the first woman to offer oral arguments before the Supreme Court. In addition she ran for President in 1884 and 1888 as the Equal Rights Party candidate.

Her impact on the legal system, however, was not limited to these "firsts." As an attorney, she assisted many clients and affected the outcome of their cases. The last case in which she participated in full argument was the United States v. Cherokee Nation. In it, she represented nearly 6,000 Cherokee whose ancestors had been forced to relocate westward after passage of the Indian Removal Act of 1835. Partly through her efforts, in 1906 (when Lockwood was 76) the Cherokee were awarded damages totaling nearly $5 million.

Note

The document featured in this article comes from the Records of the U.S. Senate, Record Group 46, and is housed in the National Archives Building in Washington, DC.

For More Information

Norgren, Jill. "Before it was Merely Difficult: Belva Lockwood's Life in Law and Politics." *Journal of the Supreme Court*, 1999. Available online at www.stanford.edu/group/WLHP/articles/Bnorgren.pdf.

TEACHING ACTIVITIES

1. Write the title "A Bill to Relieve Certain Legal Disabilities of Women" and the year 1878-79 on the board and ask students what they think the bill referred to. Record their suggestions on the board.

2. Distribute copies of the document to students or project it on an overhead screen. Ask one student to read it aloud while the others follow along. Lead a class discussion by posing the following questions: What type of document is it? What is the date of the document? Who created it? For what purpose?

3. Inform students that the bill was signed into law in February 1879 due in large part to the efforts of Belva A. Lockwood, a Wash-

ington DC attorney. Provide students with copies of the background essay, ask them to read it and write a one-page biography of Lockwood. Or, suggest that they conduct additional research into the lives of the other individuals mentioned in the article and write a one-page biography about one of them. Possibilities include Charlotte E. Ray, Representative Albert G. Riddle, Senator Aaron Sargent, Judge Charles Nott, Chief Justice Waite, and Samuel R. Lowery.

4. Remind students that in Lockwood's four-page brief in support of the bill she referred Congress to the Declaration of Independence, Article Four of the Constitution, and the 14th Amendment. Divide students into three groups, assign each group one of these documents, ask them to read the document, and determine how its contents may have been used by Lockwood in support of the bill to admit women to the Bar of the Supreme Court. Encourage a spokesperson from each group to share their conclusions with the class.

5. Divide students into small groups and assign each group to conduct research into another Supreme Court first using library and Internet resources. Possibilities include the first oral arguments by a woman, the first African American admitted to the bar, the first African American appointed to the court, and the first woman appointed to the court. Ask students to present their findings in a newspaper article or a news broadcast performed for the class.

6. Explain to students that admission to the Supreme Court's bar was one of many milestones achieved by women. Encourage students to refer to their text books, Internet, and library resources and create a time line listing ten events: what they judge to be the five most significant milestones achieved by women prior to and following passage of the 19th Amendment. Encourage volunteers to share their time lines with the class.

7. Invite students to research other parts of the world today and find out what are the restrictions placed on individuals based on gender. Lead a class discussion from the students' findings.

National Archives Document Citation

H.R. 1077: A Bill to Relieve Certain Legal Disabilities of Women; Women, Legal Disabilities of, February, 1878; Accompanying Papers of the 45th Congress; 45th Congress; Records of the U.S. House of Representatives, Record Group 233; National Archives Building, Washington, DC.

Article Citation

Potter, Lee Ann. "A Bill to Relieve Certain Legal Disabilities of Women." *Social Education* 66, 2 (March 2002): 117-120.

Glidden's Patent Application for Barbed Wire, 1874

Life in the American West was reshaped by a series of patents for a simple tool that helped ranchers tame the land: barbed wire. Nine patents for improvements to wire fencing were granted by the U.S. Patent Office to American inventors, beginning with Michael Kelly in November 1868 and ending with Joseph Glidden in November 1874. Barbed wire not only simplified the work of the rancher and farmer, but it significantly affected political, social, and economic practices throughout the region. The swift emergence of this highly effective tool as the favored fencing method influenced life in the region as dramatically as the rifle, six-shooter, telegraph, windmill, and locomotive.

Barbed wire was extensively adopted because it proved ideal for western conditions. Vast and undefined prairies and plains yielded to range management, farming, and ultimately, widespread settlement. As the use of barbed wire increased, wide open spaces became less wide, less open, and less spacious, and the days of the free roaming cowboy were numbered. Today, cowboy ballads remain as nostalgic reminders of life before barbed wire became an accepted symbol of control, transforming space to place and giving new meaning to private property.

Before the invention of barbed wire, the lack of effective fencing limited the range of farming and ranching practices, and with it, the number of people who could settle in an area. Wooden fences were costly and difficult to acquire on the prairie and plains, where few trees grew. Lumber was in such short supply in the region that farmers were forced to build houses of sod. Likewise, rocks for stone walls–commonly found in New England–were scarce on the plains. Shrubs and hedges, early substitutes for wood and rock fencing materials, took too long to grow to become of much use in the rapidly expanding West. Barbed wire was cheaper, easier, and quicker to use than any of these other alternatives.

Without fencing, livestock grazed freely, competing for fodder and water. Where working farms existed, most property was unfenced and open to foraging cattle and sheep. Once a year, cattle owners, unhindered by fenced property lines, led their herds on long cattle drives, eventually arriving at slaughter-houses located near urban railheads for shipping convenience. The appearance of barbed wire meant the end of both the open range and the freedom of the rancher and cowboy, an event lamented in the Cole Porter song "Don't Fence Me In."

Wire fences used before the invention of the barb consisted of only one strand of wire, which was constantly broken by the weight of cattle pressing against it. Michael Kelly made a significant improvement to wire fencing with an invention that "twisted two wires together to form a cable for barbs–the first of its kind in America," according to Henry D. and Frances T. McCallum, the authors of *The Wire That Fenced the West*. Known as the "thorny fence," Kelly's double-strand design made the fence stronger, and the painful barbs taught cattle to keep their distance.

Predictably, other inventors sought to improve upon Kelly's designs; among them was Joseph Glidden, a farmer from De Kalb, IL. In 1873 and 1874, patents were issued for various designs to strengthen Kelly's invention, but the recognized winner in this series of improvements was Glidden's simple wire barb locked onto a double-strand wire. Glidden's invention made barbed wire more effective not only because he described a method for locking the barbs in place, but also because he developed the machinery to mass-produce the wire. His invention also survived court challenges from other inventors. Glidden's patent, prevailing in both litigation and sales, was soon known as "the winner." Today, it remains the most familiar style of barbed wire.

The widespread use of barbed wire changed life on the Great Plains dramatically and permanently. Land and water once open to all was fenced off by ranchers and homesteaders with predictable results. Cattlemen, increasingly cut off from what they regarded as common-use resources in such territories

UNITED STATES PATENT OFFICE.

JOSEPH F. GLIDDEN, OF DE KALB, ILLINOIS.

IMPROVEMENT IN WIRE FENCES.

Specification forming part of Letters Patent No. **157,124**, dated November 24, 1874; application filed October 27, 1873.

To all whom it may concern:

Be it known that I, JOSEPH F. GLIDDEN, of De Kalb, in the county of De Kalb and State of Illinois, have invented a new and valuable Improvement in Wire Fences; and that the following is a full, clear, and exact description of the construction and operation of the same, reference being had to the accompanying drawings, in which—

Figure 1 represents a side view of a section of fence exhibiting my invention. Fig. 2 is a sectional view, and Fig. 3 is a perspective view, of the same.

This invention has relation to means for preventing cattle from breaking through wire fences; and it consists in combining, with the twisted fence wires, a short transverse wire, coiled or bent at its central portion about one of the wire strands of the twist, with its free ends projecting in opposite directions, the other wire strand serving to bind the spur-wire firmly to its place, and in position, with its spur ends perpendicular to the direction of the fence-wire, lateral movement, as well as vibration, being prevented. It also consists in the construction and novel arrangement, in connection with such a twisted fence-wire, and its spur-wires, connected and arranged as above described, of a twisting-key or head-piece passing through the fence-post, carrying the ends of the fence-wires, and serving, when the spurs become loose, to tighten the twist of the wires, and thus render them rigid and firm in position.

In the accompanying drawings, the letter B designates the fence-posts, the twisted fence-wire connecting the same being indicated by the letter A. C represents the twisting-key, the shank of which passes through the fence-post, and is provided at its end with an eye, b, to which the fence-wire is attached. The outer end of said key is provided with a transverse thumb-piece, c, which serves for its manipulation, and at the same time, abutting against the post, forms a shoulder or stop, which prevents the contraction of the wire from drawing the key through its perforation in said post.

The fence-wire is composed at least of two strands, a and z, which are designed to be twisted together after the spur-wires have been arranged in place.

The letter D indicates the spur-wires. Each of these is formed of a short piece of wire, which is bent at its middle portion, as at E, around one only of the wire strands, this strand being designated by the letter a. In forming this middle bend or coil several turns are taken in the wire, so that it will extend along the strand-wire for a distance several times the breadth of its diameter, and thereby form a solid and substantial bearing-head for the spurs, which will effectually prevent them from vibrating laterally or being pushed down by cattle against the fence-wire. Although these spur-wires may be turned at once around the wire strand, it is preferred to form the central bend first, and to then slip them on the wire strand, arranging them at suitable distances apart. The spurs having thus been arranged on one of the wire strands are fixed in position and place by approaching the other wire strands z on the side of the bend from which the spurs extend, and then twisting the two strands a z together by means of the wire key above mentioned, or otherwise. This operation locks each spur-wire at its allotted place, and prevents it from moving therefrom in either direction. It clamps the bend of the spur-wire upon the wire a, thereby holding it against rotary vibration. Finally, the spur ends extending out between the strands on each side, and where the wires are more closely approximated in the twist, form shoulders or stops s, which effectually prevent such rotation in either direction.

Should the spurs, from the untwisting of the strands, become loose and easily movable on their bearings, a few turns of the twisting-key will make them firm, besides straightening up the fence-wire.

What I claim as my invention, and desire to secure by Letters Patent, is—

A twisted fence wire having the transverse spur-wire D bent at its middle portion about one of the wire strands a of said fence-wire, and clamped in position and place by the other wire strand z, twisted upon its fellow, substantially as specified.

JOSEPH F. GLIDDEN.

Witnesses:
G. L. CHAPIN,
J. H. ELLIOTT.

Document 1.24a1 Glidden's Patent Application for Barbed Wire, 1874. [National Archives]

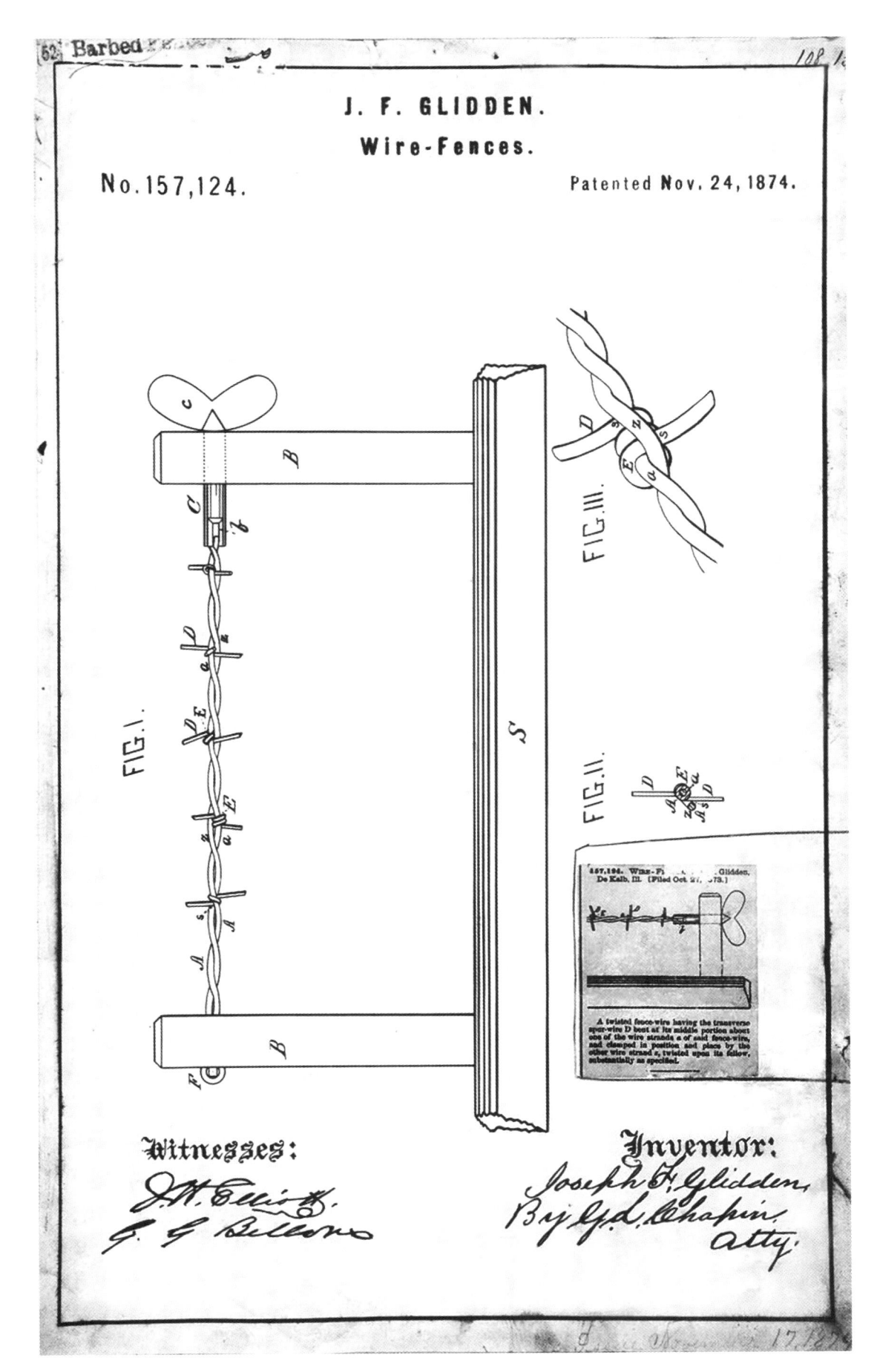

Document 1.24a2 Glidden's Patent Application for Barbed Wire, 1874. [National Archives]

as Texas, New Mexico, Colorado, and Wyoming, first filed land-use petitions and then waged fierce range wars against the property-owning farmers. Gradually, there was a discernible shift in who controlled the land and thus wielded the superior power.

Living patterns of nomadic Native Americans were radically altered, as well. Further squeezed from lands they had always used, they began calling barbed wire "the Devil's rope." Fenced-off land meant that more and more cattle herders–regardless of race–were dependent on the dwindling public lands, which rapidly became overgrazed. The harsh winter of 1886, culminating in a big January 1887 blizzard, wreaked further havoc on the cattle market: Losses totaled more than $20 million in Wyoming alone. In effect, large-scale, open-range cattle enterprises disappeared.

While barbed wire symbolized the range wars and the end of widespread open grazing land for livestock in the American West, it also became a widely used commodity elsewhere, especially during land warfare. In early European history, pointed spears or palisades circumferentially surrounded many castles for protection. Barbed wire rapidly replaced these and other devices used to protect people and property from unwanted intrusion. Military usage of barbed wire formally dates to 1888, when British military manuals first encouraged its use.

During the Spanish American War, Teddy Roosevelt's Rough Riders chose to defend their camps with the help of barbed wire. In turn-of-the-century South Africa, five-strand fences were linked to blockhouses sheltering British troops from the encroachment of Boer commandos. During World War I, barbed wire was used as a military weapon. It was a formidable barrier along the front, stretching from Switzerland to the English Channel. Even now, barbed wire is widely used to protect and safeguard military installations and to establish territorial boundaries. It has also emerged as a commonly recognized instrument for prisoner confinement; the image of a corpse caught on the wires of a concentration camp fence has become the emblem of war's ravages. Today, barbed wire is often part of the containment wall of prisons all over the world.

Other less emotionally charged uses of barbed wire fencing exist in industry. Used on construction and storage sites and around warehouses, barbed wire protects supplies and persons and keeps out unwanted intruders. In any event, it has proved both highly useful and highly significant in altering traditional practices during both war and peace.

Glidden's patent, No. 157124, was issued November 24, 1874. The patent application and related papers are found in the Records of the Patent and Trademark Office, Record Group 241.

TEACHING ACTIVITIES

Document Analysis

1. Divide students into pairs, and ask them to take turns "free-associating" or describing aloud any words or images they associate with barbed wire. Then ask them to discuss ways in which this object has become a symbol of the romance of the old West, war and destruction, and confinement.

2. Project a transparency of the patent drawing on an overhead projector, read the written description aloud, and then ask the students the following questions: For whom was the drawing intended? Why was it created? What is the inventor actually seeking to patent? What are the strengths of the invention? How well does the written description depict the physical design and intended use? What aspects of the description need enhancement?

3. Ask students to consider what skills were required for the inventor to design these improvements to wire and what skills were required to manufacture, market, and sell the product. Ask the students to connect these skills to professions and technical fields, and list them on the chalkboard. As an optional follow-up, ask some students to create advertisements for barbed wire. Help them locate a reproduction copy of a 19th-century Sears Roebuck catalog. Project copies of student designs and pages from the catalog that advertise barbed wire on an overhead projector, and ask the class to compare the two sets of designs.

Writing and Defining a Position

4. Divide the class into four groups, and instruct each group to research and prepare a position on the invention as follows: first group, cowboys or herders; second, farmers; third, Native Americans; and fourth, wire manufacturers. Convene a community meeting to discuss the various viewpoints of each group regarding the safety, privacy, and other issues related to the invention.

Comparing Written and Visual Descriptions

5. Ask students to write a description of an improvement for an object they use regularly in the classroom, such as a pencil sharpener, chalkboard, or desk. Pair the students, and instruct them to take turns reading the description aloud to their partners, who must draw their impressions of what the object looks like. Ask them to assess the accuracy of the results and to explore reasons why the visual and verbal descriptions matched or failed to match. Then discuss with the class why the patent office requires both written and visual descriptions of patent applications.

Relating Personal Experiences

6. Collecting barbed wire is a popular hobby. The Barbed Wire Museum in Canyon, TX, has over 200 specimens of barbed wire in its collection. Ask your students what their encounters with barbed wire have been. Also ask them how they would account for the continued fascination with barbed wire.

Creative Interpretation

7. Locate the words and a recording of Cole Porter's song "Don't Fence Me In." Ask the class to identify the point of view of the singer as you project the words from a transparency and play the recording. Ask students to translate the images raised by the songwriter in another medium, such as a drawing, pantomime, poem, or dance. Encourage some students to take another viewpoint related to the changes produced by barbed wire and to express those feelings in an appropriate medium.

Further Research Activity

8. Ask for volunteers to research other inventions or improvements to inventions that significantly influenced the changing landscape of the American West, such as the rifle, six-shooter, telegraph, windmill, and locomotive. Arrange for these students to conduct a panel discussion for the class on the effects of these improvements on life in the West.

National Archives Document Citation
Glidden's Patent Application for Barbed Wire, 1874; Patent File No. 157124; Patented Files; Records of the Patent and Trademark Office, Record Group 241; National Archives at College Park, College Park, MD.

Article Citation
Ray, Emily and Wynell Schamel. "Glidden's Patent Application for Barbed Wire." *Social Education* 61, 1 (January 1997): 52-55.

Documents Related to the Disputed Election of 1876, 1876

The election of 1876 between Democrat Samuel L. Tilden and Republican Rutherford B. Hayes occurred at a precarious time. The end of the Civil War had brought economic expansion that unfortunately was short-lived. A devastating depression followed the Panic of 1873, causing the closure of banks and businesses, and widespread strikes, unemployment, and homelessness. President Ulysses S. Grant, a war hero, was unable to guide the nation through the economic crisis. Scandals in his administration undermined his ability to lead and further eroded confidence in his presidency.

Adding to the anxiety of the times, hopes for a national reunion on the eve of the centennial of the American Revolution were threatened by strong sectional differences. Blacks were voting Republican in the traditionally Democratic South. White southerners were eager for Radical Reconstruction to end and for federal troops to leave the region. Northern Republicans were concerned about the election of former Confederates to Congress and attempts to limit the civil rights of blacks in the South.

The Democrats selected New York Governor Samuel J. Tilden as their choice for president. Tilden was well known for having been instrumental in prosecuting corrupt politicians in New York. He had amassed a fortune as a corporate lawyer, railroad reorganizer, and land and stock speculator. He was a Jeffersonian Democrat and believed in a high standard of morals for government officials. Thomas A. Hendricks of Indiana was selected as the vice-presidential candidate.

Delegates to the Republican convention, amidst disagreement and doubt, selected Rutherford B. Hayes of Ohio as their candidate. Hayes was a Harvard trained lawyer, with a creditable military record as a Union army general. As a member of the House of Representatives, he had supported Reconstruction and campaigned for giving blacks the right to vote in Ohio as well as in the South. He was a three-term governor of Ohio and was known as a loyal party member and a reformer. His running mate was William A. Wheeler of New York.

During the campaign, the Democrats focused on the corruption in the southern "carpetbagger" governments and the scandals in Grant's administration. They stressed Tilden's honesty and history of being a reformer. The Republicans similarly emphasized Hayes' pledge to work for civil service reform and his willingness to end Reconstruction in the South.

On election night, newspapers reported Tilden the winner. He had, after all, received about 3 percent, or 250,000 more popular votes than Hayes. He did not, however, receive the majority of votes from the Electoral College.

The Electoral College was invented by the framers of the Constitution as a compromise between those who favored letting Congress select the executive and those who advocated a direct popular election. Originally, the plan for the Electoral College included the eight major points described in Article II, section 1 of the Constitution:

1. Each state would be allocated a number of electoral votes equal to the sum of its senators and representatives in Congress.
2. Each state legislature would decide the method for choosing electors in its respective state.
3. Electors would meet in their own state capitals and each cast two votes on one ballot.
4. The president of the Senate would open and count the electoral votes before a joint session of Congress.
5. The candidate who received the largest number of votes and who won a majority of the Electoral College would become president.
6. The candidate who received the second largest number of votes would become vice president.
7. In the case of a tie between candidates or if no one received a majority of the electoral votes, the House of Representatives would choose the president from the candidates. Voting would be by state, each state having one vote, with a majority needed for a choice to be made.

In the case of a tie between two or more candidates having the second-largest number of votes, the Senate would choose the vice president from among them.

The framers of the Constitution carefully crafted the Electoral College, hoping that it would provide an effective system for electing the president. But the system was not long in use before the first of several problems with its structure was revealed. This occurred in the election of 1800 as a result of the rise of political parties.

In 1800, the two political parties nominated their candidates for president and vice president, and in each state, chose a slate of electors to vote for their party's candidates. Voters in the general election cast their ballots not for the candidates themselves, but for electors. The Democratic Republicans nominated Thomas Jefferson and Aaron Burr, and the Federalists nominated John Adams and Charles Pinckney, for president and vice president, respectively. Jefferson and Burr won the election, both receiving 73 electoral votes, while Adams received 65, Pinkney 64, and John Jay one vote. Since Burr and Jefferson tied, both receiving a majority, the choice was sent to the House of Representatives. The House cast 36 ballots before it finally chose Jefferson. This election highlighted the problem with the double-voting system as described in the Constitution, and led to demands for an amendment requiring separate votes for president and vice president. The 12th Amendment was approved by Congress in 1803, and ratified in time for the next election in 1804.

The only other time a president was selected by the House of Representatives occurred in the election of 1824, when no candidate for president received a majority of the electoral votes. In that election, Andrew Jackson received 99 electoral votes, John Adams 84, William Crawford 41, and Henry Clay 37. Jackson also led in the popular vote. In accordance with the 12th Amendment, the top three candidates' names were placed before the House, where the votes controlled by Clay would decide the election. Clay's support went to Adams, who was thus elected president even though Jackson had more electoral votes and a larger popular vote. Clay was eventually appointed secretary of state by Adams.

The election of 1876 proved to be the next major challenge to the electoral system. Although Tilden won the popular vote, he had only 184 undisputed electoral votes (one vote shy of the 185 majority then required to be elected). Hayes had 165 elector votes. There were 20 contested electoral votes.

One of the contested electoral votes came from a disqualified elector in Oregon. It was readily resolved in Hayes' favor. The other disputed electoral votes came from Florida (4), Louisiana (8), and South Carolina (7). In these states, the Republican-controlled election boards claimed Hayes as the winner, while the Democrats maintained that the actual winner was Tilden. Each of these three states submitted two conflicting certificates of election. Tilden needed only one of these states to become president, while Hayes needed all three. The Constitution provides for the House to choose a president if no candidate wins a majority of the Electoral College. The Democratic majority in the House would have elected Tilden.

In December, following the election, Congress reconvened in a state of stalemate. The Republican-controlled Senate and the Democrat-controlled House quarreled over who should determine which electoral returns from the three southern states to accept. The 12th Amendment states only that "the President of the Senate shall, in the presence of the Senate and the House of Representatives, open all the certificates and the votes shall then be counted."

The Republicans in the Senate argued in favor of the Senate's right to count the disputed electoral votes, while the Democrats in the House argued that only the two houses acting together could determine which votes were legitimate. Eventually, the Senate and House created committees to consider compromise solutions. Meeting in January 1877, the congressional committees recommended creating a nonpartisan electoral commission composed of five representatives (three Democrats and two Republicans), five senators (two Democrats and three Republicans), and five members of the Supreme Court. The Supreme Court Justices (two were known to be Republicans and two were Democrats) were to select a fifth justice. Everyone understood an independent would be selected. When Supreme Court Justice David Davis, an independent who it was presumed would become the fifth member from the Supreme Court, resigned from the Court to take a seat in the Senate, the position was filled by a Republican. Thus, there were eight Republicans and seven Democrats on the commission.

The fifteen-member commission was to hear legal arguments from each side and then determine whether or not to further investigate the circumstances of the disputed elections. Many citizens from the three states wrote to their congressmen and senators urging them to accept or reject the disputed

State of Louisiana, ss.

We, the undersigned, Electors of President and Vice-President of the United States of America for the next ensuing regular term of the respective offices thereof, being Electors duly and legally appointed by and for the State of _Louisiana_ as appears by the annexed list of Electors, made, certified and delivered to us by the direction of the Executive of the State, having met and convened in the City of New Orleans and the seat of government at the Hall of House of Representatives, in pursuance of the laws of the United States, and also in pursuance of the laws of the State of Louisiana, on the first Wednesday, the sixth day of December, in the year of our Lord one thousand eight hundred and seventy-six.

Do hereby Certify: That being so assembled and duly organized, we proceeded to vote by ballot, and balloted first for such President, and then for such Vice-President, by distinct ballots.

And we further Certify: That the following are two distinct lists; one of the votes for President, and the other of the votes for Vice-President.

List of Persons Voted for as President with the Number of Votes for each.

NAMES OF PERSONS VOTED FOR.	NUMBER OF VOTES.
SAMUEL J. TILDEN, Of the State of New York.	Eight votes

List of all Persons Voted for as Vice-President with the Number of Votes for each.

NAMES OF PERSONS VOTED FOR	NUMBER OF VOTES.
THOMAS A. HENDRICKS, Of the State of Indiana.	Eight votes

In Witness Whereof, we have hereunto set our hands.

Done at the Hall of the House of Representatives in the City of New Orleans, and State of Louisiana, the sixth day of December, in the year of our Lord one thousand eight hundred and seventy six, and of the United States of America the one hundred and first.

Document 1.25a Electoral Ballot from Louisiana (rejected), December 6, 1876. [National Archives]

State of Louisiana
Executive Department.

New Orleans Nov. 20th 1876

Hon Z Chandler
  Sec'y of Interior
    Washington DC

Sir

I have this day forwarded to you by telegraph the annexed enquiry,

  New Orleans Nov 20/76

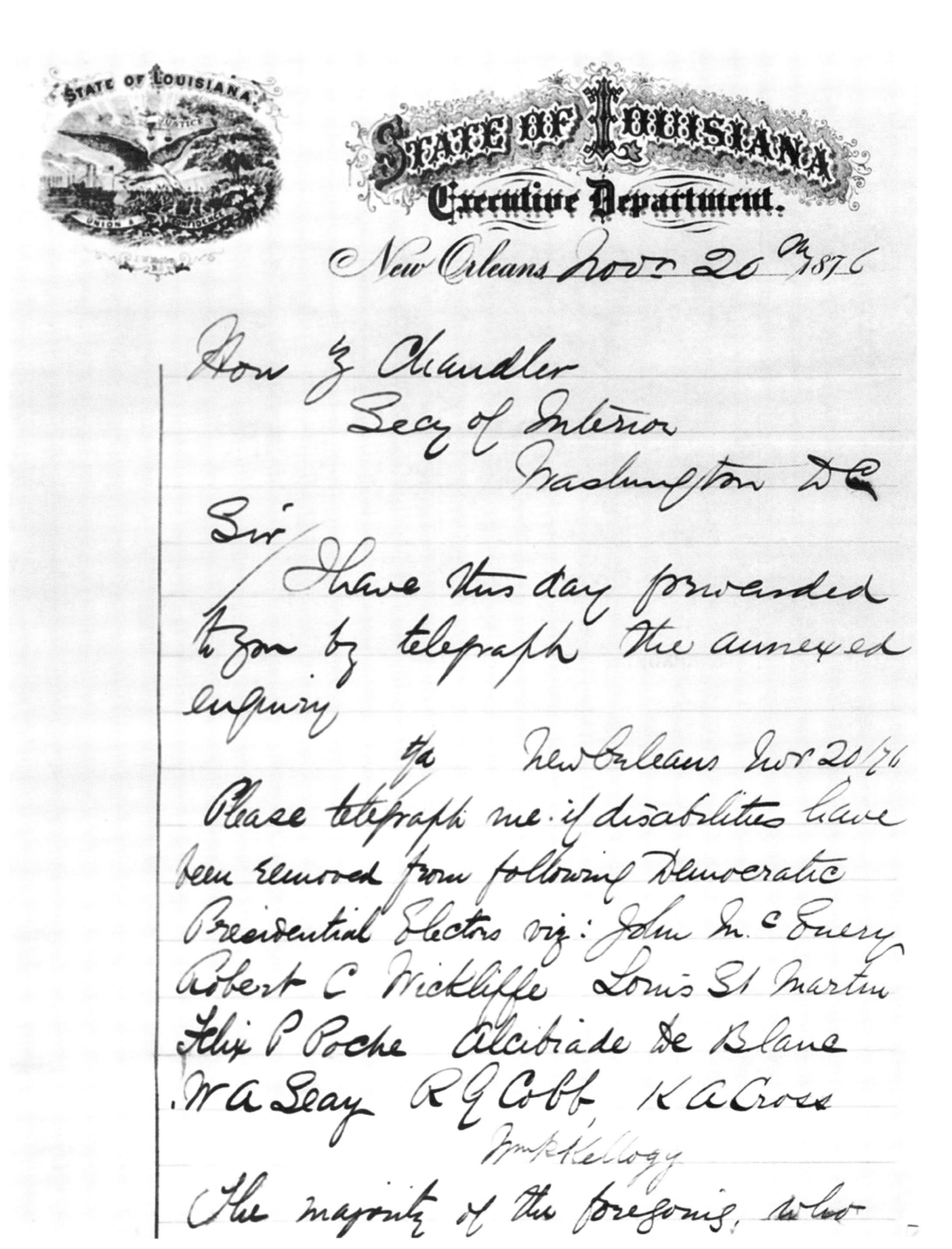

Please telegraph me if disabilities have been removed from following Democratic Presidential Electors viz: John McEnery Robert C Wickliffe Louis St Martin Felix P Poche Alcibiade De Blanc W A Seay R G Cobb K A Cross
  Wm K Kellogg

The majority of the foregoing, who

Document 1.25b1 Letter from Executive Department, State of Louisiana, November 20, 1876. [National Archives]

are on the democratic ticket as Presidential electors in this State, held more or less prominent positions in the Confederacy & unless their disabilities have been removed by Congress are ineligible

Very respy
Yr obdt Servt
Wm P Kellogg.

Document 1.25b2 Letter from Executive Department, State of Louisiana, November 20, 1876. [National Archives]

votes. Many special interest groups recruited signatures on petitions from citizens in their congressional districts and forwarded them to Congress.

Private negotiations between Democrats and Republicans now took place in an attempt to keep the disputed election from erupting into violence. Meeting at the Wormley Hotel in Washington, D.C., at the end of February, Hayes supporters agreed that, if elected, Hayes would withdraw all federal troops from the South, appoint a southerner to the Cabinet, and assist in the rebuilding of the war-torn South. Tilden refused to speak out against the behind-the-scenes negotiations, warning his party's firebrands that another civil war would "end in the destruction of free government."

Congress began the electoral ballot count on February 1, 1877. When the ballots from Florida were reached, two envelopes claiming to be the official set of ballots were in the box. The problem was referred to the commission. By a partisan vote of 8 to 7, the commission decided not to investigate the Florida returns any further, and accepted those signed by Florida's Republican governor for Hayes. The House (with a Democratic majority) rejected the commission's findings, but the Republican Senate approved. Hayes received Florida's votes.

The same 8 to 7 commission vote followed by Senate approval gave Hayes the votes from Louisiana and South Carolina.

On March 2, Senate pages marched in procession to the House chamber, carrying two mahogany boxes filled with electoral ballots. The House galleries were filled with excited citizens when, at 4 in the morning, the ballots were counted and Hayes and Wheeler were declared elected.

Ten years later, in 1887, legislation was passed that gives final authority to each state to decide on the legality of a set of electoral votes. This legislation, which is still current, also requires a concurrent majority of both the Senate and the House of Representatives to reject any electoral vote.

The first document featured in this article is the electoral ballot from Louisiana that was rejected by the commission. It is drawn from the Records of the U.S. Senate, Record Group 46. The second featured document is a letter from William Kellogg, the Republican Governor of Louisiana, calling the electors into question. It is drawn from the Records of the House of Representatives, Record Group 233.

Note: This article is based on two lesson plans developed by Gerri Soffa, teacher at Dodson Middle School in Rancho Palos Verdes, CA, and Mary Frances Greene, assistant principal at Avoca West Elementary School in Glenview, IL.

TEACHING ACTIVITIES

1. Direct students to read Article II, section 1, clauses 2 and 3 of the United States Constitution, and the 12th Amendment. Ask students to explain the major components of the Electoral College System. List these on the board.

2. Provide students with copies of the two featured documents. Lead a class discussion using the following questions: What types of documents are they? Who are the authors? When were they written? What is the purpose of the documents? How are they related to each other? How do they relate to the Electoral College?

3. Make a transparency of the accompanying chart showing the electoral votes by state in the 1876 presidential election and project it for students to view. Ask students to determine how many votes each candidate received and how many votes were needed to receive a majority. Next, direct students to look at the votes recorded for the state of Louisiana. Ask them to compare the information on the chart with the information provided in the first featured document. Explain to students that the electoral votes for South Carolina, Florida, Louisiana, (and one Oregon vote) had been disputed. Ask students to determine what the outcome of the election would have been if Tilden had received the votes from these states. Direct students to read, or provide them with information from, the background essay about how the election of 1876 was finally decided.

The Disputed Election of 1876

STATE	ELECTORAL VOTES	CANDIDATE
Alabama	10	Tilden
Arkansas	6	Tilden
California	6	Hayes
Colorado	3	Hayes
Connecticut	6	Tilden
Delaware	3	Tilden
Florida	4	Hayes
Georgia	11	Tilden

Illinois	21	Hayes
Indiana	15	Tilden
Iowa	11	Hayes
Kansas	5	Hayes
Kentucky	12	Tilden
Louisiana	8	Hayes
Maine	7	Hayes
Maryland	8	Tilden
Massachusetts	13	Hayes
Michigan	11	Hayes
Minnesota	5	Hayes
Mississippi	8	Tilden
Missouri	15	Tilden
Nebraska	3	Hayes
Nevada	3	Hayes
New Hampshire	5	Hayes
New Jersey	9	Tilden
New York	35	Tilden
North Carolina	10	Tilden
Ohio	22	Hayes
Oregon	3	Hayes
Pennsylvania	29	Hayes
Rhode Island	4	Hayes
South Carolina	7	Hayes
Tennessee	12	Tilden
Texas	8	Tilden
Vermont	5	Hayes
Virginia	11	Tilden
West Virginia	5	Tilden
Wisconsin	10	Hayes

Total Electoral Votes 369

4. Inform students that the election of Hayes is often referred to as part of the Compromise of 1877. Democrats in Congress agreed to the election of Hayes in exchange for the end of Reconstruction. They were promised the withdrawal of troops from the South, the appointment of at least one southerner to the cabinet, and substantial appropriations for Southern internal improvements. Direct students to conduct research into these three promises. Ask them to find out when and to what extent they were fulfilled. Ask them to find out what this compromise boded for the rights of black people in the South.

5. Divide students into three groups, and assign the groups to research the role played by the (1) states, (2) Congress, and (3) the National Archives in the current Electoral College process. Ask a representative from each group to report its findings to the class. (Note: the Federal Register's Electoral College Home Page at http://www.archives.gov/federal_register/electoral_college/electoral_college.html and the web site of the Federal Election Commission at www.fec.gov, provide valuable information.)

6. Assign small groups of students to research possible alternatives to the Electoral College (e.g., direct popular election, district plan, proportional plan, and national bonus plan). After each group reports its findings to the class, lead a discussion comparing and contrasting these plans. Challenge students to write persuasive speeches describing which process of electing the president they prefer and why. Ask volunteers to read their speeches.

Note: Additional activities related to the Electoral College are available online in the National Archives Digital Classroom at www.archives.gov/digital_classroom.

National Archives Document Citation

Electoral Ballot from Louisiana (rejected), December 6, 1876; (SEN44A-K1); 44th Congress; Records of the U.S. Senate, Record Group 46; National Archives Building, Washington, DC.

Letter from Executive Department., State of Louisiana, November 20, 1876; 1 of 4 Folders (HR44A-F39.2); 44th Congress; Records of the U.S. House of Representatives, Record Group 233; National Archives Building, Washington, DC.

Article Citation

Schamel, Wynell, Lee Ann Potter, and Katherine Snodgrass. "Documents Related to the Disputed Election of 1876." *Social Education* 64, 5 (September 2000): 286-292.

Native American Education, 1876

In February 1876 Reverend George Ainslie, Presbyterian missionary to the Nez Percés, wrote a letter to Professor F.V. Hayden, renowned leader of explorations in the West and Southwest, requesting Government assistance in providing copies of the Lord's Prayer, the Ten Commandments, and the Apostle's Creed in all the Indian languages. That letter is featured in this article.

Viewed from the context of Supreme Court decisions since the 1940s, this request is a clear breach of the First Amendment principle of separation of church and state. At the time the letter was written, however, the U.S. Government and church-sponsored missionary boards were joined in a partnership for the "civilizing" of Native Americans. Since colonial times, the missionary responsibility to convert and moralize Native Americans with government support was a clear and accepted policy of both church and government. Missionary programs were interrupted by the Revolutionary War and again by the Civil War, but from the close of the Revolution, past the turn of the century, and throughout most of the 19th century, missionary developments expanded and gained support and power. At no time was the program stronger than during President Ulysses Grant's administration, when a full partnership between the Government and the missions was set forth under the Peace Policy of 1868. Grant, however, strongly opposed public funds for sectarian schools and supported the Blaine amendment prohibiting the teaching of religion in public schools.

Grant's Peace Policy was established following a congressional investigation into the state of Indian affairs. The objectives of the policy, according to historian Pierce Beaver, were "the pacification of the Indians through just and fair dealing, the appointment of able and honest Indian agents devoted to Indian improvement and nominated by the religious societies, settlement of the tribes on reservations and within Indian Territory as far as possible, fostering their progress in 'civilization' through education, and thus neutralizing them as an obstacle to white settlement of the western country." Grant's ultimate goal was citizenship for the Indians.

The establishment and maintenance of schools were an important part of the efforts to "civilize" the Indians. Generally, public education has been a state-controlled institution, but a principal exception was the education of reservation Indians who were "wards of the Government" rather than citizens. Schools, therefore, along with other Indian affairs, fell under the jurisdiction of the Department of the Interior, the agency Reverend Ainslie appeals to in his letter.

Though the Constitution gives control of Indian affairs to Congress, the administration of those affairs has been delegated to the President by legislation that divided Indian territory into two districts, each with a superintendent who reported to the Secretary of War. Later, as Indian affairs became more complex, other provisions allowed the President to appoint agents, promote civilization, and secure friendship. Legislation of 1818 defined the procedure by which superintendents and agents were to be nominated by the President and appointed with the advice and consent of the Senate. In the meantime, the Department of the Interior, which was created in 1849, assumed responsibility for the Bureau of Indian Affairs, whereby the bureau passed from military to civilian control. The argument for the transfer was expressed by Secretary of the Treasury Robert Walker in his annual report to Congress:

The duties now performed by the Commissioner of Indian Affairs are most numerous and important, and must be vastly increased with the great number of tribes scattered over Texas, Oregon, New Mexico, and California, and with the interesting progress of so many of the tribes in Christianity, knowledge, and civilization. The duties do not necessarily appertain to war, but to peace, and to our domestic relations with those tribes placed by the Constitution under the charge of this Government.

Except for a short period when Army officers

Rochester Minnesota
Feb. 29th 1876

Prof. F. V. Hayden
Dear Sir

Enclosed you will find the Lord's Prayer in Nez Perces and one of their Hymns interlined as you desired. I will also mail to you a copy of Catechism.

I expect to morrow the Proof sheets of the Gospel of John. When the work is ready I will send you a copy.

I have written to James Reuben, asking him to write a History of his Tribe and giving him an outline for an Introduction and fourteen Chapters comprising everything of interest in regard to their History — Habits — Civilization — Language &c. If he consents to write — when I get his MS. I will rewrite and forward to you. I am confident he will write an interesting history.

It would make an interesting vol. to have the Lord's Prayer — the Ten Commandments and the Apostle's Creed in all the Indian Languages. Why may we not aim at this? I can collect a considerable number. Perhaps the Department of the Interior could make provision for a thorough collection.

Very Truly Yours
Geo. Ainslie

served as agents, Indian agencies have been served by appointees from civilian life. Indian agents were notorious for cheating Indians, diverting goods and appropriations for their own advancement. Representative James A. Garfield described the problem in 1869 as follows: "No branch of the national government is so spotted with fraud, so tainted with corruption, so utterly unworthy of a free and enlightened government, as this Indian Bureau."

In an attempt to improve the appointments during Grant's administration, links between religious denominations and the Government strengthened. Agents were selected upon the recommendation of religious denominations with a certain number of agencies being assigned to each denomination. According to a special report issued by the Bureau of Education in 1888, "The intent of this distribution of agencies was to enlist the active sympathy of the several religious organizations in the Indian work, and to obtain men specially qualified by disposition and character for the peculiar service desired."

Reports from the Commissioner of Indian Affairs during this time include tables of statistics with such categories as numbers of schools, scholars, and teachers; denomination in charge of schools; amount contributed by religious society; and numbers of missionaries, school buildings, church buildings, Indians brought immediately under the civilizing influence of the agency, and Indians who have learned to read. The schools included day schools and boarding schools in Indian country and boarding schools in communities outside the Indian reservations. The general policy of the Government schools was to teach Indian children to speak, read, and write the English language and to instruct them in arithmetic, geography, U.S. history, farming and trades for the boys, and housekeeping for the girls. In addition, religious training was required.

Education and religious training were fostered by funds from the Native Americans themselves, from church funds, and from Government appropriations. The major church-related missions were the American Missionary Association (Congregational), which was the first national foreign missionary society, as well as Catholic, Presbyterian, Friends, Protestant Episcopal, Methodist, Baptist, Moravian, Reformed Dutch, Christian, Lutheran, and Unitarian. Reports of the operations of the Government and missionary societies under the Indian peace policy describe the "civilizing" progress in terms of literary accomplishments, church attendance, "citizens' dress," house accommodations, and extent of farming and stock raising. The Cherokee were the most successful farmers and stockraisers. All of the so-called Five Civilized Tribes–the Cherokee, Choctaws, Chickasaws, Creeks, and Seminoles–established a republican government, set up school systems, and made rapid progress in literacy and agriculture, thus proving to most leaders of the time that Indians could be conditioned to "live as white men." It was also commonly believed that civilization followed conversion to Christianity.

Overt control of agent appointments by missionary societies ended when Secretary of the Interior H.M. Teller under President Chester Arthur excluded mission boards from administering the agencies. Secretary Teller announced in 1882 that he would not consult the religious organizations because "I know no reason why government officials should be selected for one class of government employment by religious bodies and not by all."

By 1889 a majority of the schools were controlled and operated by the Indian Bureau. Only four boarding schools remained by contract in the hands of religious societies, although they received Government assistance in the form of supplies and clothing. A contract school was one wherein the Government paid a stated sum for each pupil, and the religious society provided the teachers, the building, and other expenses. Gradually the church-state partnership decreased in the administration of Indian education, but some entanglements of tribal funding and mission land and buildings persisted. Although Commissioner of Indian Affairs Gen. Thomas J. Morgan was himself a Baptist minister, he promoted a comprehensive, compulsory, nonsectarian education program conforming to the laws of the several States in his 1889 annual report. It was not until the passage of the Indian Reorganization Act of 1934, however, that the Government policy was dramatically changed, returning control to tribal governments and ending compulsory attendance of Indian children at Christian classes and worship services.

It is not surprising that in 1876 Rev. George Ainslie believed that the Department of the Interior would be amenable to translating religious literature into various Indian languages. His request is addressed to geologist Ferdinand V. Hayden, who led several significant expeditions to the Dakota Badlands, Yellowstone, and Colorado's Mesa Verde as a scientist for the U.S. Geological Survey.

In his letter, Ainslie mentions James Reuben, a Nez Percé youth, who according to Ainslie was "quite gifted and master of English to a remarkable degree" and a good candidate for writing a history of his tribe. He also mentions several religious writings that he and fellow missionary Henry S. Spalding translated into the Nez Percé language. Ainslie was a student of the Nez Percé language and wrote a grammar for it.

The original Ainslie letter is located in the Records of the U.S. Geological Survey, Record Group 57, Geological and Geographical Survey of the Territories (Hayden Survey), Letters Received 1867-1879, vol. A-B.

TEACHING ACTIVITIES

Document Analysis

1. Ask students to read the document closely and answer the following questions:
   a. Who wrote the letter?
   b. To whom was the letter written?
   c. When was the letter written?
   d. Why, according to the author, was the letter written?
   e. What is the tone of the letter?
   f. What request does the author make?
   g. Given Supreme Court decisions since 1948, how is his request a breach of the First Amendment separation of Church and state?
   h. Why do you suppose the author expects the Department of Interior to accommodate his request?

   Lead a class discussion of the student responses.

Analysis of Grant's Peace Policy

2. Using the information in the article and other research sources, students should answer these questions:
   a. What was the purpose of the policy?
   b. How did it work?
   c. How was it a violation of the separation of church and state?
   d. Why was it enacted?
   e. What were its accomplishments and its failures?
   f. How did it conflict with Grant's policy for common schools?

Map Work

3. Ask students to mark the location of the various Indian reservations on a blank map of the United States. Instruct them to plot the missions that conducted schools on the reservations. Ask students to present oral reports on the history of Indian mission schools and Government support. Assign segments of time to several students to cover the developments by the colonial companies in Virginia and New England, by Secretary of War Henry Knox and President James Monroe after the Revolution, by the Five Civilized Tribes, by Presidents Grant and Rutherford Hayes after the Civil War, by the Dawes Act of 1887, and by the Indian Reorganization Act of 1934.

Storytelling

4. Ask students to study the personality and events in the lives of F.V. Hayden, U.S. Grant, Chief Joseph, Jeremiah Evarts, and T.J. Morgan. In a role-playing exercise, students should assume the personality of each man and tell the story of the Indians, education, and the Federal Government from his viewpoint.

Position Paper

5. Assign students to write a position paper in response to the following question: Had Native Americans been given a reasonable amount of land and adequate subsidies and allowed to maintain their way of life, might they have accepted the reservation policy and ceased hostility?

Research Options

6. For further research, students might examine these related topics: the plight of the Nez Percés, the friction between church and Government over the removal of the Cherokee, Native American cultural history, Native American religion, the Constitution and the Indians, Indian citizenship, the Blaine amendment to prohibit teaching of religion in public schools and using public funds for sectarian schools, the Hampton and Carlisle Indian Schools, the Protestant-Roman Catholic conflict over Indian schools, and major church-state issues that are currently affecting public and private schools.

National Archives Document Citation

Letter from Rev. George Ainslie to Professor F.V. Hayden, February 29, 1876; Records of the "Hayden Survey," Letters Received, Vol. A-B, 1871-1879; Records of the U.S. Geological Survey, Record Group 57; National Archives at College Park, College Park, MD.

Article Citation

Mueller, Jean West and Wynell Burroughs Schamel. "Native American Education." *Social Education* 54, 5 (September 1990): 267.

Alexander Graham Bell's Telephone Patent, 1876

On his 29th birthday, Alexander Graham Bell's patent application for the telephone was formally received and approved by the United States Patent Office. Four days later, on March 7, 1876, U.S. Patent No. 174,465 for the telephone, one of the most valuable patents ever issued, was granted to Bell. Both the drawing, which is included in this article, and the written application are located in the Records of the Patent and Trademark Office, Record Group 241.

Bell's family history is a part of the story of his invention of the telephone. Born in Edinburgh, Scotland, on March 3, 1847, he was a third-generation elocutionist and speech therapist. Aleck (as he was called by his family) was influenced by both his grandfather Alexander Bell, an expert on elocution and drama, and his father Alexander Melville Bell, the inventor of a renowned system of writing down speech symbols called Visible Speech (the model for the method used by Professor Higgins to improve Eliza's speech in George Bernard Shaw's play *Pygmalion*). Following graduation from the Royal High School in Edinburgh at the age of 14, Aleck lived in London for a year with his grandfather. Under his grandfather's influence, he abandoned his dream of becoming a pianist in favor of a career in speech, "the turning point in my whole life," according to Bell. A working association with his father led him to use Visible Speech techniques to teach speech to the deaf, the occupation Bell most closely identified himself with throughout his lifetime. Bell outpaced both father and grandfather with his own accomplishments, however, and earned the distinction he longed for from age 11 when he added Graham to his name in an effort to distinguish himself from his namesakes.

Bell and his parents sailed to America in 1870 after tuberculosis claimed the lives of his two brothers and illness was threatening his own health. They settled in Ontario, Canada, for a two-year trial but never returned to live in Great Britain. Interest in teaching Visible Speech to the deaf brought Bell to Boston in 1871 to teach at the School of the Deaf (later the Horace Mann School). The development of the telephone was a direct result of his deep personal interest in helping deaf students. This work was recognized by his friend and student Helen Keller when she dedicated her autobiography, *The Story of My Life*, "to Alexander Graham Bell who taught the deaf to speak." No doubt the deafness of both his mother and his wife, Mabel, increased his commitment to alleviating communication problems faced by the deaf.

Although Bell's talents and skills with musical and vocal sounds were necessary for developing the telephone, he lacked the knowledge of electricity essential for translating his theory of the electric-speaking telephone into a working model. He solved this problem in 1874 when he discovered Thomas A. Watson in a Boston electrical workshop. Watson, a bright young electrician, became Bell's dedicated assistant and is immortalized in the now famous, though disputed, first words spoken over the telephone, "Mr. Watson, come here; I want to see you!"

Inventions and Patents

The art of inventing requires a special set of talents, interest, temperament, and environment. According to the biographer Robert V. Bruce, Bell was born with the talents and temperament, his upbringing gave him the interest, and chance brought him to Boston where he encountered the intellectual, technical, and economic environment that made the invention of the telephone possible. It was the Federal Government, however, that provided the legal environment to protect Bell's invention and ensure that the invention was understood by all parties concerned, such as manufacturers, patent agents, and other inventors. Through power granted by the Constitution, Congress set up the patent process that resulted in the issuance of 30 patents associated with Bell and protected his most lucrative and contested invention, the telephone.

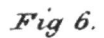

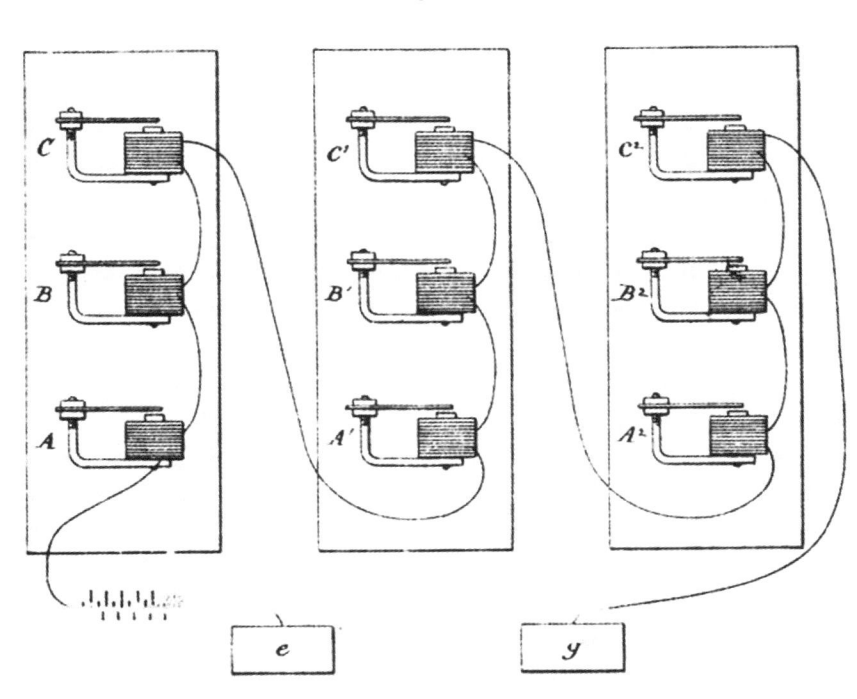

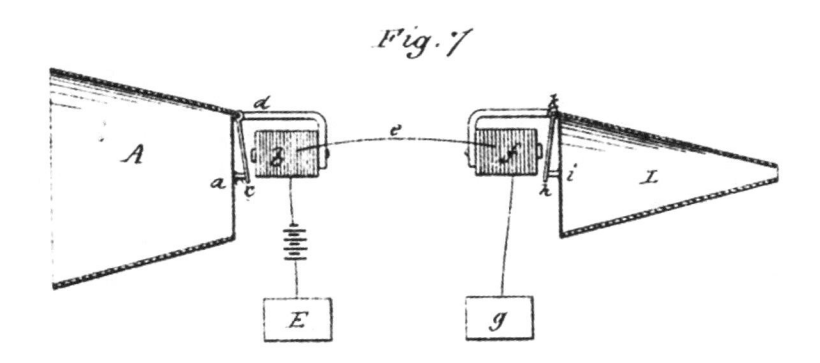

Document 1.27 Alexander Graham Bell's Telephone Patent, 1876. [National Archives]

The Role of the Federal Government

Article I, section 8, of the Constitution grants Congress the power "To promote the Progress of Science and useful Arts, by securing for limited Times to Authors and Inventors the exclusive Right to their respective Writings and Discoveries"–that is, to issue copyrights and patents. To establish a process for such activity, Congress passed the first patent legislation in 1790, which guaranteed certain rights to inventors and granted the authority to issue patents to the executive branch. As a result, the U.S. Patent Office was established to review, approve, and register applications for patents. Applications consist of a written description called a specification, a drawing, and until 1880, a model of the invention. During the years between the Civil War and the end of the 19th century, the U.S. Patent Office granted more than half a million patents, including those for Bell's telephone, George Eastman's camera, and Thomas Edison's electric lightbulb. In the words of writer Alistair Cooke, it was "the heyday of the Ingenious American."

Success of the Telephone

The Centennial Exposition, held in Philadelphia in 1876, was organized to celebrate the first 100 years since the signing of the Declaration of Independence and featured examples of the technological progress of the era. Among the scientists demonstrating their inventions at the exposition was A. Graham Bell, who received a centennial award for the telephone. Although his invention received the highest praise from the chairman of the judges, Sir William Thomson, a notable scientist responsible for the first successful transatlantic cable, it was not until later that the scientific community saw the commercial possibilities of Bell's invention. Until World War I, the telegram continued to be the most widely used means of quick communication. Since then, the telephone has become so essential in our lives that Marshall McLuhan was moved to describe its history in these words: "The telephone began as a novelty, became a necessity and is regarded as an absolute right."

TEACHING ACTIVITIES

Choose or adapt from the following suggestions activities based on Bell's patent drawing of the telephone. The activities are arranged by topic or discipline, not by grade level or ability.

Introduction

1. Make a transparency of the document. Display it for the class, and ask the students the following questions: What do you think this is? Is there anything familiar on this document? What is the date of this document? Whose names appear on this document?

   Then ask them to find out all they can about the document before the next class day.

Government

2. Discuss with your students the purposes and procedures for securing a patent. Ask them to find the authority for granting patents in a copy of the Constitution.

History

3. Assign students to find all they can about Alexander Graham Bell and the invention of the telephone, or tell them the story as recorded in the accompanying note to the teacher. Ask the students to tell the story of Bell and his invention using the relay method, whereby you or a student begins the story, then pass it on to the next person, and so on until the story is completed.

Science

4. Record on the chalkboard objects that operate by electricity as the students list them orally. With the help of a science teacher or a visiting electrician, ask students to construct a model of an electrical circuit. Display Bell's patent drawing and ask the students to compare their circuits with the drawing.

Writing

5. Ask students to design a new product to benefit industry in the United States and then write an application for a patent keeping in mind that a patent application requires a certified declaration of a new and useful improvement with reasons why the product should be manufactured, a written description of the invention, a drawing of the invention, and until 1880, a model of the invention.

Vocabulary

6. Write the two Greek words "tele," meaning afar, and "phone," meaning voice, on the chalkboard. Ask students to write as many words as they can think of that use one or the other of these Greek words. Use the list as a spelling and vocabulary quiz.

Social change

7. Ask students to imagine that they are transported back in time and space to the United States in 1876. Using the jigsaw method of group activity, divide the students into five groups. With each group concentrating on a different category—such as modes of travel, roads and bridges, means of communication, common household items, and types of work—ask them to describe what sort of world they see around them. Reassemble the groups so that the new groups contain at least one person from each of the original five. Ask all the students to report their descriptions in their reorganized group. Then, as a class, discuss how the telephone and its sister inventions have changed the way we live since 1876, revolutionizing communications, industry, and society itself. Remind your students that the late 19th century was an age of letter writing, when the telegraph was the swiftest means of communication, and intrusions such as wiretapping, telephone solicitations, and crank telephone calls were unforeseen nuisances. Consider also the dramatic changes the invention meant for women, moving thousands from the kitchen stove to the switchboard.

National Archives Document Citation

Alexander Graham Bell's Telephone Patent, 1876; Patent File No. 174465: Patented Files; Records of the Patent and Trademark Office, Record Group 241; National Archives at College Park, College Park, MD.

Article Citation

Schamel, Wynell Burroughs and Jean West. "Alexander Graham Bell's Telephone Patent." *Social Studies and the Young Learner* 4, 2 (November/December 1991): 1-4.

1.28

Mapping a Mystery:
The Battle of Little Bighorn, 1877

The Battle of Little Bighorn is a study in contrasts. In the East, reports of the defeat vied in newspaper headlines with hoopla about the celebration of the Nation's centennial. A great Indian victory ultimately led to Indian subjugation. Cavalry commanders who saved their troops were disciplined rather than commended. "Custer's Last Stand" is one of the best-recognized episodes in American history, yet very little is known about the events of that hot summer day. What was a minor episode in military history has become an enduring topic of study and debate.

In terms of documentation and verification, Little Bighorn presents a complex challenge to the historian. The salient difficulty is that neither Lt. Col. George Armstrong Custer nor a single man of the five companies under his command lived to tell his story of the day. Reliable accounts of the 7th Cavalry's actions end at a point 4 miles from Last Stand Hill where Capt. Frederick W. Benteen was ordered to scout bluffs to the south of Custer's advance and Maj. Marcus A. Reno was ordered west across the river to attack an Indian encampment. From official reports filed immediately following the battle and in testimony recorded some months later at the court of inquiry that absolved Major Reno of misconduct, the modern researcher can get a good grasp of what happened at the Reno-Benteen entrenchment. However, this information sheds little light on the events of the late afternoon of June 25, 1876, that resulted in the massacre of Custer's contingent. Even though Reno and other witnesses heard shots to the north, their view was obscured by dust, trees, bluffs, and distance. They did not know of their comrades' fates until relieved on June 26 by troops led by Gen. Alfred H. Terry and Col. John Gibbons.

General Terry attempted immediately to reconstruct onsite the events that had led to the debacle, but the investigation was hasty because he feared renewed Indian attack and getting wounded survivors to medical stations was urgent. On the afternoon of the 26th and part of the 27th, Lt. Edward MacGuire of the Corps of Engineers and his assistant, Sgt. Charles Becker, sketched the battle site. They took compass bearings to construct a plat, made stick measurements of the locale by walking over much of the 10,000 acres of the battlefield, and recorded distances with an odometer cart. The dead were located and identified, when possible, by burial parties and MacGuire included some of this information on his map. Other evidence collected was less absolute. Because Reno and Benteen's men had left their positions when rescued, MacGuire interviewed them to determine their placement and movements during the engagement. When they observed Terry's column, the Indians left, breaking up their camp and removing most of their dead. MacGuire studied lodge pole holes and hearths to reconstruct the Indian encampment, and hoofprints, crushed grass, and artifacts to figure out their movements. It was as good a map as could be made under the circumstances, but MacGuire knew it was not fully accurate, as he testified at the Reno inquiry. "This map, except with regard to the relative position of points is a survey made with transit and chain," he admitted.

It is important to recall that there were surviving eyewitnesses to the swirl of action on Last Stand Hill–the Sioux and Cheyenne warriors. As they surrendered or were captured and placed on reservations, government officials interviewed them. Their accounts trickled in beginning in August 1876. Understandably, many were reluctant to provide details of their roles. Sioux warrior Red Horse said, "I don't like to talk about that fight. If I hear any of my people talking about it, I always move away." Most Indian accounts were relayed in sign language, interpreted by translators, and summarized by reporting agents. Through this process, the Indian accounts were filtered by the white man. In spite of his reluctance, on February 27, 1877, at the Post Cheyenne Agency, Red Horse gave one of the most detailed reports of the Indian side of the battle, which

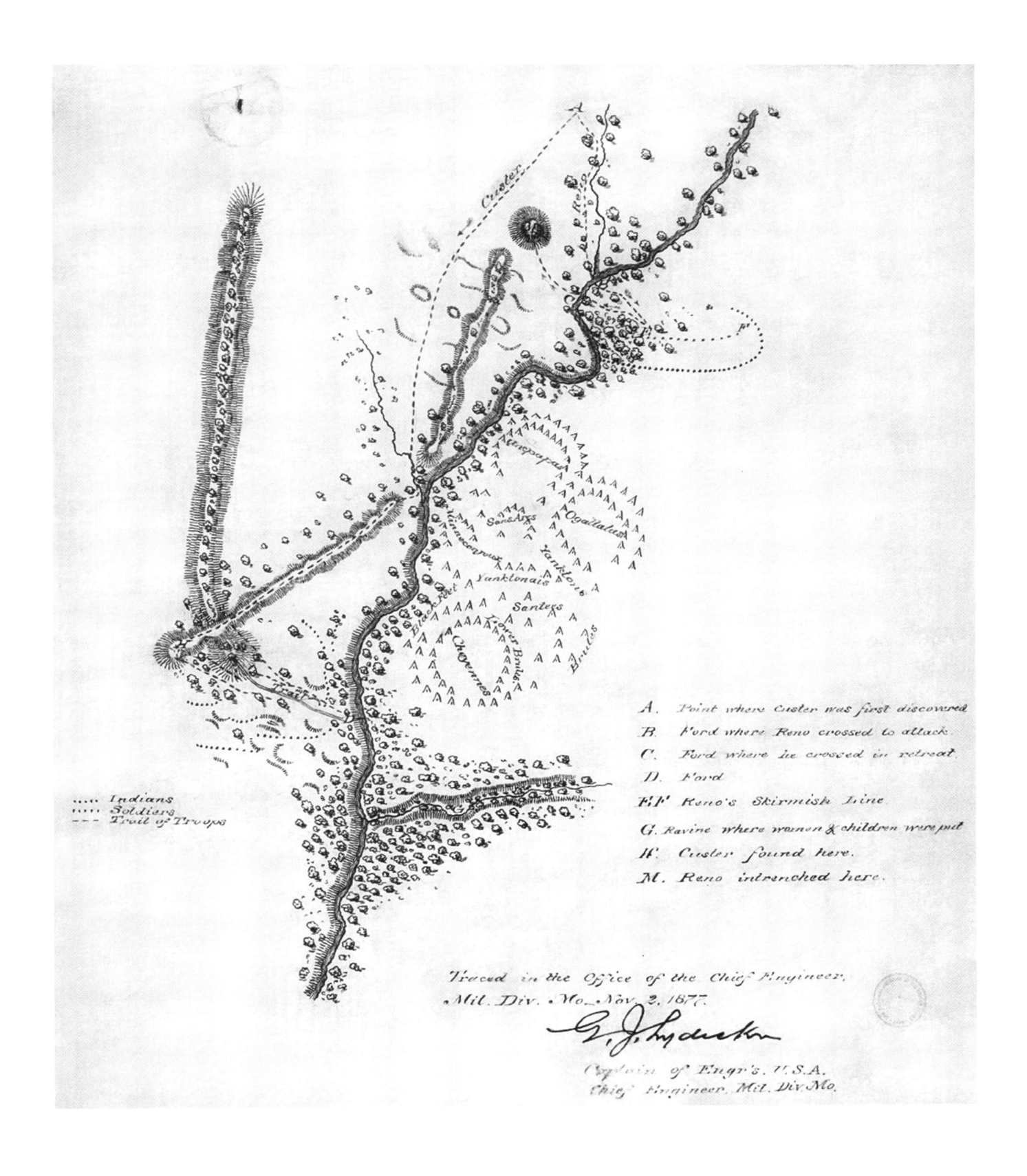

Document 1.28 The Lydecker Sketch of the Battle of Little Bighorn, November 2, 1877. [National Archives]

was subsequently included in a report by Col. W. H. Wood. Five years later, at the request of surgeon Charles McChesney, Red Horse also drew a series of pictographs of the battle.

A report filed by Lt. W. P. Clark, 2d Cavalry, was incorporated into an assessment of the battle by his commander and was forwarded to the headquarters of the Military Division of the Missouri in Chicago. Clark had collected information from Indian witnesses to the battle with the help of interpreters and had obtained an Indian sketch of the site. Clark's commander was not convinced of the reliability of Indian information and warned headquarters that "the narrative of the Indians should be received with a considerable degree of allowance and some doubt, as Indians generally make their descriptions to conform to what they think are the wishes of those who interview them." He was skeptical of the map, too, and wrote: "General features of the enclosed topographical sketch of Custer's battlefield are correct, but I doubt if the Indian who made it was in the fight as he puts the main attack on Custer's party upon the wrong [side?] of the ridge." After the report was received in Chicago, Capt. Garrett J. Lydecker of the Engineers was ordered to trace the Indian map. His tracing was attached to the report and sent on to the Adjutant General's Office, which received both items on November 6, 1877. Lydecker's tracing of the Indian's map, however imperfect, names the remnants of tribes resisting enclosure on the reservation, including Blackfeet, Cheyenne, and seven tribes of the Sioux Nation, and provides additional information about the conduct of the battle. For that reason, it is the featured document in this article.

The MacGuire map, Lydecker tracing, official Army reports, telegrams, court testimony, and newspaper articles based on official information are all part of the National Archives' collection of material related to the Sioux Wars. Although contemporary with the event, they are not particularly objective, verifiable, or complete; the historian cannot definitively recreate the battle of Little Bighorn. A prairie fire in 1983 enabled the National Park Service to conduct the first major scientific excavation of the site. The general outlines of contemporary reports were confirmed by the thousands of artifacts uncovered and ballistic studies of spent bullets and cartridges. Still, the specifics of this event, like many in history, continue to elude us.

The Lydecker sketch is kept in the Records of the Adjutant General's Office, 1780's-1917, Record Group 94, Miscellaneous File, #53 1/2. It is a black ink tracing, measuring 11 5/8 by 13 3/8 inches, with Indian movements noted in red, soldiers' in blue. Additional information can be found in National Archives Microfilm Publication M666, roll 273 (reports filed by the expeditionary force) and M592, rolls 1 and 2 (the Reno Court of Inquiry).

TEACHING ACTIVITIES

Map Analysis

1. Ask students to review their textbooks' account of the battle of Little Bighorn or a general article in another reference book. Duplicate and distribute a copy of the map and the map Analysis Worksheet (see Appendix H) to each student.

Mapping Activity

2. Divide the class into small groups of two or three students each. Ask each group to make a map of an event that occurred in their school or neighborhood during the past year. The map should be accurate spatially and include standard aids to the map reader such as scale, orientation, and key. It should be based on research and interviews–the memory of the group members requires additional verification–and these should be listed in a bibliography attached to the map. Subjects for this activity might include:

   - The first series of downs at the first home football game of the past season

   - The order and progress of the homecoming parade

   - The arrangement of tables and entertainment at a prom including location of refreshments, chaperones, and the movements of the prom queen and her escort

   - The arrangement of graduation ceremonies, a flow pattern of the procession, and an indication of speakers, faculty, valedictorian, and guests.

Further Research

3. You may wish to instruct students to examine other maps and read additional primary and secondary accounts of the battle of Little Bighorn, then write a paragraph with their own evaluations of the accuracy of the Lydecker map. Secondary resources might include:

   Capps, Benjamin. *The Indians.* New York: Time-Life Books, 1973.

   Graham, Col. W. A. *The Custer Myth.* 1953. Reprint. Lincoln: University of Nebraska, 1986.

   Jordan, Robert P. "Ghosts on the Little Bighorn." *National Geographic* 170, no. 6 (December 1986): 787.

   Stewart, Edgar I. *Custer's Luck.* Norman: University of Oklahoma Press, 1955.

   U.S. Department of the Interior. National Park Service. *Custer Battlefield.* Washington, DC, 1987.

   Utley, Robert. *Cavalier in Buckskin.* Norman: University of Oklahoma Press, 1988.

National Archives Document Citation

The Lydecker Sketch of the Battle of Little Bighorn, November 2, 1877; #53 1/2; Miscellaneous File; Records of the Adjutant General's Office, 1780's-1917, Record Group 94; National Archives Building, Washington, DC.

Article Citation

Mueller, Jean West and Wynell Burroughs Schamel. "Mapping a Mystery: The Battle of Little Bighorn." *Social Education* 54, 2 (February 1990): 104-106.

NUMBERED LIST of ARTICLES

This list enumerates all the articles included in volumes 1 through 4 of TEACHING WITH DOCUMENTS. The articles in volume 1 are numbered 1.1 - 1.28. The articles in volume 2 are numbered 2.1 - 2.32. The articles in volume 3 are numbered 3.1 - 3.26. The articles in volume 4 are numbered 4.1- 4.27. The articles in the four volumes are arranged chronologically by the date of the document.

Volume I

1.1 "The Alternative of Williamsburg": A British Cartoon on Colonial American Violence, 1775
1.2 Navigation Act Broadside, 1785
1.3 Delaware's Ratification of the U.S. Constitution, 1787
1.4 The Wording of the First Amendment Religion Clauses, 1789
1.5 Jefferson's Letter to Washington Accepting the Position of Secretary of State, 1790
1.6 The 1820 Census of Manufactures, 1820
1.7 Maps of Salem, Massachusetts, 1822
1.8 Census of Cherokees in the Limits of Georgia, 1835
1.9 U.S. Court of Claims Deposition of Kish um us tubbee, 1837
1.10 General Orders Pertaining to Removal of the Cherokees, 1838
1.11 A Ship's Manifest, 1847
1.12 Lincoln's Spot Resolutions, 1848
1.13 Lincoln's Letter to Siam, 1861
1.14 Robert E. Lee's Resignation from the U.S. Army, 1861
1.15 Letter to Giuseppe Garibaldi, 1861
1.16 Circular from the Surgeon General's Office, 1862
1.17 The Fight for Equal Rights: A Recruiting Poster for Black Soldiers in the Civil War, ca. 1862
1.18 The Homestead Act of 1862, 1862
1.19 *Ex parte Milligan* Letter, 1864
1.20 Civil Rights Mini-Unit, 1865 - 1978
1.21 Reconstruction, the Fourteenth Amendment, and Personal Liberties, 1866 and 1874
1.22 1869 Petition: The Appeal for Woman Suffrage, 1869
1.23 A Bill to Relieve Certain Legal Disabilities of Women, 1872
1.24 Glidden's Patent Application for Barbed Wire, 1874
1.25 Documents Related to the Disputed General Election of 1876, 1876
1.26 Native American Education, 1876
1.27 Alexander Graham Bell's Telephone Patent, 1876
1.28 Mapping a Mystery: The Battle of Little Bighorn, 1877

Volume II

2.1 Patents and Inventions in American History, 1846, 1871, 1880, 1906
2.2 Resolution of the "Indian Question," 1880
2.3 Little House in the Census: Almanzo and Laura Ingalls Wilder, 1880 and 1900
2.4 The Statue of Liberty Deed of Presentation, 1884
2.5 Cache Note from Peary's North Greenland Expedition of 1892, 1892
2.6 Documents Related to the Pledge of Allegiance, 1892 - 1954
2.7 Petition for a Fair Representation of African Americans at the World's Columbia Exposition, 1892
2.8 Sierra Club Petition to Congress Protesting the Proposed Diminution of Yosemite National Park, 1892
2.9 Petition for the Rights of Hopi Women, 1894
2.10 *Plessy v. Ferguson* Mandate, 1896
2.11 The 1897 Petition Against the Annexation of Hawaii, 1897
2.12 The Spanish-American War and the Philippine Insurrection, 1898
2.13 Legacy of Health: Documentary Photographs of the Panama Canal Construction, 1900-1920
2.14 Immigration Patterns, Public Opinion, and Government Policy, 1900 - 1921
2.15 Land Auction Photograph, ca. 1904
2.16 Photographs of Children at Work, ca. 1908
2.17 Chinese Exclusion Forms, 1913
2.18 Censoring the Mails, 1916
2.19 German Propaganda Leaflets, 1917
2.20 Zimmermann Telegram, 1917
2.21 The First Amendment: The Finished Mystery Case and World War I, 1918
2.22 1919 Presidential Proclamation to Schoolchildren About the Red Cross, 1919
2.23 Black Soldiers in World War I Poster, 1919
2.24 The Red Scare and Attorney General Palmer, 1920
2.25 Schools for Americanization Poster, 1920
2.26 Lincoln Memorial Photograph, 1920
2.27 The Protection of Working Children, 1922

2.28 Photographs of Ellis Island: The High Tide of Immigration, 1923

2.29 A Telegram From Persia, 1924

2.30 Questionnaire on Moral Problems, ca. 1924

2.31 A Political Cartoon About the Wickersham Committee, 1920s

2.32 Letter From Concerned Mother, 1929

Volume III

3.1 Letter to President Franklin Roosevelt on Employment of Women, 1933

3.2 Letter of Appeal to President Franklin Roosevelt, 1933

3.3 Roosevelt and Hitler - A Comparison of Leadership, 1933

3.4 The Inquiry into the Education of Don Henry and His Subsequent Death in the Spanish Civil War, 1936

3.5 A Statement on Separation of Powers, 1937

3.6 A 1939 Letter of Protest: Controversy Over Public Art During the New Deal, 1939

3.7 Eleanor Roosevelt's Letter to the DAR, 1939

3.8 "A Date Which Will Live in Infamy": The First Typed Draft of Franklin D. Roosevelt's War Address, 1941

3.9 Memorandum re the Enlistment of Navajo Indians, 1942

3.10 Correspondence concerning Women and the Army Air Forces in World War II, 1942

3.11 Declaration of Intention and Petition for Naturalization, 1942, 1948

3.12 Inflation Poster, 1942

3.13 Rights in Time of Crisis: American Citizens and Internment, 1943

3.14 Interned Japanese-American Theme, 1943

3.15 Victory Garden Poster, 1943

3.16 D-day Message from General Eisenhower to General Marshall, 1944

3.17 FDR Campaign Poster, 1944

3.18 Fire Prevention Posters: The Story of Smokey Bear, 1944

3.19 Nazi Medical Experiment Report: Evidence from the Nuremberg Medical Trial, 1944

3.20 Correspondence Urging Bombing of Auschwitz during World War II, 1944

3.21 Decision at Yalta: Anna Roosevelt's Diary, 1945

3.22 Letter Proposing Candidates for the First U.N. Assembly, 1945

3.23 Telegram From Ho Chi Minh to Harry S. Truman, 1946

3.24 Letter on Behalf of Raoul Wallenberg, 1947

3.25 Press Release on the Recognition of State of Israel, 1948

3.26 President Harry S. Truman's Diary, 1949

Volume IV

4.1 Peace Propaganda Cartoon, 1950

4.2 Truman's Firing of General Douglas MacArthur During the Korean War, 1951

4.3 "Out of Fear and into Peace": President Eisenhower's Address to the United Nations, 1953

4.4 Frontiers in Civil Rights: Dorothy E. Davis, et. al. versus County School Board of Prince Edward County, Virginia, 1954

4.5 The Arrest Records of Rosa Parks, 1955

4.6 Letter About Federalism, 1956

4.7 Jackie Robinson, President Eisenhower, and the Little Rock Crisis, 1957

4.8 Letter From Elvis Presley Fans, 1958

4.9 Archives and Baseball Cards, 1959

4.10 State Department Briefing Notebook for President Eisenhower, 1959

4.11 Letter to Senator Kennedy on Religious Tests, 1960

4.12 Alabama Voters Literary Test, 1960s

4.13 A Cartoonist's View of the Eisenhower Years, 1961

4.14 The Space Race - President Kennedy's Telegram to Khrushchev, 1961

4.15 John Glenn's Space Flight, 1962

4.16 The Bill of Rights: Due Process and Rights of the Accused: Clarence Earl Gideon's Petition *in forma pauperis*, 1962

4.17 President Kennedy's Speech on James Meredith, 1962

4.18 *Abington* v. *Schempp* - The Establishment Clause, 1962

4.19 UFO Sighting Report, 1962

4.20 The 1963 March on Washington, 1963

4.21 The Reaction of Beatles' Fans to Immigration Law, 1964

4.22 Tonkin Gulf Resolution, 1964

4.23 The 26th Amendment and Youth Voting Rights, 1971

4.24 Letter from House Minority Leader Gerald R. Ford to President Richard M. Nixon, 1973

4.25 Watergate and the Constitution, 1974

4.26 President Nixon's Letter of Resignation, 1974

4.27 Due Process and Student Rights: Syllabus of the Goss v. Lopez Decision, 1975

APPENDIX A: TYPES of DOCUMENTS

This chart is a listing of articles in the four volumes of TEACHING WITH DOCUMENTS that feature the following types of documents. [See page 154 for a numbered list of the articles.]

Baseball cards	4.9
Cache note	2.5
Census	1.6, 1.8, 2.3
Diaries & Journals	1.4, 3.21, 3.26
Editorial/political cartoons	1.1, 2.31, 4.1, 4.13
Foreign language documents	2.4, 2.5, 3.19
Gov't proclamations/resolutions/reports	1.3, 1.4, 1.10, 1.12, 1.16, 1.20, 1.21, 1.23, 1.25, 2.4, 2.6, 2.10, 2.17, 2.22, 2.27, 3.8, 3.16, 3.19, 3.25, 4.2, 4.5, 4.10, 4.12, 4.18, 4.22, 4.23, 4.25, 4.27
Graphs/charts	1.8, 1.11, 2.3, 2.14, 3.13
Letters	1.5, 1.10, 1.13, 1.14, 1.15, 1.19, 1.20, 1.26, 2.12, 2.14, 2.18, 2.21, 2.24, 2.32, 3.1, 3.2, 3.4, 3.6, 3.7, 3.9, 3.10, 3.20, 3.22, 3.24, 4.6, 4.7, 4.8, 4.11, 4.19, 4.20, 4.21, 4.24, 4.25, 4.26
Literary works	2.28, 3.14
Maps	1.7, 1.28, 2.8
Patents	1.24, 1.27, 2.1
Petitions	1.20, 1.21, 1.22, 2.7, 2.8, 2.9, 2.11, 4.16
Photographs/paintings	1.20, 2.6, 2.13, 2.15, 2.16, 2.26, 2.28, 3.6, 4.4, 4.15
Posters/broadsides/leaflets	1.2, 1.17, 2.19, 2.23, 2.25, 3.4, 3.12, 3.15, 3.17, 3.18
Press release and news article	2.14, 3.25
Resolutions/statements by private organization	1.20, 2.2, 3.5
Speech transcripts	3.8, 4.3, 4.17
Surveys/forms/interviews/depositions	1.8, 1.9, 1.18, 2.3, 2.17, 2.30, 3.11, 4.12
Telegrams	2.20, 2.29, 3.3, 3.23, 3.25, 4.14

APPENDIX B: DISCIPLINES and SUBJECT AREAS

These charts list the articles in the four volumes of TEACHING WITH DOCUMENTS that contain teaching suggestions related to the following disciplines or subject areas. [See page 154 for a numbered list of the articles.]

American History	all
Art/Music/Literature	1.1, 1.12, 1.13, 1.17, 1.24, 1.27, 2.3, 2.4, 2.5', 2.8, 2.9, 2.14, 2.17, 2.28, 3.4, 3.6, 3.16, 3.18, 3.24, 4.8, 4.13, 4.19, 4.21,
*Civics/Government	1.1, 1.3, 1.4, 1.5, 1.9, 1.12, 1.14, 1.18, 1.19, 1.20, 1.21, 1.23, 1.25, 2.6, 2.7, 2.8, 2.9, 2.11, 2.12, 2.14, 2.16, 2.17, 2.18, 2.21, 2.24, 3.3, 3.4, 3.5, 3.6, 3.13, 3.18, 3.22, 4.2, 4.3, 4.4, 4.5, 4.6, 4.16, 4.17, 4.20, 4.22, , 4.23, 4.24, 4.25, 4.27
Economics	1.1, 1.2, 1.6, 1.8, 1.17, 1.18, 1.24, 1.27, 2.9, 2.14, 2.15, 2.16, 2.27, 3.6, 3.12, 3.15, 4.9, 4.14
Foreign Language	2.4, 2.5, 3.3, 3.9, 3.19
Geography	1.5, 1.7, 1.9, 1.10, 1.12, 1.13, 1.18, 1.26, 1.28, 2.3, 2.4, 2.5, 2.8, 2.11, 2.12, 2.13, 2.14, 2.15, 2.20, 3.14, 3.21, 3.25, 4.9, 4.14
*Language Arts/Writing	1.3, 1.4, 1.8, 1.9, 1.12, 1.14, 1.15, 1.17, 1.20, 1.21, 1.22, 2.5, 2.8, 2.10, 2.12, 2.16, 2.19, 2.21, 2.28, 3.2, 3.4, 3.5, 3.7, 3.8, 3.14, 3.16, 3.18, 3.21, 3.26, 4.3, 4.8, 4.10, 4.12, 4.13, 4.16
Math	1.6, 1.7, 1.8, 1.18, 2.3, 2.4, 2.14, 2.16, 2.27, 2.30, 3.13, 4.9
Science	1.16, 1.24, 1.27, 2.1, 2.5, 2.8, 2.28, 3.18, 3.19, 3.21, 4.3, 4.14, 4.15, 4.19
World History	1.1, 1.2, 1.11, 1.13, 1.15, 1.24, 2.4, 2.5, 2.7, 2.12, 2.14, 2.20, 2.21, 2.28, 2.29, 3.3, 3.4, 3.8, 3.10, 3.16, 3.19, 3.20, 3.21, 3.22, 3.23, 3.24, 3.25, 4.1, 4.3, 4.10, 4.19, 4.22

* *Basically all of the articles relate to civics and government and to language arts and writing, but especially the articles listed.*

Teaching With Documents   157   THE COLONIAL PERIOD TO 1879

APPENDIX C: THEMATIC CHART

This chart lists articles from the four volumes of TEACHING WITH DOCUMENTS that contain information and teaching suggestions related to the following themes. [See page 154 for a numbered list of the articles.]

Citizenship	1.1, 1.11, 1.14, 1.18, 1.20, 1.21, 1.22, 1.26, 2.6, 2.7, 2.9, 2.21, 2.22, 2.25, 3.11, 3.13, 4.7, 4.16, 4.23, 4.27
Civil Rights/Liberties	1.1, 1.4, 1.9, 1.12, 1.17, 1.20, 1.21, 1.22, 1.26, 2.6, 2.7, 2.9, 2.10, 2.21, 2.24, 3.4, 3.13, 3.14, 3.22, 4.4, 4.5, 4.7, 4.16, 4.20, 4.27
Civil War	1.14, 1.15, 1.17
Congress	1.1, 1.4, 1.12, 1.18, 1.20, 1.21, 1.22, 1.23, 1.27, 2.4, 2.6, 2.7, 2.8, 2.27, 3.5, 4.22, 4.23
Constitution	1.3, 1.4, 1.5, 1.6, 1.19, 1.21, 1.22, 1.27, 2.1, 2.6, 2.21, 2.27, 3.5, 3.13, 4.6, 4.11, 4.12, 4.16, 4.18, 4.23, 4.24, 4.25, 4.27
Economics/Industry	1.1, 1.2, 1.6, 1.8, 1.11, 1.24, 1.27, 2.15, 2.16, 2.17, 2.27, 3.1, 3.6, 3.12, 3.15
Explorers/Exploration	1.26, 2.5, 4.15
Family Life	1.8, 1.9, 2.3, 2.9, 2.32, 3.1, 3.2
Federalism	1.3, 1.14, 1.20, 1.21, 2.6, 2.10, 2.27, 4.6, 4.7, 4.17
Foreign Policy	1.1, 1.2, 1.5, 1.13, 2.12, 2.13, 3.22, 3.23, 3.25, 4.3
Global Studies (20th c)	see World History Standards chart
Holocaust	3.19, 3.20, 3.24
Immigration	1.11, 2.4, 2.14, 2.17, 2.25, 2.28, 3.11, 3.14
Inventors/Inventions	1.24, 1.27, 2.1
Military Issues	1.6, 1.10, 1.12, 1.14, 1.15, 1.17, 1.19, 1.28, 2.12, 2.19, 2.21, 2.23, 3.8, 3.9, 3.10, 3.13, 3.16, 3.20, 4.2, 4.8, 4.22
Minority Studies	1.8, 1.9, 1.17, 1.20, 1.21, 1.26, 1.28, 2.2, 2.7, 2.9, 2.10, 2.17, 2.21, 2.23, 2.25, 3.7, 3.9, 3.13, 3.14, 4.4, 4.5, 4.6, 4.7, 4.9, 4.12, 4.17, 4.20

APPENDIX C: THEMATIC CHART (continued)

Presidency	1.5, 1.12, 1.13, 1.17, 1.19, 1.25, 2.6, 2.26, 3.1, 3.2, 3.3, 3.5, 3.8, 3.17, 3.21, 3.22, 3.24, 3.25, 3.26, 4.2, 4.3, 4.6, 4.7, 4.8, 4.9, 4.10, 4.11, 4.13, 4.14, 4.17, 4.23, 4.25, 4.26
Propaganda	1.1, 1.2, 1.17, 2.19, 3.4, 3.18
Public Policy	1.9, 1.18, 1.20, 1.21, 1.26, 2.2, 2.8, 2.9, 2.10, 2.14, 2.16, 2.17, 2.18, 2.21, 2.25, 2.27, 2.30, 3.1, 3.2, 3.13, 4.3
Religious Freedom	1.4, 1.26, 2.6, 2.21, 2.30, 4.11, 4.18
Supreme Court	1.19, 1.20, 1.23, 2.6, 2.10, 2.21, 2.27, 3.5, 3.13, 4.6, 4.16, 4.18, 4.27
Voting Rights	1.20, 1.22, 4.23
Westward Expansion	1.8, 1.9, 1.12, 1.18, 1.24, 1.26, 1.28, 2.2, 2.3, 2.8, 2.9, 2.11, 2.15, 2.17
Women's Studies	1.16, 1.22, 1.23, 2.3, 2.9, 2.32, 3.1, 3.2, 3.7, 3.21, 3.22
World War II	3.3, 3.8, 3.10, 3.12, 3.13, 3.14, 3.15, 3.16, 3.17, 3.18, 3.19, 3.20, 3.21, 3.24
Youth Roles/Issues	2.3, 2.6, 2.16, 2.22, 2.27, 2.30, 2.32, 3.4, 3.14, 4.4, 4.8, 4.9, 4.17, 4.21, 4.23, 4.27

APPENDIX D: NATIONAL STANDARDS for U.S. HISTORY

This chart identifies the articles in the four volumes of TEACHING WITH DOCUMENTS that connect primary sources and related teaching activities to the National Standards for U.S. History, grades 5-12. Note the absence of articles for the first two eras since the primary sources featured in the articles are official documents of the federal government, which had its beginnings in the late 18th century. [See page 154 for a numbered list of the articles.]

ERA 1: THREE WORLDS MEET (BEGINNINGS TO 1620)

Standard 1: Comparative characteristics of societies in the Americas, Western Europe, and Western Africa that increasingly interacted after 1450.

1A	Student understands the patterns of change in indigenous societies in the Americas up to the Columbus voyages.	No TWD
1B	Student understands changes in Western European societies in the age of exploration.	No TWD
1C	Student understands developments in Western African societies in the period of early contact with Europeans.	No TWD
1D	Student understands the differences and similarities among Africans, Europeans, and Native Americans who converged in the western hemisphere after 1492.	No TWD

Standard 2: How early European exploration and colonization resulted in cultural and ecological interactions among previously unconnected peoples.

2A	Student understands the stages of European oceanic and overland exploration, amid international rivalries, from the 9th to 17th centuries.	No TWD
2B	Student understands the Spanish and Portuguese conquest of the Americas.	No TWD

ERA 2: COLONIZATION AND SETTLEMENT (1585-1763)

Standard 1: Why the Americas attracted Europeans, why they brought enslaved Africans to their colonies, and how Europeans struggled for control of North America and the Caribbean.

1A	Student understands how diverse immigrants affected the formation of European colonies.	No TWD
1B	Student understands the European struggle for control of North America.	No TWD

Standard 2: How political, religious, and social institutions emerged in the English colonies.

2A	`Student understands the roots of representative government and how political rights were defined.	No TWD
2B	Student understands religious diversity in the colonies and how ideas about religious freedom evolved.	No TWD
2C	Student understands social and cultural change in British America.	No TWD

APPENDIX D: NATIONAL STANDARDS for U.S. HISTORY ((continued))

Standard 3: How the values and institutions of European economic life took root in the colonies, and how slavery reshaped European and African life in the Americas.

3A	Student understands colonial economic life and labor systems in the Americas.	No TWD
3B	Student understands economic life and the development of labor systems in the English colonies.	No TWD
3C	Student understands African life under slavery.	No TWD

ERA 3: REVOLUTION AND THE NEW NATION (1754-1820s)

Standard 1: The causes of the American Revolution, the ideas and interests involved in forging the revolutionary movement, and the reasons for the American victory.

1A	Student understands the causes of the American Revolution.	1.1
1B	Student understands the principles articulated in the Declaration of Independence.	No TWD
1C	Student understands the factors affecting the course of the war and contributing to the American victory.	No TWD

Standard 2: The impact of the American Revolution on politics, economy, and society.

2A	Student understands revolutionary government-making at national and state levels.	1.1
2B	Student understands the economic issues arising out of the Revolution.	1.2
2C	Student understands the Revolution's effects on different social groups.	1.1

Standard 3: The institutions and practices of government created during the Revolution and how they were revised between 1787 and 1815 to create the foundation of the American political system based on the U.S. Constitution and the Bill of Rights.

3A	Student understands the issues involved in the creation and ratification of the U.S. Constitution and the new government it established.	1.3, 1.4, 1.5
3B	Student understands the guarantees of the Bill of Rights and its continuing significance.	1.3, 1.4, 2.6, 3.13
3C	Student understands the development of the Supreme Court's power and its significance from 1789 to 1820.	No TWD
3D	Student understands the development of the first American party system.	No TWD

ERA 4: EXPANSION AND REFORM (1801-1861)

Standard 1: United States territorial expansion between 1801 and 1861, and how it affected relations with external powers and Native Americans.

1A	Student understands the international background and consequences of the Louisiana Purchase, the War of 1812, and the Monroe Doctrine.	No TWD

APPENDIX D: NATIONAL STANDARDS for U.S. HISTORY (continued)

1B	Student understands federal and state Indian policy and the strategies for survival forged by Native Americans.	1.8, 1.9, 1.10
1C	Student understands the ideology of Manifest Destiny, the nation's expansion to the Northwest, and the Mexican-American War.	1.12, 1.13

Standard 2: How the industrial revolution, increasing immigration, the rapid expansion of slavery, and the westward movement changed the lives of Americans and led toward regional tensions.

2A	Student understands how the factory system and the transportation and market revolutions shaped regional patterns of economic development.	1.6
2B	Student understands the first era of American urbanization.	No TWD
2C	Student understands how antebellum immigration changed American society.	1.11
2D	Student understands the rapid growth of the "peculiar institution" after 1800 and the varied experience of African Americans under slavery.	No TWD
2E	Student understands the settlement of the West.	1.9, 1.18

Standard 3: The extension, restriction, and reorganization of political democracy after 1800.

3A	Student understands the changing character of American political life in the "age of the common man".	No TWD
3B	Student understands how the debates over slavery influenced politics and sectionalism.	1.14

Standard 4: The sources and character of cultural, religious, and social reform movements in the antebellum period.

4A	Student understands the abolitionist movement.	1.22
4B	Student understands how Americans strived to reform society and create a distinct culture.	No TWD
4C	Student understands changing gender roles and the ideas and activities of women reformers.	1.16, 1.22, 1.23

ERA 5: CIVIL WAR AND RECONSTRUCTION (1850-1877)

Standard 1: The causes of the Civil War.

1	Student understands how the North and South differed and how politics and ideologies led to the Civil War.	1.14

Standard 2: The course and character of the Civil War and its effects on the American people.

2A	Student understands how the resources of the Union and Confederacy affected the course of the war.	1.14, 1.15, 1.16, 1.17
2B	Student understands the social experience of the war on the battlefield and homefront.	1.16, 1.17, 1.19

APPENDIX D: NATIONAL STANDARDS for U.S. HISTORY (continued)

Standard 3: How various reconstruction plans succeeded or failed.

3A	Student understands the political controversy over Reconstruction.	1.20, 1.25
3B	Student understands the Reconstruction programs to transform social relations in the South.	1.20
3C	Student understands the success and failures of Reconstruction in the South, North, and West.	1.20, 1.21

ERA 6: THE DEVELOPMENT OF THE INDUSTRIAL U. S. (1870-1900)

Standard 1: How the rise of corporations, heavy industry, and mechanized farming transformed the American people.

1A	Student understands the connections among industrialization, the advent of the modern corporation, and material well-being.	1.27, 2.1
1B	Student understands the rapid growth of cities and how urban life changed.	No TWD
1C	Student understands how agriculture, mining, and ranching were transformed	1.18, 1.24, 2.15
1D	Student understands the effects of rapid industrialization on the environment and the emergence of the first conservation movement.	2.8, 2.9

Standard 2: Massive immigration after 1870 and how new social patterns, conflicts, and ideas of national unity developed amid growing cultural diversity.

2A	Student understands the sources and experiences of the new immigrants.	2.4, 2.14, 2.17
2B	Student understands "scientific racism", race relations, and the struggle for equal rights.	1.20, 2.7, 2.10, 2.14
2C	Student understands how new cultural movements at different social levels affected American life.	2.6, 2.14

Standard 3: The rise of the American labor movement and how political issues reflected social and economic changes.

3A	Student understands how the "second industrial revolution" changed the nature and conditions of work.	2.16
3B	Student understands the rise of national labor unions and the role of state and federal governments in labor conflicts.	No TWD
3C	Student understands how Americans grappled with social, economic, and political issues.	1.22, 1.23, 1.25, 2.16

Standard 4: Federal Indian policy and United States foreign policy after the Civil War.

4A	Student understands various perspectives on federal Indian policy, westward expansion, and the resulting struggles.	1.26, 1.28, 2.2, 2.3, 2.9

APPENDIX D: NATIONAL STANDARDS for U.S. HISTORY (continued)

4B	Student understands the roots and development of American expansionism and the causes of the Spanish-American War.	2.5, 2.12

ERA 7: THE EMERGENCE OF MODERN AMERICA (1890-1930)

Standard 1: How Progressives and others addressed the problems of industrial capitalism, urbanization, and political corruption.

1A	Student understands the origin of the Progressives and the coalitions they formed to deal with issues at the local and state levels.	2.16, 2.27
1B	Student understands Progressivism at the national level	2.16, 2.27
1C	Student understands the limitations of Progressivism and the alternatives offered by various groups.	2.7, 2.18

Standard 2: The changing role of the United States in world affairs through World War I.

2A	Student understands how the American role in the world changed in the early 20th century.	2.11, 2.13
2B	Student understands the causes of World War I and why the U.S. intervened.	2.19, 2.20
2C	Student understands the impact at home and abroad of the U.S. involvement in World War I.	2.14, 2.18, 2.19, 2.21, 2.22, 2.23, 2.28

Standard 3: How the United States changed from the end of World War I to the eve of the Great Depression.

3A	Student understands social tensions and their consequences in the postwar era.	2.14, 2.17, 2.23, 2.24, 2.25, 2.28, 2.30, 2.31, 2.32
3B	Student understands how a modern capitalist economy emerged in the 1920s.	No TWD
3C	Student understands how new cultural movements reflected and changed American society.	2.25
3D	Student understands politics and international affairs in the 1920s.	2.24, 2.26, 2.29, 2.31

ERA 8: THE GREAT DEPRESSION AND WORLD WAR II (1929-1945)

Standard 1: The causes of the Great Depression and how it affected American society.

1A	Student understands the causes of the crash of 1929 and the Great Depression.	No TWD

APPENDIX D: NATIONAL STANDARDS for U.S. HISTORY (continued)

1B	Student understands how American life changed during the 1930s.	1.20, 3.1, 3.2, 3.4, 3.6, 3.7

Standard 2: How the New Deal addressed the Great Depression, transferred American federalism, and initiated the welfare state.

2A	Student understands the New Deal and the presidency of Franklin D. Roosevelt.	3.2, 3.3, 3.6, 3.17
2B	Student understands the impact of the New Deal on workers and the labor movement.	3.1
2C	Student understands opposition to the New Deal, the alternative programs of its detractors, and the legacy of the New Deal.	3.5, 3.6

Standard 3: The causes and course of World War II, the character of the war at home and abroad, and its reshaping of the U.S. role in world affairs.

3A	Student understands the international background of World War II.	3.3, 3.4, 3.8, 3.19, 3.20
3B	Student understands World War II and how the Allies prevailed.	3.9, 3.16, 3.19, 3.20
3C	Student understands the effects of World War II at home.	2.6, 3.10, 3.12, 3.13, 3.14, 3.15, 3.18

ERA 9: POSTWAR UNITED STATES (1945 to early 1970s)

Standard 1: The economic boom and social transformation of postwar United States.

1A	Student understands the extent and impact of economic changes in the postwar period.	No TWD
1B	Student understands how the social changes of the postwar period affected various Americans.	1.20, 3.11, 3.26, 4.8, 4.9, 4.21
1C	Student understands how postwar science augmented the nation's economic strength, transformed daily life, and influenced the world economy.	4.3, 4.14, 4.15, 4.19

Standard 2: How the Cold War and conflicts in Korea and Vietnam influenced domestic and international politics.

2A	Student understands the international origins and domestic consequences of the Cold War.	3.21, 3.24, 4.1, 4.3, 4.10, 4.14

APPENDIX D: NATIONAL STANDARDS for U.S. HISTORY (continued)

2B	Student understands U.S. foreign policy in Africa, Asia, the Middle East, and Latin America.	3.25, 4.2
2C	Student understands the foreign and domestic consequences of U.S. involvement in Vietnam.	3.23, 4.22

Standard 3: Domestic policies after World War II.

3A	Student understands the political debates of the post-World War II era.	4.6, 4.13
3B	Student understands the "New Frontier" and the "Great Society".	4.11, 4.14

Standard 4: The struggle for racial and gender equality and the extension of civil liberties.

4A	Student understands the "Second Reconstruction" and its advancement of civil rights.	1.20, 4.5, 4.6, 4.7, 4.12, 4.17, 4.20
4B	Student understands the women's movement for civil rights and equal opportunities.	3.22
4C	Student understands the Warren Court's role in addressing civil liberties and equal rights.	1.20, 4.4, 4.16, 4.18

ERA 10: CONTEMPORARY UNITED STATED (1968 to the present)

Standard 1: Recent developments in foreign policy and domestic politics.

1A	Student understands domestic politics from Nixon to Carter.	4.23, 4.24, 4.25, 4.26, 4.27
1B	Student understands domestic politics in contemporary society.	No TWD
1C	Student understands major foreign policy initiatives.	No TWD

Standard 2: Economic, social, and cultural developments in contemporary United States.

2A	Student understands economic patterns since 1968.	No TWD
2B	Student understands the new immigration and demographic shifts.	No TWD
2C	Student understands changing religious diversity and its impact on American institutions and values.	No TWD
2D	Student understands contemporary American culture.	No TWD
2E	Student understands how a democratic polity debates social issues and mediates between individual or group rights and the common good.	1.20

APPENDIX E:
NATIONAL STANDARDS for WORLD HISTORY

This chart identifies the articles in the four volumes of TEACHING WITH DOCUMENTS that connect primary sources and related teaching activities to the National Standards for World History, grades 5-12. Note the absence of articles for the first six eras since the primary sources featured in the articles are official documents of the U.S. government, which had its beginnings in the late 18th century. [See page 154 for a numbered list of the articles.]

ERA 7: AN AGE of REVOLUTIONS, 1750-1914

Standard 1: The causes and consequences of political revolutions in the late 18th and early 19th centuries.

1A	Student understands how the French Revolution contributed to transformation of Europe and the world.	No TWD
1B	Student understands how Latin American countries achieved independence in the early 19th century.	No TWD

Standard 2: The causes and consequences of the agricultural and industrial revolutions, 1700-1850.

2A	Student understands the early industrialization and the importance of developments in England.	1.1, 1.2
2B	Student understands how industrial economies expanded and societies experienced transformations in Europe and the Atlantic basin.	1.2
2C	Student understands the causes and consequences of the abolition of the trans-Atlantic slave trade and slavery in the Americas.	1.20

Standard 3: The transformation of Eurasian societies in an era of global trade and rising European power, 1750-1870.

3A	Student understands how the Ottoman Empire attempted to meet the challenge of Western military, political, and economic power.	No TWD
3B	Student understands Russian absolutism, reform, and imperial expansion in the late 18th and 19th centuries.	No TWD
3C	Student understands the consequences of political and military encounters between Europeans and peoples of South and Southeast Asia.	1.13
3D	Student understands how China's Qing dynasty responded to economic and political crises in the late 18th and the 19th centuries.	1.12
3E	Student understands how Japan was transformed from feudal shogunate to modern nation-state in the 19th century.	No TWD

Standard 4: Patterns of nationalism, state-building, and social reform in Europe and the Americas, 1830-1914.

4A	Student understands how modern nationalism affected European politics and society.	No TWD

APPENDIX E: NATIONAL STANDARDS for WORLD HISTORY (continued)

4B	Student understands the impact of new social movements and ideologies on 19th-century Europe.	1.16, 1.20, 1.22, 2.16
4C	Student understands cultural, intellectual, and educational trends in 19th-century Europe.	No TWD
4D	Student understands the political, economic, and social transformations in the Americas in the 19th century.	1.5, 1.6, 1.7, 2.9, 2.10

Standard 5: Patterns of global change in the era of Western military and economic dominance, 1800-1914.

5A	Student understands connections between major developments in science and technology and the growth of industrial economy and society.	1.24, 1.28, 2.16
5B	Student understands the causes and consequences of European settler colonization in the 19th century.	1.8. 1.9, 2.2, 2.3, 2.13
5C	Student understands the causes of European, American, and Japanese imperial expansion.	2.5, 2.11
5D	Student understands transformations in South, Southeast, and East Asia in the era of the "new imperialism".	1.13
5E	Student understands the varying responses of African peoples to world economic developments and European imperialism.	No TWD

Standard 6: Major global trends from 1750-1914.

6	Student understands major global trends from 1750-1914.	1.3, 1.11, 2.2, 2.4, 2.14, 2.17

ERA 8: A HALF-CENTURY of CRISIS and ACHIEVEMENT, 1900-1945

Standard 1: Reform, revolution, and social change in the world economy of the early century.

1A	Student understands the world industrial economy emerging in the early 20th century.	1.22, 2.16, 2.27, 3.1
1B	Student understands the causes and consequences of important resistance and revolutionary movements in the early 20th century.	3.4

Standard 2: The causes and global consequences of World War I.

2A	Student understands the causes of World War I.	2.20
2B	Student understands the global scope, outcome, and human costs of the war.	2.19, 2.21, 2.22, 2.23
2C	Student understands the causes and consequences of the Russian Revolution of 1914.	2.24

APPENDIX E: NATIONAL STANDARDS for WORLD HISTORY   (continued)

Standard 3: The search for peace and stability in the 1920s and 1930s.

3A	Student understands postwar efforts to achieve lasting peace and social and economic recovery.	2.29
3B	Student understands economic, social, and political transformations in Africa, Asia, and Latin America in the 1920s and 1930s.	2.29
3C	Student understands the interplay between scientific or technological innovations and new patterns of social and cultural life between 1900 and 1940.	No TWD
3D	Student understands the interplay of new artistic and literary movements with changes in social and cultural life in various parts of the world in the post-war decades.	3.6
3E	Student understands the causes and global consequences of the Great Depression.	3.1, 3.2, 3.3, 3.5

Standard 4: The causes and global consequences of World War II.

4A	Student understands the causes of World War II.	3.3, 3.4, 3.8
4B	Student understands the global scope, outcome, and human costs of the war.	3.10, 3.14, 3.16, 3.19, 3.20, 3.21, 3.24, 3.25

Standard 5: Major global trends from 1900 to the end of World War II.

5	Student understands major global trends from 1900 to the end of World War II.	2.25, 3.3

ERA 9: THE 20ᵀᴴ CENTURY SINCE 1945: PROMISES and PARADOXES

Standard 1: How post-World War II reconstruction occurred, new international power relations took shape, and colonial empires broke up.

1A	Student understands major political and economic changes that accompanied post-war recovery.	3.22, 3.25
1B	Student understands why global power shifts took place and the Cold War broke out in the aftermath of World War II.	3.23, 4.1, 4.10, 4.14, 4.22
1C	Student understands how African, Asian, and Caribbean peoples achieved independence from European colonial rule.	No TWD

Standard 2: The search for community, stability, and peace in an interdependent world.

2A	Student understands how population explosion and environmental changes have altered conditions of life around the world.	No TWD

APPENDIX E: NATIONAL STANDARDS for WORLD HISTORY (continued)

2B	Student understands how increasing economic interdependence has transformed human society.	No TWD
2C	Student understands how liberal democracy, market economies, and human rights movements have reshaped political and social life.	1.20, 3.22, 4.7, 4.17, 4.23
2D	Student understands major sources of tensions and conflict in the contemporary world and efforts that have been made to address them.	No TWD
2E	Student understands major worldwide scientific and technological trends of the second half of the 20th century.	4.3, 4.14, 4.19
2F	Student understands worldwide cultural trends of the second half of the 20th century.	4.8

Standard 3: Major global trends since World War II.

3	Student understands major global trends since World War II.	1.20, 3.22, 3.25, 4.3, 4.23

APPENDIX F:
NATIONAL STANDARDS for CIVICS and GOVERNMENT

This chart identifies the articles in the four volumes of TEACHING WITH DOCUMENTS that connect primary sources and related teaching activities to the National Standards for Civics and Government for upper grades. [See page 154 for a numbered list of the articles.]

I. WHAT ARE CIVIC LIFE, POLITICS, AND GOVERNMENT?

A. What is civic life? What is politics? What is government? Why are government and politics necessary? What purposes should government serve?

1	Students should be able to explain the meaning of the terms civic life, politics, and government.	all
2	Students should be able to explain the major arguments advanced for the necessity of politics and government.	all
3	Students should be able to evaluate, take, and defend positions on competing ideas regarding the purposes of politics and government and their implications for the individual and society.	all

B. What are the essential characteristics of limited and unlimited government?

1	Students should be able to explain the essential characteristics of limited and unlimited governments.	1.19, 3.3, 3.19, 3.24
2	Students should be able to evaluate, take, and defend positions on the importance of the rule of law and on the sources, purposes, and functions of law.	1.19, 3.3, 4.17. 4.25, 4.26
3	Students should be able to explain and evaluate the argument that civil society is a prerequisite of limited government.	1.20, 1.22, 1.26, 2.2, I 2.7, 2.8, 2.16, 2.25, 2.30, 3.7
4	Students should be able to explain and evaluate competing ideas regarding the relationship between political and economic freedoms.	1.2, 1.24, 1.27, 2.15

C. What are the nature and purposes of constitutions?

1	Students should be able to explain different uses of the term of "constitution" and to distinguish between governments with a constitution and a constitutional government.	1.3
2	Students should be able to explain the various purposes served by constitutions.	1.4, 1.20, 1.22, 4.23, 4.25
3	Students should be able to evaluate, take, and defend positions on what conditions contribute to the establishment and maintenance of constitutional government.	1.3, 3.3, 4.6, 4.24, 4.25

Teaching With Documents

APPENDIX F: NATIONAL STANDARDS for CIVICS and GOVERNMENT (continued)

D. What are the alternative ways of organizing constitutional governments?

1	Students should be able to describe the major characteristics of systems of shared powers and of parliamentary systems.	1.12, 2.6, 3.5, 4.23, 4.25, 4.26
2	Students should be able to explain the advantages and disadvantages of federal, confederal, and unitary systems of government.	1.3, 4.6
3	Students should be able to evaluate, take, and defend positions on how well alternative forms of representation serve the purposes of constitutional government.	1.20, 1.22, 4.23

II. WHAT ARE THE FOUNDATIONS OF THE AMERICAN POLITICAL SYSTEM?

A. What is the American idea of constitutional government?

1	Students should be able to explain central ideas of American constitutional government and their history.	1.3, 1.4, 3.5, 4.25
2	Students should be able to explain the extent to which Americans have internalized the values and principles of the Constitution and attempted to make its ideals realities.	1.20, 1.22, 2.18, 2.21, 3.13, 4.7, 4.16, 4.27

B. What are the distinctive characteristics of American society?

1	Students should be able to explain how [certain] characteristics tend to distinguish American society from most other societies.	1.8, 1.20, 1.26, 2.3, 2.4, 2.6, 2.14, 2.15, 2.21, 2.25, 2.26, 2.28, 2.30, 4.11, 4.18
2	Students should be able to evaluate, take, and defend positions on the importance of voluntarism in American society.	1.16, 1.26, 2.22, 3.15
3	Students should be able to evaluate, take, and defend positions on the contemporary role of organized groups in American social and political life.	1.20, 2.2, 2.8, 2.30, 3.7
4	Students should be able to evaluate, take, and defend positions on issues regarding diversity in American life.	1.8, 1.9, 1.11, 1.20, 2.4, 2.9, 2.14, 2.17, 2.25, 2.28

APPENDIX F: NATIONAL STANDARDS for CIVICS and GOVERNMENT (continued)

C. What is American political culture?

1	Students should be able to explain the importance of shared political and civic beliefs and values to the maintenance of constitutional democracy in an increasingly diverse American society.	2.4, 2.25
2	Students should be able to describe the character of American political conflict and explain factors that usually tend to prevent it or lower its intensity.	1.4, 1.14, 1.17, 1.20, 1.22, 2.24, 2.27, 3.7, 4.11, 4.17

D. What values and principles are basic to American constitutional democracy?

1	Students should be able to explain the meaning of the terms "liberal" and "democracy" in the phrase "liberal democracy."	1.3, 1.20, 2.10
2	Students should be able to explain how and why ideas of classical republicanism are reflected in the values and principles of American constitutional democracy.	1.12, 4.25, 4.26
3	Students should be able to evaluate, take, and defend positions on what the fundamental values and principles of American political life are and their importance to the maintenance of constitutional democracy.	1.4, 2.4, 2.6, 2.21
4	Students should be able to evaluate, take, and defend positions on issues in which fundamental values and principles may be in conflict.	1.19, 2.18, 2.21, 2.23, 3.13
5	Students should be able to evaluate, take, and defend positions about issues concerning the disparities between American ideals and realities.	1.17, 1.20, 1.22, 2.7, 2.10, 2.17, 2.23, 3.10, 3.14, 4.7, 4.12, 4.17

III. HOW DOES THE GOVERNMENT ESTABLISHED BY THE CONSTITUTION EMBODY THE PURPOSES, VALUES, AND PRINCIPLES OF AMERICAN DEMOCRACY?

A. How are power and responsibility distributed, shared, and limited in the government established by the United States Constitution?

1	Students should be able to explain how the U.S. Constitution grants and distributes power to national and state government and how it seeks to prevent the abuse of power.	1.3, 1.20, 1.21, 1.25, 2.6, 3.5, 4.6, 4.12
2	Students should be able to evaluate, take, and defend positions on issues regarding the distribution of powers and responsibilities within the federal system.	1.14, 1.20, 4.6, 4.12

APPENDIX F: NATIONAL STANDARDS for CIVICS and GOVERNMENT (continued)

	B. How is the national government organized and what does it do?	
1	Students should be able to evaluate, take, and defend positions on issues regarding the purposes, organization, and functions of the institutions of the national government.	all
2	Students should be able to evaluate, take, and defend positions on issues regarding the major responsibilities of the national government for domestic and foreign policy.	2.16, 2.27, 3.8, 4.22
3	Students should be able to evaluate, take, and defend positions on issues regarding how government should raise money to pay for its operations and services.	No TWD

	C. How are state and local governments organized and what do they do?	
1	Students should be able to evaluate, take, and defend positions on issues regarding the proper relationship between the national government and the state and local governments.	4.6, 4.12
2	Students should be able to evaluate, take, and defend positions on issues regarding the relationships between state and local governments and citizen access to those governments.	No TWD
3	Students should be able to identify the major responsibilities of their state and local governments and evaluate how well they are being fulfilled.	No TWD

	D. What is the place of law in the American constitutional system?	
1	Students should be able to evaluate, take, and defend positions on the role and importance of law in the American political system.	1.20, 1.21, 2.6, 4.25
2	Students should be able to evaluate, take, and defend positions on current issues regarding the judicial protection of individual rights.	1.21, 3.13, 4.16, 4.27

	E. How does the American political system provide for choice and opportunities for participation?	
1	Students should be able to evaluate, take, and defend positions about how the public agenda is set.	1.22, 3.1, 3.2, 4.13
2	Students should be able to evaluate, take, and defend positions about the role of public opinion in American politics.	3.12, 3.17, 4.11
3	Students should be able to evaluate, take, and defend positions on the influence of the media on American political life.	1.2, 2.18, 2.31, 3.8, 4.17
4	Students should be able to evaluate, take, and defend positions about the roles of political parties, campaigns, and elections in American politics.	1.21, 1.25, 3.17
5	Students should be able to evaluate, take, and defend positions about the contemporary roles of associations and groups in American politics.	1.20, 2.8, 2.16

APPENDIX F: NATIONAL STANDARDS for CIVICS and GOVERNMENT (continued)

6	Students should be able to evaluate, take, and defend positions about the formation and implementation of public policy.	1.20, 2.8, 2.16, 2.27

IV. WHAT IS THE RELATIONSHIP OF THE UNITED STATES TO OTHER NATIONS AND TO WORLD AFFAIRS?

A. How is the world organized politically?

1	Students should be able to explain how the world is organized politically.	3.25
2	Students should be able to explain how nation-states interact with each other.	1.12, 1.13, 2.17, 2.20, 3.8, 3.19, 3.23, 3.25, 4.10, 4.14, 4.22
3	Students should be able to evaluate, take, and defend positions on the purposes and functions of international organizations in the world today.	3.22, 4.3

B. How do the domestic politics and constitutional principles of the United States affect its relations with the world?

1	Students should be able to explain the principal foreign policy positions of the United States and evaluate their consequences.	1.12, 2.12, 2.20, 3.4, 3.20, 3.21, 3.25, 4.22
2	Students should be able to evaluate, take, and defend positions about how U.S. foreign policy is made and the means by which it is carried out.	1.12, 2.12, 2.29, 3.8, 4.10, 4.22
3	Students should be able to evaluate, take, and defend positions on foreign policy issues in light of American national interests, values, and principles.	3.4, 3.19, 3.24, 3.25

C. How has the United States influenced other nations, and how have other nations influenced American politics and society?

1	Students should be able to evaluate, take, and defend positions about the impact of the American political ideas on the world.	2.11, 2.13, 3.24
2	Students should be able to evaluate, take, and defend positions about the effects of significant international political developments on the United States and other nations.	2.19, 2.20, 2.24, 3.4, 4.1
3	Students should be able to evaluate, take, and defend positions about the effects of significant economic, technological, and cultural developments in the United States and other nations.	1.27, 4.8, 4.9

APPENDIX F: NATIONAL STANDARDS for CIVICS and GOVERNMENT (continued)

4	Students should be able to evaluate, take, and defend positions about what the response of American governments at all levels should be to world demographic and environmental developments.	2.8, 2.14, 2.17, 2.28
5	Students should be able to evaluate, take, and defend positions about what the relationship of the United States should be to international organizations.	3.22, 4.3

V. WHAT ARE THE ROLES OF THE CITIZEN IN AMERICAN DEMOCRACY

A. What is citizenship?

1	Students should be able to explain the meaning of citizenship in the United States.	2.25, 3.14
2	Students should be able to evaluate, take, and defend positions on issues regarding the criteria used for naturalization.	2.14, 2.28, 3.11

B. What are the rights of citizens?

1	Students should be able to evaluate, take, and defend positions on issues regarding personal rights.	1.3, 1.4, 1.21, 4.16
2	Students should be able to evaluate, take, and defend positions on issues regarding political rights.	1.20, 1.21, 1.22, 4.7, 4.27
3	Students should be able to evaluate, take, and defend positions on issues regarding economic rights.	1.18, 1.24, 1.27, 2.9
4	Students should be able to evaluate, take, and defend positions on the relationships among personal, political, and economic rights.	1.6, 1.18, 2.16, 2.27
5	Students should be able to evaluate, take, and defend positions on issues regarding the proper scope and limits of rights.	1.19, 2.18, 2.21, 2.24, 3.4

C. What are the responsibilities of citizens?

1	Students should be able to evaluate, take, and defend positions on issues regarding personal responsibilities of citizens in American constitutional democracy.	2.30, 2.32
2	Students should be able to evaluate, take, and defend positions on issues regarding civic responsibilities of citizens in American constitutional democracy.	1.5, 1.16, 4.4, 4.5, 4.7, 4.21

APPENDIX F: NATIONAL STANDARDS for CIVICS and GOVERNMENT (continued)

D. What civic dispositions or traits of private and public character are important to the preservation and improvement of American constitutional democracy?

1	Students should be able to evaluate, take, and defend positions on the importance to American constitutional democracy of dispositions that lead individuals to become independent members of society.	1.12, 4.7, 4.17
2	Students should be able to evaluate, take, and defend positions on the importance to American constitutional democracy of dispositions that foster respect for individual worth and human dignity.	3.7
3	Students should be able to evaluate, take, and defend positions on the importance to American constitutional democracy of dispositions that incline citizens to public affairs.	1.5, 1.20, 3.22
4	Students should be able to evaluate, take, and defend positions on the importance to American constitutional democracy of dispositions that facilitate thoughtful and effective participation in public affairs.	1.22, 1.23

E. How can citizens take part in civic life?

1	Students should be able to evaluate, take, and defend positions on the relationship between politics and the attainment of individual and public goals.	1.14, 1.21, 3.4, 4.7, 4.17
2	Students should be able to explain the difference between political and social participation.	1.16
3	Students should be able to evaluate, take, and defend positions about the means that citizens should use to monitor and influence the formation and implementation of public policy.	1.20, 1.22, 3.10, 3.17, 4.7
4	Students should be able to evaluate, take, and defend positions about the functions of leadership in a American constitutional democracy.	1.5, 3.3, 3.26
5	Students should be able to explain the importance of knowledge to competent and responsible participation in American democracy.	all

APPENDIX G:
NATIONAL ARCHIVES and RECORDS ADMINISTRATION

National Archives and Records Administration
700 Pennsylvania Avenue, NW
Washington, DC 20408-0001
202-501-5400
Email: inquire@nara.gov

National Archives and Records Administration
8601 Adelphi Road
College Park, MD 20740-6001
301-837-2000
Email: inquire@nara.gov

Regional Records Services Facilities

NARA Northeast Region (Boston)
380 Trapelo Road
Waltham, MA 02452-6399
781-647-8104

NARA Northeast Region (Pittsfield)
10 Conte Drive
Pittsfield, MA 01201-8230
413-445-6885

NARA Northeast Region (New York City)
201 Varick Street, 12th Floor
New York, NY 10014-4811
212-337-1300

**NARA Mid Atlantic Region
(Center City Philadelphia)**
900 Market Street
Philadelphia, PA 19107-4292
215-597-3000

**NARA Mid Atlantic Region
(Northeast Philadelphia)**
14700 Townsend Road
Philadelphia, PA 19154-1096
215-617-9027

NARA Southeast Region
1557 St. Joseph Avenue
East Point, GA 30344-2593
404-763-7474

NARA Great Lakes Region (Chicago)
7358 South Pulaski Road
Chicago, IL 60629-5898
773-581-7816

NARA Great Lakes Region (Dayton)
3150 Springboro Road
Dayton, OH 45439-1883
937-225-2852

NARA Central Plains Region (Kansas City)
2312 East Bannister Road
Kansas City, MO 64131-3011
816-926-6272

NARA Central Plains Region (Lee's Summit)
200 Space Center Drive
Lee's Summit, MO 64064-1182
816-478-7079

NARA Southwest Region
501 West Felix Street
P.O. Box 6216
Fort Worth, TX 76115-0216
817-334-5525

NARA Rocky Mountain Region
Denver Federal Center, Building 48
P.O. Box 25307
Denver, CO 80225-0307
303-236-0804

NARA Pacific Region (Laguna Niguel)
24000 Avila Road
P.O. Box 6719
Laguna Niguel, CA 92607-6719
949-360-2641

NARA Pacific Region (San Francisco)
1000 Commodore Drive
San Bruno, CA 94066-2350
650-876-9009

NARA Pacific Alaska Region (Seattle)
6125 Sand Point Way, NE
Seattle, WA 98115-7999
206-526-6507

NARA Pacific Alaska Region (Anchorage)
654 West Third Avenue
Anchorage, AK 99501-2145
907-271-2443

NARA National Personnel Records Center
(Civilian Personnel Records)
111 Winnebago Street
St. Louis, MO 63118-4199
314-538-5722

NARA National Personnel Records Center
(Military Personnel Records)
9700 Page Avenue
St. Louis, MO 63132-5100
314-538-4247

Presidential Libraries

Herbert Hoover Library
210 Parkside Drive
P.O. Box 488
West Branch, IA 52358-0488
319-643-5301
Email: hoover.library@nara.gov

Franklin D. Roosevelt Library
511 Albany Post Road
Hyde Park, NY 12538-1999
845-229-8114
Email: roosevelt.library@nara.gov

Harry S. Truman Library
500 West U.S. Highway 24
Independence, MO 64050-1798
816-833-1400
Email: truman.library@nara.gov

Dwight D. Eisenhower Library
200 Southeast Fourth Street
Abilene, KS 67410-2900
785-263-4751
Email: eisenhower.library@nara.gov

John Fitzgerald Kennedy Library
Columbia Point
Boston, MA 02125-3398
617-929-4500
Email: kennedy.library@nara.gov

Lyndon Baines Johnson Library
2313 Red River Street
Austin, TX 78705-5702
512-916-5137
Email: johnson.library@nara.gov

Nixon Presidential Materials Staff
Office of Presidential Libraries
National Archives at College Park
8601 Adelphi Road
College Park, MD 20740-6001
301-837-3290
Email: nixon@nara.gov

Gerald R. Ford Library
1000 Beal Avenue
Ann Arbor, MI 48109-2114
734-741-2218
Email: ford.library@nara.gov

Gerald R. Ford Museum
303 Pearl Street, NW
Grand Rapids, MI 49504-5353
616-451-9263

Jimmy Carter Library
Delete One Copenhill
441 Freedom Parkway
Atlanta, GA 30307-1498
404-331-3942
Email: carter.library@nara.gov

Ronald Reagan Library
40 Presidential Drive
Simi Valley, CA 93065-0600
805-522-8444/800-410-8354
Email: reagan.library@nara.gov

George Bush Library
1000 George Bush Drive
P.O. Box 10410
College Station, TX 77842-0410
979-260-9552
Email: bush.library@nara.gov

Clinton Presidential Materials Project
1000 LaHarpe Boulevard
Little Rock, AR 72201
501-254-6866
Email: clinton.library@nara.gov

APPENDIX H:
DOCUMENT ANALYSIS WORKSHEETS

Cartoon Analysis Worksheet

	Visuals	*Words* (not all cartoons include words)
LEVEL ONE:	1. List the objects or people you see in the cartoon.	1. Identify the cartoon caption and/or title. 2. Locate three words or phrases used by the cartoonist to identify objects or people within the cartoon. 3. Record any important dates or numbers that appear in the cartoon.
LEVEL TWO:	2. Which of the objects on your list are symbols? 3. What do you think each symbol means?	4. Which words or phrases in the cartoon appear to be the most significant? Why do you think so? 5. List adjectives that describe the emotions portrayed in the cartoon.
LEVEL THREE:	A. Describe the action taking place in the cartoon. B. Explain how the words in the cartoon clarify the symbols. C. Explain the message of the cartoon. D. What special interest groups would agree/disagree with the cartoon's message? Why?	

Designed and developed by the Education Staff, National Archives and Records Administration, Washington, DC 20408.

Teaching With Documents   THE COLONIAL PERIOD TO 1879

Map Analysis Worksheet

1. TYPE OF MAP (check one):

    _____ Raised relief map
    _____ Topographic map
    _____ Political map
    _____ Contour-line map
    _____ Natural resource map
    _____ Military map
    _____ Bird's-eye view
    _____ Artifact map
    _____ Satellite photograph/mosaic
    _____ Pictograph
    _____ Weather map
    _____ Other ( )

2. PHYSICAL QUALITIES OF THE MAP (check one or more):

    _____ Compass
    _____ Handwritten
    _____ Date
    _____ Notations
    _____ Scale
    _____ Name of mapmaker
    _____ Title
    _____ Legend (key)
    _____ Other

3. DATE OF MAP: _____
4. CREATOR OF MAP: _____
5. WHERE WAS THE MAP PRODUCED? _____
6. MAP INFORMATION

    A. List three things in this map that you think are important:

        1. _____
        2. _____
        3. _____

    B. Why do you think this map was drawn?
        _____
        _____

    C. What evidence in the map suggests why it was drawn?
        _____
        _____

    D. What information does the map add to the textbook's account of this event?
        _____
        _____

    E. Does the information in this map support or contradict information that you have read about this event? Explain.
        _____
        _____

    F. Write a question to the mapmaker that is left unanswered by this map.
        _____
        _____

Designed and developed by the Education Staff, National Archives and Records Administration, Washington, DC 20408.

Teaching With Documents THE COLONIAL PERIOD TO 1879

Photograph Analysis Worksheet

Step 1. Observation

A. Study the photograph for 2 minutes. Form an overall impression of the photograph and then examine individual items. Next, divide the photo into quadrants and study each section to see what new details become visible.

B. Use the chart below to list people, objects, and activities in the photograph.

PEOPLE	OBJECTS	ACTIVITIES

Step 2. Inference

Based on what you have observed above, list three things you might infer from this photograph.

_____

_____

_____

Step 3. Questions

A. What questions does this photograph raise in your mind?

_____

_____

B. Where could you find answers to them?

_____

Designed and developed by the Education Staff, National Archives and Records Administration, Washington, DC 20408.

Teaching With Documents   THE COLONIAL PERIOD TO 1879

Poster Analysis Worksheet

1. What are the main colors used in the poster?

2. What symbols (if any) are used in the poster?

3. If a symbol is used, is it
   a. clear (easy to interpret)?
   b. memorable?
   c. dramatic?

4. Are the messages in the poster primarily visual, verbal, or both?

5. Who do you think is the intended audience for the poster?

6. What does the Government hope the audience will do?

7. What Government purpose(s) is served by the poster?

8. The most effective posters use symbols that are unusual, simple, and direct. Is this an effective poster?

Designed and developed by the Education Staff, National Archives and Records Administration, Washington, DC 20408.

Written Document Analysis Worksheet

1. TYPE OF DOCUMENT (check one):

    _____ Newspaper

    _____ Letter

    _____ Patent

    _____ Memorandum

    _____ Map

    _____ Telegram

    _____ Press release

    _____ Report

    _____ Advertisement

    _____ Congressional record

    _____ Census report

    _____ Other

2. UNIQUE PHYSICAL QUALITIES OF THE DOCUMENT (check one or more):

    _____ Interesting letterhead

    _____ Handwritten

    _____ Typed

    _____ Seals

    _____ Notations

    _____ "RECEIVED" stamp

    _____ Other

3. DATE(S) OF DOCUMENT: _____

4. AUTHOR (OR CREATOR) OF THE DOCUMENT: _____

    POSITION (TITLE): _____

5. FOR WHAT AUDIENCE WAS THE DOCUMENT WRITTEN? _____

6. DOCUMENT INFORMATION (There are many possible ways to answer A-E.)

    A. List three things the author said that you think are important:

        1. _____

        2. _____

        3. _____

    B. Why do you think this document was written?

        _____

        _____

    C. What evidence in the document helps you know why it was written? Quote from the document.

        _____

        _____

    D. List two things the document tells you about life in the United States at the time it was written:

        _____

        _____

    E. Write a question to the author that is left unanswered by the document:

        _____

        _____

Designed and developed by the Education Staff, National Archives and Records Administration, Washington, DC 20408.

Teaching With Documents   THE COLONIAL PERIOD TO 1879